MEMORIES OF AFRICA

Jessica B. Harris, Series Editor

MEMORIES OF AFRICA

Home and Abroad in the United States

Toyin Falola

University Press of Mississippi / Jackson

The University Press of Mississippi is the scholarly publishing agency of
the Mississippi Institutions of Higher Learning: Alcorn State University,
Delta State University, Jackson State University, Mississippi State University,
Mississippi University for Women, Mississippi Valley State University,
University of Mississippi, and University of Southern Mississippi.

www.upress.state.ms.us

The University Press of Mississippi is a member
of the Association of University Presses.

Copyright © 2023 by University Press of Mississippi
All rights reserved

First printing 2023

∞

Library of Congress Cataloging-in-Publication Data

Names: Falola, Toyin, author.
Title: Memories of Africa : home and abroad in the United States / Toyin Falola.
Other titles: Atlantic migrations and the African diaspora.
Description: Jackson : University Press of Mississippi, 2023. |
Series: Atlantic migrations and the African diaspora |
Includes bibliographical references and index.
Identifiers: LCCN 2022053807 (print) | LCCN 2022053808 (ebook) |
ISBN 9781496843494 (hardback) | ISBN 9781496843487 (trade paperback) |
ISBN 9781496843470 (epub) | ISBN 9781496843463 (epub) |
ISBN 9781496843456 (pdf) | ISBN 9781496843449 (pdf)
Subjects: LCSH: African diaspora. | Globalization—Africa. |
Africans—United States. | African Americans—Intellectual life. |
Pan-Africanism. | Transnationalism. | Autobiography—Black authors. |
Africa—Emigration and immigration.
Classification: LCC DT16.5 .F353 2023 (print) | LCC DT16.5 (ebook) |
DDC 304.8096—dc23/eng/20221220
LC record available at https://lccn.loc.gov/2022053807
LC ebook record available at https://lccn.loc.gov/2022053808

British Library Cataloging-in-Publication Data available

Dedicated to
Professors Aribidesi Usman and Bola Sotunsa
for their humanistic vision and caring

CONTENTS

Acknowledgments ix

Preface. xi

Chapter 1. (Shifting) Spaces and (Fixed) Crossroads:
The African Diaspora and the Imaginations of Africa 3

Chapter 2. Culture and Cultural Politics in Cherno Njie's
Sweat Is Invisible in the Rain 40

Chapter 3. The Representation of Tradition and Modernity in
Emmanuel Babatunde's *Kelebogile* 62

Chapter 4. Deriving Meaning: Nuances of Language, Nodes of
Orality, and Sense of Communitarianism in Michael Afolayan's
Fate of Our Mothers 91

Chapter 5. The Density of Cultures: A. B. Assensoh's *Journeys* 108

Chapter 6. Migrant (Un)Homeliness: Universalism and Global
Identity in the Memoirs of A. B. Assensoh and Cherno Njie 133

Chapter 7. Contrasting Experiences of Old and New Homes in the
New African Diaspora Memoirs 158

Conclusion. From Slave Narratives to Freedom Narratives:
A Genealogy of Immigrant Stories. 177

Notes 207

Bibliography 225

Index 235

ACKNOWLEDGMENTS

This book has grown out of decades of my interest in memoirs. I suppose my professional career as an academic has facilitated this interest. I teach memoirs. I teach memory. I combine memoirs and memory to teach about a particular past. I teach films as well. Films connect to memoirs and memories as people move texts to visuals. Thus, my first gratitude must go to my students at various times and generations.

The second gratitude goes to the various authors who have written their memoirs and autobiographies. Going into print to reveal someone's life requires motives. Some are genuine; some are designed to clarify; some are pure factions. To politicians, it is to explain their successes and failures. Those represented in this book used the memoirs to talk about their cultures, places in spaces, relocation, and challenges. I thank them for writing their memoirs, without which this book would not have been possible. The authors have written on hidden ideas inside of them and visible ideas outside of their bodies. The analyses in this book combine what they reveal about themselves and others to talk about the more essential ideas of Africa and its diaspora.

My readers and critics are the third category of people, especially Segun Atolagbe, Bola Dauda, and Miriam Odeyemi, all based in Ibadan, Nigeria. I am impressed by the commitment of Joshua Agbo, Oladejo Afolayan, and Olajumoke Jacob-Haliso, who read various aspects of this book. Segun Atolagbe and 'Tayo Keyede worked hard to do the final preparation for the press. Michael Efionayi worked with me on the photographs, a process of recreation.

Finally, I appreciate the efforts of Professor Tunde Adeleke, director of the African Studies Center, Iowa State University, who encouraged me to publish with the University of Mississippi Press. I thank the editors and staff of the University of Mississippi Press, notably Lisa McMurtray, for making this book a reality.

PREFACE

A memoir is a literary piece of an individual's personal history, enveloped within certain themes and relevant people, places, and events. It is not synonymous with its sister work, autobiography, because it does not merely detail a timeline of a person's life. Rather, it provides the reader with a commentary on life lessons, societal philosophy, and interpersonal relationships with others. It also does not have to be entirely fact-based. For instance, a memoirist can sprinkle in fictional characters that represent certain individuals or circumstances to better demonstrate a particular message to the reader. Even with some possible fiction engrained in the story, the focus of the memoir is essentially on the memoirists' personal truth. This personal truth can teach a reader about him- or herself and about a piece of the human condition. Consequently, memoirs are important because they contain emotional and psychological accounts of history and humanity that others can relate to or learn from.

The book aims to expand African Diaspora studies to include African migrant memoirs and African migrant memoirists because such works and people can capture important themes and events of the early and modern African Diaspora. Reading African Diaspora memoirs written since the beginning of the transatlantic slave trade through the twenty-first century can show a reader how African migrant experiences and identities have changed over time and how African migrant experiences can teach much about African resilience and identity. Memoir accounts are significant sources of knowledge because they are not meant to be objective, as no historical account can ever be. Memoirists do not try to write as though they are unbiased figures; they describe their life and surrounding events with emotion and reflection. It is their emotion and reflection that make their storytelling and history-telling more "natural," "real," and "human." Their emotion and reflection also make for a compelling historical source, for these memoirists personally experienced a moment that would eventually become history.

While many compelling African migrant memoirs have been written and noteworthy research has been done on African American memoirs and memoirists, there remains a gap in the literature on the studies of African migrant memoirs and memoirists. There is also a gap in the literature on a direct comparison of old and new African migrant memoirs and the connections between the two. Indeed, it is thought-provoking to observe that most African slaves coming to the United States came from Western Africa and that many modern African memoirists also come from Western Africa. Therefore, scholars can use Western African memoirs over time, as well as other secondary sources, to propose theories on how the African migrant experience has changed or even, in some ways, remained the same. These same scholars can also use African migrants' own accounts to give a testament to the African migrant work ethic, determination, and resilience. Ultimately, this book, in its studies of various African migrant memoirs and memoirists, seeks to fill the gap in the literature and to honor African migrants over the centuries.

It is also worth noting that this book has been produced in a unique political climate. Today, many African migrants coming into the United States have been incredibly successful in their respective fields. Many have brought knowledge from advanced degrees or applied their talents and intellect to American universities. They have also contributed to the diversity of the country. However, at the same time, President Trump's "America First" rhetoric—as racial, dangerous, and offensive as it is—threatens African immigrants' and all immigrants' way of life. Consequently, this book allows for a humanization of African migrants and the assurance that African migrant voices will not be erased despite the prevailing political uncertainty and fear.

In this book, I have crafted literary analyses of various African migrant memoirs and used secondary scholarly sources to testify to migration phenomena and the usefulness of memoir as an artistic medium. In doing so, I illustrate how African migrants' experiences can inform scholars about many aspects of the African Diaspora. For instance, African migrants' stories can reveal how African migrants have to navigate between physical and psychological spaces. African migrants leave their homes (often without choice) and maneuver between their home country and host country identities, adapt to their new environment and decide which home traditions should be kept and which should be disposed of. This opens up further theories about the connection between diaspora and space that the literary analyses of the various memoirs eked out. The impact and challenges of the construction of diasporas by these African migrants are revisited, which helps to vividly understand the anxieties and coping strategies they develop to navigate the physical and psychological spaces in new landscapes.

I have attempted to open up further theoretical axes and connections between the concept of diaspora and the notion of spatiality, which is not only about dispersion and migration, but of necessary entanglements and inclusion of indigenous people to address the dynamics of contesting identities in contemporary societies. Additionally, African migrants' stories can depict many poignant details about cultural, political, religious, and societal differences between African regions. They can also say much about Africans' perceptions of colonial and postcolonial power structures and how these structures have necessarily impacted their worldviews over time.

Indeed, the stories told by African migrants themselves provide scholars with a unique opportunity to see the world of the African Diaspora "from the inside." African migrant memoirs are significant because they provide a history for non-African readers and a mirror for African readers. This book can also be useful for history students studying the impact of the African Diaspora and for literature students who study how fiction and fact can be blended to form a work full of rich metaphors, themes, and lessons. I hope that this book will create a catalyst for scholars to dig and delve deeper into African migrant memoirs when studying the African Diaspora and migration patterns more generally.

I offer this book as a tribute to the African migrant memoirists who so masterfully crafted their stories. This book also serves as a portal for readers to see and feel the complex, painful, beautiful, and triumphant experiences of African migrants. Let us celebrate and revere the wisdom of these voices and all that they have to teach us.

MEMORIES OF AFRICA

Chapter 1

(SHIFTING) SPACE AND (FIXED) CROSSROADS

The African Diaspora and the Imaginations of Africa

INTRODUCTION

The diaspora is a midpoint between two places for African migrants and their ability to imagine and reimagine Africa. This relationship can be examined through specific ideas, such as Du Bois's double consciousness, Homi Bhabha's Third Space, and Victor Turner's liminal space. By addressing the idea of the diaspora, one can explore the context-sensitive relationship between the African Diaspora and the Black Diaspora. The diaspora is a configurable space that can be conceptually framed as a Third Space, drawing on Bhabha and Turner's ideas, which makes it possible to centralize the lives of migrants and recognize their identity and experiences as shifting, persistently contested by dominant forces, and the product of persons who are trapped between two spaces: ideal and lived. In this context, the idea of home is sedentary and mobile, grounded and ungrounded, and simultaneously physical and amorphous. This foregrounds how the imaginations of Africa in the African Diaspora are dependent on the experiences that define the diaspora as the space of constant instability, liminality, struggle, shifts, and negotiations.

THE DIASPORA

Diaspora, as a term, has a taxonomic function: it is often used to label migrant settlers in new destinations who raise new generations while maintaining ties with their homeland. Reflecting on Africa and its image and ambassadors outside Africa—especially in connection to diasporic discourses—requires touching on monumental historical phases. These include slavery and its impact on the formation of Black[1] spaces[2] within and outside of the African continent. Transatlantic slavery was a hideous, shameful, devastating force that is mostly in Africa's past, but it continues to wreak havoc on the spirits, souls, and bodies of Blacks at home and abroad. It is like a vengeful spirit that reaches across temporal and spatial boundaries to torment Black lives. The events that shipped millions of Africans across the Atlantic involuntarily, dehumanizing them in unimaginable ways, left indelible patterns rippling across the sociocultural, political, and ontological formations emerging from these major demographic and geographic shifts. About 12.8 million Africans are estimated to have been shipped across the Atlantic, although the number is higher when including the individuals who died during the journey. This demographic shift was a massive subtraction from Africa and a substantial addition to the Americas, and it induced long-lasting cultural alterations and wide-ranging societal changes.

On a very basic level, slavery changed the demographic and cultural diversity of Blacks at home and abroad.[3] Enslaved Africans had their expressive cultures and knowledge systems transferred with them from Africa, arriving in America with an assortment of cultural ideologies that shaped the fabric of the diaspora. It became a place of cultural synthesis, hybridism, and miscellany.[4] These plastic expressions and their guiding philosophies became modes of survival and resistance, continually reworked to fit the spatial and experiential demands of the new inhabited regions that would eventually become the Black Diaspora. These transported cultural expressions, often coded as channels of resistance and hidden from the exploitative scrutiny and reproach of slave masters, became significantly different from their original forms—they were inadvertently "diasporically re-worlded."[5]

The Black Diaspora was created through this process of forceful removals, abrupt emplacements, and radical alienation. It harbored tensions between ideas of the past and ideals of the present, as conflicts between the past and the future required practical ways to navigate the resulting ideological distance. The demographic constitution of continental Africa and the diaspora bore the burden of slavery's intrusion, and both spaces calcified around the fissures that it created. These fissures are more than ideological—they manifest physically and define what it means to be Black, African, and "at home," as well as what those mean for those in the diaspora or migrants located within either or both spaces. Going by popular figures and knowledge of transatlantic slavery, the forced Black Diaspora represents the first major African migratory concentration outside the continent. The formation of this Black Diaspora had rippling effects on the construction of other diasporas like the

African Diaspora. For context, migration in present-day Africa dates back to the fourth century in Mali.[6]

The relations that shape the spaces of home and diaspora—as sites of European injustices/encroachment and as sites inhabited by the descendants of enslaved Africans—mimicked, revised, and reproduced in varying degrees the tensions and estrangements that created the diaspora. Years after the transatlantic slave experience, its ghost still torments the present and threatens its configuration. This is partly due to the continuing survival of the subtle, potent structures that induced and supported colonialism and the slave trade. It is also due to the persistent inequalities that shaped the circumstances of the past and continue to exert their influence over the present. The diaspora is a site of struggle shaped by decades of history involving intrusion, removals, and displacements visited on the Black body from within and without. The enslavement of Africans had guilty parties on both sides of the Atlantic, meaning that inter-racial tensions, borne of misunderstanding and mistrust, also added to the character of the diaspora.

To speak in the terms of Du Bois, the souls of Black folk are subjected to repressive forces from within and without. Attacked by seemingly unstoppable forces from both sides of the continental divide, these souls can only be assuaged by the fickle promise that lies in protean and quixotic assurances of racial ties, Blackness, and connections to home, otherwise known as roots. These are unstable cleavages, subjected to continual revision by cultural elites exploiting profitable and self-serving formations. The meaning of Blackness is highly sociocultural, contestable, and depends on the context within which it is deployed. However, "Africa as motherland" has been rejected by advocates who oppose the idea of returning diasporic Blacks to Africa. These malleable identity structures owe much of their definition to the forces that created, engineered, and facilitated the transatlantic incident, or they owe their essence to the consequences of such cataclysmic events.

The factors directly responsible for colonialism and slavery in Africa can be traced to Europe, fueled by ideologies that glamorized European modernism. Once Europe was accepted as the benchmark against which all cultural standards are measured, the evil enterprise was supported as a civilizing mission. Capitalism and the control and mobilization of resources, while not tied to any single period in history, are principal features of the modern-day state. They have become political staples due to their particularly emphatic stress on competition and the formation of group identities related to resource acquisition. After the ideological machineries of Western Europe were at full throttle, all the frauds of state practices and the shortcomings of capitalism as an economic philosophy were embraced as stable modern phenomena. The creation of the diaspora followed the competition for resources, which was the impulse behind slavery. This ideology is ingrained into the fabric of the diaspora as a space of identity contest and construction; it is the foundation upon which it was set, evident in the lives of its inhabitants.

When tensions peak—especially when those tensions were created by a history of forced migration, estrangement, ideological disparity, longing, and competition for resources—the outcome manifests as space-specific experiential conditions. These conditions shape the imagined ideas of belonging and nonbelonging as well as the conceptions of home and abroad. Group ideologies are developed that characterize spaces as alien, hostile, or welcoming.

The African Diaspora is a space where negotiations of identity and belonging take place in front of a backdrop of ideas viewing Africa as home. African migration and resettlement can be examined within a frame composed of the rich history of mobility, physical shifts, and epistemological reconfiguration supporting the idea of the diaspora as "home away from home," considering how this weighs on African migrants and their relationship with Africa as the motherland. Migrants exist within a bifurcated reality that affects their construction of home and the localization of reminiscent homemaking practices.

This chapter explores how the realities of host spaces—as either hostile or hospitable spaces—and the lived experiences of migrants instigate reconsideration of images where Africa is dominant. To achieve this, it approaches the diaspora as a midpoint between lived spaces and ideal spaces, a Third Space, where African migrants tactically renegotiate their identities. By experiencing the diaspora as a liminal space between lived and ideal spaces, African migrants shape and reshape their imagination and available narratives of Africa. These actions determine how they conceive of Africa. How does the diaspora affect and effectuate African migrants' (re)thinking of Africa? This dynamic interaction demands a great deal of contextualization to unpack the intricate situation of being trapped between spaces, the reality of the diaspora as crossroads, and the dual mindset attuned to host spaces and places of origin in order to reveal the intricacy of the relation. To set these premises in sharp focus, the idea of space can assist with comprehending and emphasizing how homemaking and identity building are bound up in spatial dynamics and how such dynamics affect migrant imaginations.

This book provides a multidimensional view of African memoirs written in the diaspora: epistemological, political, and even sociocultural. The book situates the realities of the African Diaspora in the United States in relation to their African homelands and their new homes. The memoirs examined focus on human dilemmas such as wars, political instability, and slavery. Furthermore, this book is a critical evaluation of immigrant stories, examining new intersections of texts and spaces that open up theoretical and practical possibilities in the areas of memory and memoir studies. Memoirs are more than just random stories; they are composites of experiences not just from the author but also from a community of people. The authors of these haunting, compelling memoirs are mirrored representations of the realities of individuals who had not been able to record their thoughts and experiences. The book elevates the essence of orality and language, which are at the forefront of African and Afrocentric epistemologies.

This work highlights the philosophical, historical, and cultural insights of memoirs, making contributions to several relevant debates in diaspora studies. The goal is to understand the factors that contribute to each memoir's experiences and capture aspects of lives that are unique. Historical and cultural factors make immense contributions to the experiences of the selected authors, and the book provides new ways to understand memoirs in relation to their authors' regions of origin.

This is a contribution to existing literature and dialogues on diaspora studies, African American studies, and Africana studies. The book analyzes common grounds in freedom narratives, the place of Africans in Africa and in the diaspora, the efforts made by Africans in the diaspora seeking to influence politics back home, and the influence that current Africans in the diaspora have on the next generation of Africans in the diaspora. The full agenda of this book is to examine themes such as home, culture, new home, Afropolitanism, Afrocentrism, multiculturalism, universalism, and multiple identities, which can offer new insights into the philosophical, historical, sociocultural, and political content of African memoirs written in the United States.

There is an existential interconnectedness between Africans in the diaspora, their native homelands, and the United States; the realities of all three have become interwoven and inseparable. This connection underlines all of the topics addressed and evaluated in the book. It is important to examine the connection of the context of the diaspora and how they connect to the stories to be analyzed in the book to emphasize how the African Diaspora interacts with the elements of their environment, home and abroad. Particularly, Njie highlights typical concerns of Africans in the diaspora; how they navigate new worlds while maintaining strong attachments to Africa and strong affinities with their African roots and identities. Njie's memoir shows that Africans in the diaspora become actively involved in the politics of their home countries. Ever since the slave era, the attachment of Africans in the diaspora has had a sense of nostalgia—they never abandon their fascination with the countries they leave behind.

As a major concept too, transnationalism is a social phenomenon that has shaped the memoirs examined in this book. The central idea of this work is to focus on the link between the original countries of Africans in the diaspora and their new countries of residence. According to Thomas Faist,

> Over the past decades, the concepts of diaspora and transnationalism have served as prominent research lenses through which to view the aftermath of international migration and the shifting of state borders across populations. The research has focused on delineating the genesis and reproduction of transnational social formations, as well as the particular macro-societal contexts in which these cross-border social formations have operated, such as "globalisation" and "multi-culturalism." Although both terms refer to cross-border processes, diaspora has been often used to denote religious or national groups living outside an (imagined) homeland, whereas transnationalism is often used both more narrowly—to refer to migrants' durable ties across countries—and, more widely, to capture not only communities, but all sorts of social formations, such as transnationally active networks, groups and organisations.[7]

Diaspora studies intertwine with a transnational agenda to crush boundaries, synthesizing localism and globalism, as well as maintain the specific details of individual cultures in a broader, transforming global landscape. These forces are evident in Assensoh's and Njie's memoirs. They show how individuals in the diaspora reminisce and how countries have sought help from their people in the diaspora. Africans in the diaspora have learned from their new homes, and they want to share that knowledge with their native homes. Maria Koinova discusses Africans in the diaspora in the following relevant manner:

> Socialised with liberal values in Western societies, Diasporas might be expected to be interested in promoting such values in their homelands. Indeed, this often occurs in the transnational space. Diasporas teach their extended families and friends about democratic practices, such as how to vote for local government and to develop gender equality norms—a process termed a transfer of "social remittances" ... Diasporas do not only use democratisation discourses, they also promote minimal democratic procedures in their homeland. These practices are mostly related to electoral pluralism and rotation of power of local elites rather than to liberal aspects of democratisation

associated with human, minority or gender rights. Diasporas advocate these democratic procedures for nationalist and other particularistic purposes.[8]

Individuals in the diaspora participate in the growth and development of their homelands. Members of the African Diaspora pay diasporic taxes and contribute to the development of their countries—intellectually, politically, socially, and economically.

Through the years, the African Diaspora has had affinities with Africa in many ways. The new African Diaspora can help younger generations of Africans in the diaspora to maintain those affinities. To address the concerns of Du Bois's double consciousness, there must be intentional efforts to create structures and communities to transmit the customs, values, and traditions of their African ancestry. Babatunde understands the task at hand, and acknowledging the duty of parents raising Black children, he writes:

> Kelebogile and Ayinla set out the crucial steps for their family's corporate venture as total commitment to the goal expressed, complete and total respect of each other, loyalty to every member of the family, discipline expressed in informing action with a sense of morality and accepting responsibility, inculcating the sense of decency based on mutual respect and doing to others what they would like done to them, and working hard to make their dreams for the family come through. The most basic infrastructure needed to make these desires materialize was to be fully committed to inculcating the key elements of success in America mixed with the key elements of their African culture.[9]

He also states:

> Kelebogile and Ayinla discovered a lot of recent African Immigrants who have done very well in America seemed to prefer the American white upper middle class ways of raising children as the ideal to successful existence in America. However, in this family, they chose to be selective in bringing up their children who were born in America. Since these children would go to school, university, and pick up their professions as American citizens in America, it was important they would also bring to bear the unique aspects of the culture of their parents from their lands of origin. Their children would also learn what the key elements for success in America are. Their parents would

select the best elements of American and African cultures that they would be schooled in.[10]

Babatunde has outlined the task at hand for the new diaspora. The positive values of American life and its constructive lessons must be syncretized to develop the next generation of the African Diaspora. These people can be transnational, recognizing that they should not be limited by the boundaries of a single nationality. The idea of being transnational is to have more than one identity. The task of the new diaspora is enormous. Its members must maintain affinities with their homelands while finding ways to survive in the realities of their new homes. In many ways, this situation has been constant through time.

SPACE (AFRICAN DIASPORA) AND MIGRATION

Space is integral to the construction and forging of identities, as well as the sustenance of imaginations, touching on interconnections between ideals and notions of home—it encompasses the manifest realities invalidating or ensconcing those ideals. The exploration of space can open up avenues to consider connections between spatial politics or the politics of space, understanding the ways that dominant and subaltern imagined images are created and maintained. This ties to the relation between African visions of home, the migration of Africans into diasporic spaces, and the effects of the latter on the former.

It is critical to differentiate between the terms "space" and "place." The concept of space frequently involves a shifting, time-bound, and impermanent thing, often attributed to something that is located and opened up within or without a more "grounded material and specified place."[11] The pivotal distinctions between space and place are that of temporary versus permanent, malleable versus fixed, and time-constrained versus unbounded. De Certeau's conceptualization of both terms attributes a political quality to place, viewing it as a physical sign or material symbol of those who have the power to possess, control, and secure space.[12] For de Certeau, space is the realm of the subaltern, the Other, who deploys tactics that counteract the possessive and administrative tendencies of those who are "gatekeepers" for places. These tactics, which are a result of the absence of power that comes from control, are calculated attempts to counterbalance the power of those who own places. He considers space to be a specific politicized locale within a place.

Putting it succinctly, "the space of a tactic is the space of the other."[13] Tactics are located in places controlled by others through strategies, which signifies places as self-constitutive and self-sustaining base forms. Spaces, as ensconced within places, are driven by tactical choices and sustained as a home for the disposed, powerless, and marginalized. Places are managed by strategies of control that can be political, economic, or religious. Dudgeon and Fielder, corroborating this strand of use, assert that strategies are deployed imperialistically to take and maintain control of places by higher colonialist or state powers. In contrast, the tactics of the relatively powerless are oppositional, agentive, opportunistic, momentary, and isolated—they are not state-centric and they do not translate beyond measures of resistance to create modes for visibility and survival. As such, "Relatively powerless groups have to operate tactically or simply survive and make do . . . which occurs at both an individual and collective level."[14]

Although de Certeau's postulation tends toward the highly specialized, it coincides with the more popular conception of subaltern spaces as micro- and mini-publics within larger, more policed social spaces. This echoes some of the assumptions ascribable to counter-publics, or spaces of dissent within state-owned and state-controlled spaces.[15] On another level of signification, de Certeau's position reflects Bhabha's Third Place to a substantial extent; also, it echoes Henri Lefebvre's and Relph Edwards's position on real (physical) and ideal (socio-mental) spaces. The former signifies a concrete place of social practice, and the other is an abstract socio-scape.

Ideal spaces are homes of dissent, providing the tactics necessary to subvert the strategies of control native to the real space (de Certeau's "place"). Although the terms they use have different implications, they do meet at crucial intersections to delineate types of spaces and their political implications for sociocultural life. All places are spaces constructed and guided by processes and products of sociopolitical maneuverings; de Certeau classifies these as tactics and strategies. His delineation is useful, providing general information about the politics of inhabited places and spaces, but this study must conceive of both place and space as spaces. Ideas behind delineation, such as lived spaces that contrast with the imagined or the ideal, as opposed to the real, provide more relevant distinctions. This discussion will mostly refer to spaces, providing appropriate clarification where special distinction needs to be made.

Like any space populated by people, the African Diaspora is subject to codes of conduct and rules of engagement that allow individuals to negotiate identities, forge collective bonds, and operate within the boundaries set by accepted patterns of behavior. For this reason, space is often pivotal in conditioning citizens or members of society. It is the vantage point from where individuals assess and access their portion of the universe. It also provides a frame of reference for exploring, navigating, and negotiating the differences that constitute the universe. Space, as a physical manifestation of the rules and codes governing identity and conduct, bears lasting implications on the processes of being. This reflects on space as a conditioner.

Space provides the stimuli that shape orientation and action, acting as a framework shaping inhabitants and their responses to life's demands. From this frame, collective identities can be forged and nationalist sentiments can be pushed and pursued. This is especially true when space is in its active capacity, conceived in form of spatial ties or ancestral bonds, to provide or serve as a necessary cohesive factor. Space can act or be made into a resource for mobilization, which is possible when space is seen as more than a physical property (place), constituted of malleable and fixed social features.

The institutions, practices, and cultural codes that make up space are some of these conditioning features. They demonstrate one quality of space as an abode with defined boundaries or as a signifier of a specific prevailing consciousness. They can also accommodate or promote the flowering of subaltern, marginal, or other mini-spaces as counter-public spaces—these spaces of dynamic performativity or cultural change and exchange are contoured by protean, makeshift, contrived, and shifting identities. Tactics and strategies can enable Victor Turner's liminal space as a space of "inbetweenness." Although challenged as lacking constitutive materiality,[16] this quality of spatial ambiguity and temporal dislocation makes it essential as a border space, which Bhabha describes as a "realm of the beyond"[17] and Kalua labels as the space of contest. According to Bhabha, this space is that of "borderlines of the present . . . the moment of transit where space and time cross to produce complex figures of difference and identity, past and present, inside and outside, inclusion and exclusion . . . [for] there is a sense of disorientation, a disturbance of direction, in the 'beyond.' "[18]

This space is the realm of the midpoint, consisting of border spaces or culturally invisible zones between ideal and real spaces. Kalua clarifies this connection, arguing that Bhabha's conception of the liminal space as an ambiguous space provides avenues for rejecting structures and hegemonic forces. As an abstract reality, it explains how people occupy multiple spaces and how the strategies used in negotiating their identities and dealing with existent narratives shape their realities.[19] According to Dudgeon and Fielder, Bhabha's conception of liminality as a specific realm, providing directions for his Third Space thought, is the "fissure in between ostensibly seamless [ideal space as space of fluidity] and stable places [as space of fixity]."[20] As a space, it is prone to being opened up, just as in the case of an ideal space. However, forces of control remain prominent, reminding us of the strategies of control that are native to real spaces. For Bhabha, a pure and non-heterogeneous cultural space is nonexistent—everything occurs in that space of "in-between."

Here, space refers in the general sense to the environment where everything occurs. This environment has been theorized as having an immense number of symbolic meanings[21] for exactly this reason: it ferments a multitude of essentialities and non-essentialities. Often, space is portrayed as an embodiment of the sum of those who inhabit it and the sum of their differences. A space can be the physical part of a society, a signifier of general attitude, an index of a specific portion in history; a landscape, conditioner, character,[22] or system of related living persons; or related matrixes of difference. These multiple conceptual realizations of space lead literature to approach it or conceptualize it as lived, real, or imagined space.[23]

Several conceptions of space emphasize the individual's place within it. A space is partly defined by its inhabitants or their relation to and sense of it. An individual's proximity to, reception of, and attitude toward a place goes a long way in determining how space is characterized and known. As inhabitable environments, spaces or places are less fixed in their distinctions related to how they are regarded but largely shaped through second- and third-party perception. Space, as an entity, is shaped by the perception of it, and this perception is exhibited through placement within it and ideological proximity to it. Where space is definable in relation to the perception of people, what is real and imagined (as types of places) becomes subjective—they are shaped by subjective positioning. This complication has been addressed by arguing that space is not generally fixed in its definitions or representations; it represents unity between reality (real) and perception (ideal).[24] This is a useful compromise, which Edward places in perspective while arguing that space is a bond between man and place. To him, "People are their space and a place is its people [so] to have roots in a place is to have a secure point from which to look out on the world, a firm grasp of one's own position in the order of things, and a significant spiritual and psychological attachment to somewhere in particular."[25]

Edward's position emphasizes many things, starting with the possibility of an ideal as well as a real space. Henri Lefebvre identifies the former as a mental category that is also symbolic, while the latter is a physical space of social practice—even though, as he succinctly puts it, both presume and emphasize each other—which is often the case.[26] This guidance supports the concept of space as unity between perception and reality. Knox and Marston also categorize the ideal space as semiotically constructed and the real space as a physical and social construct.[27] The second emphatic point gleaned from Edward's position is the value of individuality and human collectivity for designating the character of a place. Both enable the appreciation of the way that notions of belonging and nonbelonging, exclusivity and inclusivity, and other essentializing categories are anchored in a collective sense of identity. This can typify a particular space as welcoming or hostile. This perspective also underscores the process through which the ideal and the real character of places are attained.

Isabel Hoving offers a similar template for understanding place in her consideration of space as manifesting in real, imagined, or lived forms. Real space is a physical structure, while imagined space is psychological, reinforcing Lefebvre's categorization. There are some differences in their conceptions, but both Hoving and Lefebvre mirror Tim Cresswell's well-accepted assumption that spaces are products of social engineering.[28] Spaces are founded on principles of collectivism, such as those drawn along the lines of nationalism, racism, ethnicism, or any other social construct. Spaces exert psycho-emotional influences on inhabitants, whether or not they are potential occupants, by inducing situations of inclusion and exclusion to fulfill nationalist and cultural mandates. It has repeatedly been put forward that spaces are best treated as real and imagined, as abstract and tangible, as fixed and fluid, and not only as protean but also susceptible to redefinitions and reconstitution of their essentialism. Acknowledging that spaces work in such nondefinite manners accepts that spaces can have emotional and psychological implications for inhabitants.

By occluding fixed definitions of spaces underscored by essentializing postures or exclusionary conceptions, one can promote multiple positionalities—people experience places differently, and their views of such places can be legitimized without running the risk of being seen as an exception. A place is defined by the experiences of its people, and "people of different classes, ethnicities, ages, etc. will experience a particular place in different ways that may often be at odds with the dominant representation of that place,"[29] which demonstrates both fixity and fluidity in the construction of space. What is fixed can be altered, which emphasizes the incessant shifts of space as the midpoint between the imagined and the real. That which is real and imagined is determined by the subjective positions of a space's inhabitants.

The idea of Bhabha's Third Place is essential to understanding this union; it consolidates these thoughts by tying real and imagined spaces together. As a lived and inhabited space, replete with performances and exhibitions of the individual and collective self, the Third Space moves beyond the boundaries of materiality and immateriality. By defining this space as a place of performance and practice, Creswell and Lefebvre point our attention to a crucial point: spaces can be conceived of in ways that are radical and non-essentialized, open to multiple reimaginations, and subject to several struggles of ownership—between tactics of resistance and strategies of control, and between imaginations of nativity and performance of (non)belonging.[30] Spaces can exist as products or symbols of performance and practice, and Third Places or midpoints mediate between lived experiences and imagined expectations. This disallows any form of essentialism while allowing marginal and marginalized claims of cultural ownership to shift to the center, which delegitimizes exclusivist and homogenizing tendencies specific to lived spaces, intensifying the radical quality that shapes ideal spaces.

Bhabha's conception of the Third Place points to a place of multiple cultures and plural ownership of culture. He defines this midpoint as a space belonging to none and all, existing as a meet point of multiple cultures.[31] The Third Place is a lived space, continually shifting its essentialism and definition by accommodating reinterpretations of its material composition based on experiences and perception, which echoes its strong leaning toward idealism. To cite Claudia V. Camp, a Third Space as lived and malleable space is a "creative recombination and extension, one that builds on a Firstspace perspective that is focused on the 'real' material world and a Secondspace perspective that interprets this reality through 'imagined' representations of spatiality."[32]

Acknowledging this nature of space encourages an understanding of diasporic places as spaces in between, located only in a realm where real and imagined are perpetually trapped in a state of collision. In these places, tactics of survival are deployed against dominant imaginations, against state-sponsored oppressive mechanisms, and against indigenous standards and exclusivist codes of belonging—the momentary and continually shifting realm of the subaltern is politically located within fossilized, closed-up, strategically controlled, and imperialistically governed places. Drawing from de Certeau, the temporary and shifting nature of the diaspora makes it a zone of opportunism, "driven by tactical choices," where visibility is contested and survival is achieved through calculated risks. This space is spatially nowhere, connecting the time-shifting, impermanent, and opened-up space of the dispossessed and subaltern with the fixity and closed-up structures of a more grounded space that is controlled by imperialistic forces. In Bhabha's terms, it is the fissure between the seamless and the stable, continually threatened by authorities striving to "pin down, close, or paste over" it.

The African Diaspora is a space of multiple cultures reinventing and hybridizing themselves; it also borders the present and the past as a moment perpetually transiting across spatial and temporal boundaries. It creates tensions, differences, exclusions, inclusions, disorientation, alienation, and the disturbance of that which is perceived as real and as imaginary. Accompanying all these is the intersection of the vague, complex, radicalizing, and open nature of ideal spaces existing as micro-structures within the essentializing and fixed construction of real spaces as macro-structures, as well as the constant interruption of one by the other.

African migration to the Global South has continually increased, partly because the rate of development in the Global North is exponentially different from that of many African countries and chiefly because the forces displacing Africans from the continent have also increased. Underdevelopment in many African states is encouraging a consistent outflow of population, which largely dictates the nature and level of migration flows. Africa is seen as a continent of migration and displacements induced by privation, ordeal, trauma, and distress, as well as bloodshed and conflict between several groups.[33] The political, economic, and socioreligious conditioning affects migrants psychologically; they are forced to construct ideals from alien environments, seeking them out as improvements over their original location. Migration is an event and a process that alters personalities. Reorientating persons as individuals and in groups induces changes on psychological and sociocultural levels, manifesting as a complex and multilayered stimuli of personality change.[34]

Living conditions have immense effects on the conception of space in the framework of hostility or friendliness, as well as the extent to which inhabitants consider themselves as belonging or alienated. Prosperous nations foster higher levels of nationalism, which slows the tide of emigration. However, national prosperity also attracts immigration and encourages exclusivist sentiment—frequently in response to a perceived threat from immigrants who may compete for resources. Flahuax and Haas suggest that countries with growing economies transition from net emigration countries to net immigration countries[35] because wealth attracts immigration and decreases outward population movement.

Many African countries rank as some of the poorest nations in the world for reasons that include poor economic and fiscal policies, low life expectancy at birth, poor schooling systems, low potential for human development, and broad cross-sectional corruption. In Mozambique, about 64 percent of its citizens live below the poverty line, while their gross national income is estimated to be $1,093, and their life expectancy is 58.9 years.[36] Other African countries that consistently appear on lists of the world's poorest countries include Mali, Benin, Chad, Guinea-Bissau, Guinea, and Burkina Faso.

Several African countries rank low on the Corruption Perceptions Index (CPI), with an average regional score of 32. Despite being the fifth largest oil-producing nation globally and first in the continent, Nigeria ranks very low on the CPI. Its score is 26 out of 100.[37]

The narrative of migration in Africa has followed a north-south paradigm. African countries are continually referred to as nations in motion; the entire continent is often seen in this context. There have been counteracting arguments,[38] but most narratives cast Africa as impoverished, a conflict zone, and largely uninhabitable or unprogressive. Flahuax and Haas conclude that the continual projection of Africa in such a state betrays a lopsided rationale—it ignores Euro-American migration flows to Africa. They claim that "in recent years, irregular migration from Africa to Europe has received extensive attention. Sensationalist media reportage and popular discourses give rise to an image of an 'exodus' of desperate Africans fleeing poverty at home in search of the European 'El Dorado.' Millions of Africans are believed to be waiting to cross to Europe at the first opportunity."[39]

Some of these migration narratives may contain a grain of truth, considering the stories of desperate attempts and disastrous experiences of Africans crossing the Saharan desert to Libya in an attempt to reach Europe. Living conditions in African countries continue to engender a substantial exodus to Europe and America. However, remittances to Africa from the diaspora tell a different story from those that Flahuax and Haas identify as sensational and orchestrated. West Africa is said to be the chief beneficiary of such remittances, with Nigerians contributing about $11 billion out of the $40 billion from the African Diaspora in general.[40] To put the African situation in context, this sum exceeds the gross domestic product of some African countries—in its own right, it would rank as the twelfth most productive economy in Africa, between the Democratic Republic of Congo and Cote d'Ivoire.[41] Countries with larger economies provide migrant Africans with opportunities to remit money home. The allure of possibilities beyond the shores of Africa and the dismal circumstances of corruption and violence in African countries are the combined forces that have created the African Diaspora.

The search for an "El Dorado" has led to the creation of the African Diaspora, which has complex implications for a migrant's memories of home or understanding of what home means. Ideas of sedentariness and motility undercut one another, but they are recurrent features of popular conceptions of home. Highlighting one quality superimposes the other, given that home is experienced and conceived of contextually, although seeing home as a place of origin fixes it as immobile. Conceptions of home are tied to both nationalist and transnationalist aspirations, undergirded by the currents that uphold these base cleavages, meaning that networks and connections always exist to trace home from places of origin to places of settlement. Ideas of home are commonly proffered as fluid, dependent on experiences. In its position between more fixed and malleable positions, home is underscored by fixed and easily shifting assumptions.

Another reason for the complex conceptions of home as fixed or mobile is whether places are hostile or hospitable. This usually depends on to what extent the codes, politics, and persons of that space create an atmosphere that is welcoming or exclusionary—it creates confusion and compounds the idea of home with regard to migrants in ways that increase nationalistic, postnationalistic, and ambivalent posturing toward home. This complexity cannot be ignored, which is why Ralph and Staeheli advocate for the concept of home as dynamic and moored, mobile and sedentary. To them, "home is experienced both as a location and as a set of relationships that shape identities and feelings of belonging."[42] Although this approach corrects the assumption that home is a fixed location, which allows the exploration and foregrounding of the dynamism and experience-based value of "home," it tends to underweigh the importance of home's sedentary nature. Ralph and Staeheli put this problem in sharp relief, stating that "in highlighting the shifting and mobile meanings that migrants give to home, however, there has been a concomitant tendency to underplay the resilience of its stable, bounded and fixed interpretations."[43]

Two assumptions are necessary to proceed: 1) there is a dual consciousness of home residing within the migrant in the diaspora, consisting of the host locale and the place of origin, from which migrant views, navigates, and engages with the world; and 2) the imaginations of home or place of origin are affected or altered by the imaginations and experiences encountered in the host's space. Our knowledge of space further increases the complication of home as an indefinite thing since the concept of diaspora as home—where this is the case—is more of a Third Space. It becomes a space of negotiation and being in between, existing as an open space located amorphously within a more fixed, closed, and defined space threatening to dominate it with strategies of control. Double consciousness, a term articulated and employed by W. E. B. Du Bois as a paradigm of understanding race relations and (trans)nationalism in a multiracial and multiethnic setting, is really a triple consciousness for the African migrant. The useful question is, "where is home located?" This expression seems appropriate for the experiences of a migrant: is home the place of origin, the Third Space, or within the broader space that enables the creation of diaspora (Third Space)?

Du Bois's famous double consciousness summary of the African American condition has created room for theorizing on the Black situation in Africa. Its succinct take on the agonizing realities of race relations in America centers around the marginalization of Blacks and their exclusion from the American body politic, but its expansive philosophic base and wide-ranging discursive implications have led to its application in different contexts. It has been used to address the ugly reality of race relations in which the American creed and hegemonic repression of Blacks create conflicting responses to nationalist expectations and patriotic loyalty.[44] It has also been accepted as a succinct view of how Black identity is trapped behind estrangement, uncertainty, confusion, and duality.[45]

Robert Pack perceives double consciousness as a frame that addresses the enigma of being Black in America, or "how to be a Negro and a citizen."[46] By expanding the scope of its frame, it can account for the "existential twoness" of third-world persons existing within the boundaries of the United States. In his adaptive use of Du Bois's position, Robert Blauner uses the term "existential twoness" to explain the simultaneous imperatives of satisfying nationalistic and integrative expectations, trying to belong while also maintaining distinctive nationalistic sentiments—cultural awareness and social belonging indicate the presence of a twofold consciousness.[47] David Wight interprets double consciousness as a struggle between two kinds of nationalism, and the idea of "doubleness" reflects a "timeless lament about the potential psychological ravages of racism and oppression" in America, serving as a rallying call for cultural pluralism.[48]

Du Bois's idea had African Americans at its center, but its uses, presuppositions, and relevancies address the fundamental political and cultural schisms inherent in America as a culturally polarized space. Blauner suggests that it provides a useful frame for explaining some of the experiential tensions faced by migrants in the diaspora, especially in America. Migrants exist between cultures, asserting their identities from a place of diversity. As a starting point, the concept recognizes this dualism (expressed as binationalism, dual consciousness, or bio-focality) while creating space for recognizing the discrete experiences of migrant Africans—different from African Americans, with homes outside of the borderless space of the diaspora and the borders of America.

African migrants manifest a level of Triple Consciousness: of belonging and not-belonging to the continually shifting Third Space, of America as the space of strategies of control, and of recognizing ties with Africa as a space of origin. This has implications for migrant imaginations and views of Africa. How does the African migrant, trapped between two worlds—with the diasporic Third Place serving as the crossroad—sustain, revise, or do away with dominant and marginal assumptions of Africa as a place of origin?

Africa: Home or Abroad?

For migrants and their lived experiences, diaspora can represent their perception of places of origin, which mirrors a causative relationship. African migrants, by virtue of their exilic lives, occupy space between two cultures and experience these spaces differently; their levels of integration or acculturation in one space influence their considerations of the other. The successful ability of migrants to ground relationships, and the sort of relationships that they localize, provide feelings of belonging in their present inhabited space that determine what and where they consider home. As a space of belonging, home is not solely a fixed entity, and it is not bound to a single place. The sense of home that some migrants have is negotiable from one context to another.

The act of moving, the underlying forces that necessitate moving, and place attachments shape the ability of migrants to achieve a sense of belonging. These forces also have implications for what home is and could be. One such implication is that migrants run the risk of remembering places of origin differently if the host space is welcoming; they may remember home more fondly if their host space is hostile. Tactics of survival and integration in new spaces, and their success at negotiating room to reconstruct their identities, determine whether migrants can localize and generate feelings that foster homeliness. The multiple ways migrants succeed or fail to ground their lives in alien spaces, along with home's non-sedentary nature, inflect constructions and perceptions of home.[49] As home becomes increasingly mobile and dependent on the nature, success, and gestures of place attachment, the idea of home as location-specific to African migrants, i.e., home existing in continental Africa, is threatened.

Migrants head to Africa in search of better life experiences, suggesting dissatisfaction with their places of origin stemming from unmet desires and difficult living conditions. This claim is not absolute; African countries have transitioned post-independence to become countries of net emigration. The mass exodus from Africa to Europe and America paints an unflattering image of Africa as home. To the extent that home is defined by sets of relationships that promote belonging and inclusion, the idea of Africa as home is threatened by the constant displacement of people through the violation of civil rights and ongoing ethno-religious and state-sponsored violence.

Africa has consistently experienced large waves of cross-border movement, from the slave trade to colonialism. This was further exacerbated by protracted military misrule and warped democratic practices in several African states.[50] Because these migrations were induced by the search for better alternatives, the image of Africa was negatively affected. The idea of home as mobile and not place-specific provides better contexts—spatial-conditioned relationships and feelings of belonging determine extensively how "at home" individuals feel. Localized relationships, qualities of specific places, and spatial-based affiliations also shape the sentiments that identify places as home.

Continued violence, corruption, and other drivers of migration from Africa consistently affect African migrants' consideration of Africa as home. This is more pronounced in instances where the host space provides the resources and values that the migrants had sought. In these situations, migrants are trapped between two places politically and culturally. In exchange for avenues to acceptance, such as residency, green cards, and naturalization schemes, migrants contribute to nation-building. They can exhibit a sense of place attachment and affiliation without detaching from the cultural nationalism that is often expected from or seen in migrants in the diaspora. The extent to which migrants are accommodated in the body politic determines their attachment to the host space and their views of Africa.

The survival methods and tactics of negotiation employed by migrants within diasporic spaces often provide them with more grounded and lasting relationships in host spaces. Diasporic spaces are sites of contestation and liminality, ensuring that migrants devise ways of "grounding their lives in multiple locations."[51] This fulfills a principal feature of liminal spaces: fluidity. The existential and experiential means of survival adopted by migrants in middle realms—like the diaspora, which exists within more defined host spaces—require fluidity and motility. They must be flexible enough to negotiate cultural codes and group dynamics for acceptance and belonging.

Ralph and Staeheli have noted that mobility as a survival strategy, grounding migrants' lives in alien spaces, is inflected with gestures of attachment.[52] Since the making of home in the context of globalization is also considered in terms of being mobile, mobility is not a movement away from home by default; it could be a movement toward one. This has two implications: Africa, the geographical terrain, can remain or stop being home for African migrants, and it can become a fluid realization of home that is not constrained by geography.

One must move beyond traditional notions of what home is and what it can be to recognize the ability to negotiate liminal identities and be fluid within diasporic spaces as the migrants' tools of homemaking. In migrant spaces, especially in a transnational framework and an increasingly globalized world, home remains an experiential matter. It is vital to comprehend how migrants inhabit spaces through movement, how home-making practices in foreign spaces affect imaginations of home, and how mobility and fixity, belonging and exclusion, and displacement and emplacement define the construction of home.

David Moley argues that to comprehend how migrants make home of/in foreign worlds, one must have a balanced understanding of the limits of the orthodox contrast between geography-based and traditional notions of home and globalized home-making practices, along with an understanding of how this distinction redefines what a home could be. Migrant tactics of survival are not the presence or absence of homeliness but space-specific experiences of home—migration is not tantamount to movement from home; it is an avenue for experiencing home differently.[53] Moley describes migrant lives in relation to the idea of home as producing two different ways of experiencing home, which emphatically creates a dual awareness of home.

Given the hybrid nature of most diasporic spaces, dual awareness can lead to arguments of a pure experience of home and a tainted one, which echoes the dynamic nature of experiencing lived spaces as opposed to idealized ones. African migrants experience home in more fluid, dynamic ways than their counterparts on the continent while remaining acutely aware of the sharp differences in experience. This open-ended argument is underlined by three crucial premises: Africa is a continuous project for migrants who redefine what it means and how it is home to them; Africa can be experienced as lived and ideal space for migrants, which allows for irreconcilable tension between their notions of Africa as tangible and abstracted in specific and localized relationships between human and nonhuman forces; and Africa's image in the diaspora is shaped by experiences in the diaspora, which are tied to the role of continental Africa as an instigator of the migratory experience. Africa's position in the migratory effort and the decisions of African migrants determine how experiences of and in host spaces are evaluated.

This supports the perspective of home as simultaneously mobile and sedentary, highlighting possible views of the idea of Africa and of viewing it in the diaspora. Apart from the apparent simultaneity of the notion of Africa as a fixed and unfixed home, mobility means that Africans can ground their idea of Africa in foreign spaces. Anchoring home in set of relationships and gestures of attachment makes it possible to construct one's sense of home around materials, practices, and objects retaining the necessary familiarity for establishing homeliness. This echoes Magdalena Nowicka's argument that home can be derived from rituals, habits, and routines that are attached yet motile.[54] Home can be constructed by domesticating specific relationships that do not rely on specific features of the currently inhabited space.

The material and the physical can be employed to retain ideas and memories, fueling attachments to places of origin, even when they are physically absent. In cases like this, home is preserved through material things and evoked through the act of transiting or inhabiting liminal spaces. Recognition of these possibilities for homemaking in foreign spaces has spiked interest in understanding how migrants establish dwellings through mobility or journeying and how journeying shapes their perception and construction of home.[55] Life in the diaspora is one of constant movement, requiring migrants to locate and relocate their lives, cultures, and experiences in several ways—keeping Africa's place as home in the process.

Material possessions and symbolic relationships assist with situating home in alien spaces because they are mediumistic or "connective markers." They provide links to geographies, enabling the forging of geographically based identities. The dynamic homemaking process that migrants experience in alien spaces often threatens Africa's place as home. The diaspora is a place of constant identity shifts and a persistent battle for control between the hegemonic forces of the host space and the resilient marginalized identity of the migrant. Possessions and other cultural items aid migrants in opposing strategies of control and the hegemonic interferences that characterize the diaspora as a space of contest. Ralph and Staeheli, reflecting on Nowicka's point of view, submit that "material objects serve to both buffer individuals from the pressures of outside cultures, but also help to forge a feeling of identity and belonging somewhere, if not necessarily in the particular place they may occupy at a given moment."[56] This acknowledges the importance of materiality in (re-)locating home, understanding that homemaking is fluid and not space-specific. The activity is often contingent on reiterating, reenacting, and localizing evocative relationships, bonds, and social processes in new spaces.

Arguments have been made implicitly and explicitly in literature tracing the survival of African cultural practices: home can be a location that is not fixed. These arguments, studying diasporic spaces from the period of transatlantic enslavement of Africans to contemporary migration, presuppose that what makes Africa has been retained in the diaspora via transportation and relocation. Africanity itself is a set of assumptions about reality and unique approaches to life that are ritualized into standards of being. The reiteration of these assumptions and the practice of these rituals in evocative ways are often needed to keep Africa alive beyond the shores of the continent or beyond the limits of a geographic construct. African migrants, either as slaves or émigrés, have retained characteristics of Africa in the diaspora to create a home beyond the continent.

Identity is often fluid, and African identity does not escape this condition.[57] Because the African Diaspora is located in a space fraught with tensions of belonging and nonbelonging, the various relationships, materials, and ideas of home can fluctuate or fail to generate the required homely feeling. The unstable nature of the diaspora as a liminal and constantly shifting state can upset the expected effects of localizing or reiterating patterns of relationship to maintain ideas and feelings of home. This unstable nature can yield unexpected results; migrants that successfully negotiate or tactfully belong to the new environment may begin to have altered views of Africa. It can also create a stalemate in which migrants are caught at a crossroad of belonging, feeling that they belong neither here nor there.

Conceptions of Africa can cease to reflect the idea of home beyond that of a place that has been emigrated from. The relationships upholding the idea of a home or a localized home can change, or conflicts within the diasporic space can pressure migrants into experiencing a disconnect between idea-based and real experiences of home. In these cases, home is emphasized as simultaneously a lived and ideal space. The anxiety, disillusionment, and confusion that accompany this bifurcated consciousness are heightened, causing a shift in their imaginary construct: the host space as either a promised land or a failed promise. In many cases, this conclusion shapes the belief of what and where home is.

DIASPORA: QUIXOTIC PROMISE OR THE PROMISED LAND?

The inhabitants of a place affect how welcoming it is through the actions of those who belong to it and the migrant's success or failure at penetration and integration. As Edwards posits, people are their spaces and vice versa. A migrant's ability to successfully integrate and exist outside the fringes of the host space's dominant culture creates a sense of fixity that assures homeliness, belonging, and a level of satisfaction. In essence, migration is the pursuit of or journey toward satisfaction. It is the quest for something either missing from the place of origin or present in inadequate quantities, although this quest is not necessarily a corollary of the usual economic or political impulses for migration. Sometimes, the need to experience new places is the sole reason, and this need is shaped by the presupposition that a new place will satisfy this need. The extent to which this is achieved largely rests on how successfully the migrant can integrate into the host community, determining whether this need is met or not.

Migration is a movement toward a promise or assurance that can only be verified after arrival and through lived experiences in new places. When migration is motivated by the search for better lives elsewhere, unmet migrant desires in host spaces can create a sense of longing for the familiarity of places of origin. The uncertainty of life in the diaspora, coupled with disappointment created by culture shock, can bring rejection and exclusion into sharp contrast with a feeling of rootedness associated with places of origin (despite the lack of fulfillment that instigated the migratory effort). In such cases, familiarity and feelings of rootedness are seen as currencies of support for home attachment and attachment-making that are unavailable in diasporic places. These connotations can strengthen the idea of fixed homes, even if they were not previously seen in this light. For African migrants, it is an adaptive response to experiences in the diaspora.[58] The evocation of strong attachments to places of origin can be a reactive coping mechanism for responding to unseemly or disappointing situations.[59] Africa is prone to being idealized or reimagined by migrants as a sedentary home, forced to see it in contrast to the disillusioned reality of the diaspora.

The idealization of Africa creates an impression of dissonance in migrants for two reasons. First, the power plays and conditions that necessitated migration do not need to change for a shift in perspective to occur; migrants may only need to experience multiple rejections, exclusions, and disappointments in alien spaces before longing for the physical space of Africa. Second, the romanticized and idealized view of Africa contrasts with the lived experiences that Africans are familiar with or that they have experienced before migrating—this replicates the tension between experiencing a place as both lived and idealized space.

Where the opposite is the case, and migrants achieve inclusion within the dominant culture, reactions to Africa as lived space is open-ended, and Africa may or may not be seen in a contrary light. The migrants' ability to achieve a perfect synthesis and sustain a sense of dual nationalism—maintaining their cultural heritage while belonging or being accepted to the body politic of the host space—seemingly completes the process of homemaking outside Africa. The bifurcated consciousness is reduced to an echo since migrants achieve "belonging" without being forced to excise the cultural and racial underpinnings that define their identities. In these instances, Africa remains the home of origin, the place of emigration, and a distant land to be remembered fondly while the new space becomes home.

Arguably, Africa becomes "abroad" to these migrants, and the new space becomes the "promised land."

Migrants rarely achieve such seamless transitions and the failure to integrate, along with its associated feelings, shape how Africa is viewed and what Africa means. This position is reflected by Ralph and Staehelo, who opine that "various power geometries influence complex registers of home."[60] The failure to experience host spaces as promised lands complicates perceptions of Africa; its extant narratives can be emphasized or revised. The fact that new, foreign, or host spaces may not be considered promised lands is exemplified by the idea of the diaspora itself. The diaspora is a liminal space with its own (amorphous, ambiguous, and person-specific) rules and regulations. In fact, the vague, ambiguous, and individuated nature of the diaspora constitutes its rules.

As a space, the diaspora is a crossroads, with the migrant trapped between two worlds while inhabiting three: ideal, lived, and Third Space. Experientially, the diaspora is the Third Space. Figuratively, it represents migrants' inability to belong to the new space while conforming to essentialist ideas of what constitutes Africa and who an African is, and vice versa. Given that the Third Space of the diaspora is a fissure between both worlds, it is a realm of constant negotiation and struggle for visibility and inclusion. As a space of counter-hegemony and displacement, from host spaces and place of origin, it is the realm of action and of strategic performance driven by the inability and the need to be included. Kalua's description of "a culturally busy stage and pivot of action"[61] accentuates its liminal character. Being caught in this crossroads affects migrants' affirmation or reenvisioning of Africa as an ideal or lived space, continuing to contest the image of Africa as it is trapped with migrants in this space.

Identity is a fluid, shifting thing. As its constant negotiation and redefinition are pursued and enacted in the diaspora, they can push migrants toward culturally and politically constructed benchmarks to determine inclusion, which indicates success and fulfillment. They can also shove migrants backward, indicating failure to belong and causing the type of disillusionment that engenders reconsideration of what Africa means as home. As the terrain of action, the diaspora allows for the establishment and localization of the relationships that determine the success of integration and the construction/conception of home. These practices and relationships aid in creating identities and achieving a heightened sense of belonging.[62]

To appreciate the impact of the Third Space—as a fusion of first and second spaces, or lived and ideal spaces—as the best representation of the realities and experiences of migrants, one must appreciate the fluidity of migrant identity and the practices of identity construction, which also owe to the nature of the Third Space. While diaspora means a collision of several dimensions of home, it also means that the migrant identity, experiences, and conception of home should be seen outside essentializing ideas of what Africa is or can be or what an African is. Kalua has expounded on this perspective by advocating for a more expansive view of Africa and moving beyond essentializing definitions of who an African is. These changes will aid in appreciating African migrants as Africans whose conception of and relation to Africa as home is a product of their experiences. Their identities are not the product of a single or unique home but the result of constantly evolving relationships with different worlds, past and present. For African migrants, Africa is not solely a fixed place. It is a product of the sum of failed or successful aspirations, met and unmet desires, localized relationships, and transferred patterns of bonding between material and nonmaterial forces.

Double consciousness, multiple spatial ties, and constant reconception of home are features of migrants, which implicate African migrants as a class of Africans whose relation, imagination, and conception of Africa are responses to how they experience host spaces.

AFRICAN DIASPORA MEMOIRS AND PLURIVERSAL IDENTITIES

The diaspora is a space of identity construction and homemaking rituals for Africans, existing outside the essentializing codes of belonging that underpin the African identity. The image of Africa in the diaspora and the ways that this image is constructed or received, owing largely to the diaspora's protean nature as a persistently fluid and constantly busy midpoint between lived spaces and ideal spaces. This character of the diaspora ensures that African migrants must consistently negotiate between two worlds—between Africa and the host space or between their ideal conception of spaces and their lived reality of those spaces—to trace out their own identity. Ultimately, the diaspora is a crossroad that amplifies the dual consciousness of migrants, affecting how their visions of Africa are constructed and maintained.

Members of the African Diaspora in the United States and elsewhere are pregnant with poignant and insightful stories to be birthed. The compelling tales of those who have migrated in recent times are affected by political instability, terror, corrupt institutions, and other factors that drive them from their natal homes. Their lived experiences are shaped by the undeniable force of cultural differences. When these migrants settle in Western countries, these cultural differences are related to communitarianism, the negation of individualism, and sociocultural shifts driven by interactions with other cultures.

The realities that confront migrants in the United States can either be discouraging or intimidatingly impressive. The earliest members of the African Diaspora consisted of slaves—who were forcibly captured and relocated to the United States—and their descendants. After gaining "freedom," they recounted detailed, graphic representations of their stories in strange lands that highlighted their harsh treatment under slavery and their experience in racialized spaces. The inhumanity of slavery and oppression is at the core of their memoirs. Centuries later, the descendants of these slaves and ex-slaves have wrestled with the same challenges, dealing with the problem of maintaining their ancestral links while struggling to develop their American identities. These experiences shape their memoirs and autobiographies.

Contemporary immigrants in the United States have had to contend with the realities of their native homelands and their new homes. Those who recently migrated from Africa often find themselves juxtaposing the realities of home and abroad, invariably leading to long conversations about cultural adjustments. They usually identify differences in institutional structures that make them reminisce about home, often encouraging them to demand change in Africa. African American memoirs also focus on the notion of identity or balancing the identity of having African roots with the identity of being American. The lived experiences of the new diaspora members and their quest for survival include mistakes and misgivings. At times, they may seem dysfunctional or confused. However, the migrants' challenges are resolved by undermining the barriers posed by race and eradicating self-doubt and feelings of unworthiness, allowing them to understand the limitations of the conventional "home" and what it means to "be at home in the world."

Personal narratives reveal the quality of life for African Americans in the United States. Those who have written memoirs focus on the fight against racial discrimination, the Black rights movement, the aftermath of slavery, and the resurgence of white supremacy. There are two different realities for established African American communities and those of the new African Diaspora. The reality of African Americans in the United States is defined by the country's history of slavery and decades of subjugation in segregated spaces. However, the United States presents new opportunities for contemporary African migrants who voluntarily change their geographic location. Their historical context of migration is not the same, which shapes their memoirs in different ways. Despite their differences in motives, African memoirs in the diaspora focus on a similarly broad range of existential and epistemological issues.

STRUCTURE AND OUTLINE

Various chapters use memoirs to put the realities of Africans in the diaspora into perspective. Overall, the book dwells on culture, politics, and cultural identity in the new diaspora memoirs and homeland, with an insightful conclusion on the evolution and lineage of immigrant stories. It focuses on the nature of African memoirs and immigrant stories, identifying what constitutes African memoirs. It reviews a series of immigrant stories that provide accounts from ex-slaves and freedom fighters. The synergy of these chapters puts the features of African memoirs into context, exploring the role they occupy in our understanding of society and laying the foundation for issues discussed elsewhere in the book.

Chapter 1, which is the introduction to the volume, examines and considers divergences and convergences of intellectual efforts in memoirs written in different eras, the shifting spaces and fixed crossroads in a bid to evaluate the impact of slavery, colonialism, globalization, Afropolitanism, and other concepts on migrant lives. The central idea is that these convergences and divergences show how two civilizations and cultures have historically, philosophically, politically, and intellectually influenced one another since the transatlantic slave trade. Africans in the diaspora teach us about the concept of African identity, offering a multicultural view of citizenship that molds the particularism and modernism of African identity with the eclectic universalism of global identity. This chapter lays the foundation for closing arguments in the final segment of the book.

The first four chapters critically examine the different tropes of the new diaspora and how they negotiate concepts of home and culture in their natal land within the ambits of four memoirs written by Njie, Babatunde, Afolayan and Assensoh. Overall, the thematic preoccupations explained by the memoirists range from culture to politics to tradition and, most importantly, to movements and travels around the world in a bid to ensure and create an idea about one's homeland. The second chapter in this book is titled "Culture and Cultural Politics" and uses Cherno Njie's *Sweat Is Invisible in the Rain* to demonstrate themes and distinct regional properties while focusing on the interaction of culture and politics in contemporary memoirs. It also discusses the importance of community spirit in the life of the individual and the politics of the nation. Politics and self-governance in postcolonial

Africa began with an agenda to reinvigorate indigenous African ideologies and philosophies to influence leadership and policies. These ideas are deeply rooted in the agenda of Julius Nyerere, Kwame Nkrumah, Nnamdi Azikiwe, and Obafemi Awolowo. These pioneering nationalists fought for and demanded independence from the colonial masters.

Njie argues that indigenous philosophies were misused and misrepresented. African humanistic principles such as tolerance, honor, and a sense of community are common across all the regions in Africa. It is often believed that Africans are essentially communalistic, possessing a sense of community and shared humanism as defining aspects of their existence. Njie's memoir explores this consciousness of togetherness through the sharing of roofs and responsibilities in a Gambian community. He praises the extension of love, care, and interdependence.

Like many memoirs from Africa, Njie's work describes the lifestyles of Africans and their commitments to community. Individualism is trumped by communitarianism, which elevates the collective's interest over that of the individual. The essence and interests of the individual are not completely discarded, but they are recognized in relation to the interests of all the individuals that make up the community. These African principles and tenets are shared through aphorisms, folktales, proverbs, and other forms of oral tradition. Njie's memoir displays the importance of oral tradition—these traditions allow concepts, ideologies, and the elements of a coherent value system to be passed from one generation to another. African epistemologies and ideologies are stored in orality, which is why Njie uses Wolof proverbs and folktales to make vital points in his memoir.

Njie discusses the spiritual and religious aspects of Gambian culture, narrating how Gambians in the United States offered collective prayers for him after his arrest. He also explains that Africans seek favors from the supernatural, especially benevolent spirits. This cultural behavior was thwarted by colonialism, Christianity, and Islam. Njie's memoir shows the impact of colonialism and white dominance on the historical experience of most African nations.

Africa's history cannot be told without including the effects of colonialism; it drove African nationalists to fight for self-governance and independence. Unfortunately, African leaders could not apply indigenous principles and philosophies effectively for legislation and policies after independence. The few African leaders who managed to propose African socialism misrepresented its ideas and philosophy, turning some of them into tyrants who provoked a series of coups and civil wars.

Njie uses his memoir to address the inadequacies and dictatorship of President Yahya Jammeh of The Gambia. It points out that Jammeh's presidency—which was marked by disregard for human life and the rule of law—was a complete abandonment of indigenous African political philosophy. Jammeh promoted self-serving policies that placed his own interests above those of the nation.

Furthermore, this chapter emphasizes the need for adherence to humanistic African principles at the community, national, and continental levels. It explores Njie's demonstration of loyalty to his homeland and asserts that the greed, corruption, and immoral acts of African leaders are not representative of what it is like to be African. This chapter also examines Njie's call for Gambians and Africans to embrace traditional African ideologies and principles to bring peace, stability, and growth to the continent. Jammeh's actions show the negation of African values and ideologies, but the actions of Njie and others in the diaspora demonstrate adherence to African humanism, displayed in their attitudes of loyalty to the community's interests at the expense of their own interests.

Memoirs are used by migrants to reminisce about things that tie them to home, and members of the African Diaspora have always been perplexed by the misdeeds of people in their countries of origin. The chapter looks at the culture that played a role in shaping Njie's life, covering his childhood in Africa, his adult life in the United States, and his interactions with other Gambians at home and abroad. Tenets of culture and cultural politics are presented in various forms to understand how his culture drove his consciousness to fight for freedom. Njie criticizes people who silently tolerate misrule and emphatically declares that Gambians in the diaspora must play a role in ousting Yahya Jammeh.

Njie's narration focuses on the benefits he gained from his parents, his community, and the Wolof culture. Culture transcends values, but it can show how values and principles affect institutions and practices. Njie analyzes culture to show that elders become oral historians and diplomats for the community, serving as the link between the past, present, and future. The Wolof culture, as with many African cultures, teaches tolerance, love, and collectivism. This chapter focuses on Njie's view of communitarianism and humanism as he promotes African communal values and systems as superior to individualistic tendencies. People from other cultures find it easy to adapt to new communities that share similar values—the cultural values of African communities embrace diversity, tolerance, multiculturalism, transculturalism, and interconnectedness. Like many Africans, Njie recognizes that communitarianism and the African cultural essence are built on the idea that one's existence is affirmed through the existence of others.

The third part of this book focuses on how cultures impact the lives of Africans, most especially the portrayal of the inextricably linked ideas of tradition and modernity. Chapter 3 examines Emmanuel Babatunde's representation of tradition and modernity in *Kelebogile I Am Grateful* to explore topics that include purification rites, panegyrics, womanhood, tradition, and modernity. This chapter dwells on tradition and modernity. Babatunde's work employs materials from African traditions that were founded on a set of customs and values before colonialism and the inroads of foreign religions and languages. These include proverbs, ceremonies, initiations, beliefs, and other aspects of Yoruba culture. His narration indicates that African ways of life, along with many traditions and customs, were truncated by the introduction of colonialism, Christianity, and westernization.

This chapter also analyzes the concepts of modernity and tradition, which are drawn along the lines of different religions, epistemologies, and social formations. Babatunde's early chapters center on Yoruba customs and traditional beliefs, such as reincarnation, witchcraft, and the potency of African medicine. Just as the lives of Iya Ayinla and Kelebogile show contrasts between modernity and tradition, similar comparisons can be made for the ritual of naming children in Yoruba cultures. Yoruba names traditionally have philosophical, sociological, historical, and circumstantial inclinations. The social shift to modernity has led Yoruba people to show a preference for foreign English names that express neither the values nor the customs of Yoruba tradition.

In addition, there is the overt consideration of Yoruba homes and family structures as part of their traditions—a vast classroom that teaches values and customs. Because the family structure knits the community together, the communitarianism of Njie's memoir begins with the family and the home front. This detail is common in African traditions before westernization; the unity of the family structure was part of the indoctrination that erased individualistic tendencies. Western culture, which is touted as the paradigm of modernity, replaces African traditions with individualism, which thwarts the communitarian and humanistic spirit.

Language is another aspect of culture in which tradition and modernity are represented and analyzed. The interactions between language and orality are part of the process that passes down cultural norms, beliefs, identities, and ideologies from one generation to the next. The nature of the Yoruba language, in its orality and power, is seen in its proverbs, folklore, and other expressions. It explains that the hermeneutic use of African languages is the best way to interpret African worldviews and ideologies. Foreign languages have affected language structure in Africa, and Africans pride themselves on raising children who speak foreign languages. African languages are dismissed as hoary and incapable of intellectualism in the modern world.

Representations of modernity are pitted against African traditions to show the differences in worldviews and ideologies of the African and Western worlds. Westernization has influenced African traditions and undermined traditional customs and beliefs. However, modernity can also be a liberating force, as is evident in the lives of Iya Ayinla and Kelebogile. Babatunde's memoir shows the possibility of cooperation between Western and African cultures, which can shape Africans in Africa and in the diaspora. Modernity, as presented in Babatunde's memoir, is only a Western conception of modernity. True modernity is multilateral and multicultural.

Babatunde's memoir validates the interdependence of cultures that shape the lives of Africans in Africa—they have come in contact with African culture through birth and Western culture through colonialism. He also demonstrates how the two cultures shape the lives of Africans in the diaspora; they continue to share African culture through ancestry while forging connections with Western culture through migration. This book's chapters on Babatunde's memoir examine the impact of African and Western cultures on worldviews, beliefs, and ideologies.

Womanhood is often defined in relation to motherhood, which has led scholars to ask whether motherhood is womanhood's zenith. Many African memoirists have shared their perspectives on womanhood, and writers and social commentators often lament how women are relegated to subordinate roles in African societies. African cultures have been accused of robbing women of their essence and dignity. Although Babatunde includes many female figures in his life, Kelebogile and Iya Ayinla are the most prominent.

A different picture of womanhood is visible in Babatunde's stories of Iya Ayinla. He describes dreadful conditions for women, maintained by Imeko traditions, as he discusses how witchcraft is seen as the manifestation of malevolent powers—a barren woman is considered to be a witch. Amongst the Imeko, Babatunde describes a view of womanhood that regards women as saviors who provide children to continue lineages for their husbands. Women are cared for, respected, and nurtured because they hold the key to keeping lineages alive through their offspring.

Babatunde conceptualizes womanhood as a phenomenon with four stages: the stage from birth to puberty, the stage when they are taught the ideal characteristics of womanhood, the stage from reproduction to menopause, and the stage from menopause to death. Womanhood is viewed as a process of growth, starting at birth, in which a child is raised to be a good woman. A woman is taught how to cook, sing, and look after her family. This social construct is built around the customs and the expectations of Imeko's womenfolk, who must recite panegyrics for their husbands, cook for them, and soothe them when they are upset.

In Babatunde's work, Iya Ayinla is shown defying customs and traditions that undermine the freedom and humanity of women. Her actions were enabled by the introduction of new, foreign cultures that accommodated a more rebellious approach. A careful look at Africa's precolonial history suggests that there were previous incidents involving rebellious African women, but the introduction of colonialism, Christianity, and westernization influenced the choices made by women and the notion of womanhood.

In this book, this chapter points out that differences in time periods and regions explain the contrasts of womanhood presented in Kelebogile's story and Iya Ayinla's life; they are the children of two different ages and cultures. Kelebogile dedicated her life to defining another dimension of womanhood. The realities of women in Southern Africa can be different from those in West Africa, and this chapter identifies societal expectations and definitions for women. In places where the interaction of Western and African cultures is diminished, there is less of a platform for eradicating the subjugation of women. Western cultures and modernity have helped women to redefine their essences. Babatunde focuses on the circumstances, limitations, and pressures that women face and examines how women overcome societal obstacles and defy social constructions. It also looks to shift from using biological factors for defining women to a consideration of their human capabilities, which transcend the social construct of being women. The chapter ends with a comparative analysis of womanhood in West Africa and South Africa, shown through the lives of Kelebogile and Iya Ayinla.

The derivation of meaning in the fourth chapter of this book uses the Yoruba culture to explore the interaction between African cultures and communities. The essence of a community includes the history, beliefs, and norms that create its culture—this part examines the nuances of language and orality coupled with the features of culture and communities in Michael Oladejo Afolayan's *Fate of Our Mothers*. Chapter 4 focuses on the Yoruba world as typified in Afolayan's recollections. The full extent of the Yoruba world includes Yoruba people living in Brazil, Cuba, Jamaica, Benin Republic, and elsewhere.

Afolayan explains that the Yoruba believe in supernatural forces that explain and offer solutions to various issues and mysteries. This leads to an examination of Afolayan's use of Yoruba metaphysical concepts to depict the Yoruba world. Afolayan shows the importance of *Ori* (inner head) in the Yoruba journey through life, exploring beliefs, taboos, and superstitions. Like

Babatunde, Afolayan discusses the place of reincarnation and the afterlife in the Yoruba worldview, describing the tangible influence that the belief in reincarnation exerts over the choice of names in Yoruba culture. This chapter also examines how cultural details determine the experience of a people, considering how stories in any culture are permeated by its cultural norms, traditions, and ideologies. The experiences and stories in Afolayan's memoir are shaped by the traditions and beliefs of the Yoruba world. One such tradition is the belief in folk remedies or traditional medicine.

Also, it takes a critical look at the cultural customs and rites that deal with marriage, polygamy, and polygyny. Afolayan's work corroborates many claims from Babatunde's memoir, which is to be expected when both Afolayan and Babatunde are Yoruba. One example is the issue of womanhood and motherhood. The Yoruba world cannot be depicted without including the essence of valor that characterizes women and mothers. Afolayan shares stories that validate motherhood as the zenith of womanhood, describing women as custodians of wisdom. This chapter also considers the ideas of collectivism and communal responsibility in relation to individualist principles, seen in the ideas about communal living shown in Babatunde's and Njie's memoirs. This chapter confirms that Africans are essentially and culturally communalistic, concluding that Afolayan's memoir, *Fate of Our Mothers*, paints an apt illustration of the Yoruba through its exploration of language, religious beliefs, customs, and ideologies.

This chapter focuses on Afolayan's use of language, orality, and the sense of communitarianism. The history of Africa cannot be told without including the influence of colonialism and Western culture on the lives, languages, worldviews, and ideologies of African communities—this influence has ensured the dominance of European languages in Africa. Afolayan's use of language in the memoir is an innovative transcription of Yoruba experience through the English language, and its text includes an inherent nexus of English and Yoruba languages to emphasize lessons from the Yoruba culture. This chapter acknowledges that language gives the memoir its meaning; Afolayan uses language to depict the changing sociological world of the Yoruba people and Nigeria at large.

Afolayan's use of English and Yoruba languages pursues a distinct agenda, showing how English has become the language bridging the cultural and linguistic barriers due to Africa's multicultural formation. Afolayan uses Yoruba in the memoir to impart epistemological and moral lessons. This shows the philosophical and ideological importance of the Yoruba thought system, which remains trusted and is still in use. This employment of language gives Afolayan's memoir meaning in many senses, revealing the interconnectedness of language and orality. African languages are rooted in the orality that predates written forms of language and communication. Oral traditions are the main sources of historical, philosophical, sociological, and ideological treatises in Africa.

Consequently, it analyzes the implication of oral traditions, exploring how orality helps the author to achieve his agenda for the memoir. In the Yoruba world, language and its orality are the way in which cultural identity is ingrained in a person. The chapter considers the combination of Yoruba and English languages in Afolayan's work. Yoruba words are interpreted into English, and English words are diluted with Yoruba words, synthesizing English and Yoruba to create new words. This shows the Yoruba's creativity, overcoming the barriers of comprehending a language that is new to their culture and community. The connection of language, orality, and communitarianism helps Afolayan's work find its meaning.

The fourth chapter of the book focuses on the density of cultures in the memoir of Assensoh and the tropes that surround the idea of diversity, pluralism, and multiculturalism he assumed when he made significant journeys to different parts of the world. However, it is pertinent to note that his journey is not only to praise and appreciate the cultures of others but also to place his own culture at the forefront and can be a standard and an epitome of inspiration for other countries. The chapter focuses on these topics in A. B. Assensoh's *A Matter of Sharing* and *Migrant Stories* and delves into Assensoh's journeys, which involve struggles and encounters in several places. In *A Matter of Sharing*, the memoirist presents the devastating nature of the political situation that led to his exit from Ghana. The postcolonial realities in Ghana and other African countries were sad to witness as Assensoh saw hard-earned independence squandered by ineffective leaders. His memoir chronicles the experiences of journalists and citizens during the despotic rule of Ghana's leaders—Assensoh's life is examined, and the memoir details his arrest and detention.

It also explicates the moral and motivational attributes of Africans who have turned their adversities into opportunities. It evaluates Assensoh's journey from Europe to the United States and to Asia as voyages of pleasure and pain, capturing how the situation in postcolonial Africa created obstacles for Africans and the motivations for voluntary migration from Africa to the West. Assensoh maps a confluence between history, law, and humanities; his argument is that the history and culture of a people define the kinds of laws they establish.

Assensoh's journey to Asia can be seen as a diacritical comparative analysis of the multicultural and multilinguistic natures of Asia and Ghana. He sees these characterizations as being responsible for harmony in Asia, and the multicultural, multilinguistic, and communal attributes of African settings are equally responsible for their own harmony and peaceful coexistence. Chapter 5 emphasizes traditions, continuity, modernity, African and Western epistemologies, the politics of language, polygamy, and the family system. It also evaluates the racism experienced by Africans in the diaspora, exploring Assensoh's criticism of racism's gruesome experiences. The chapter interprets the interest of Africans who may be in a home away from home while places and spaces of nativity are apposite in their hearts and minds.

Chapters 6 and 7 critically examine and note the fluid concepts of cultural identity and homeland in the memoirs chosen for this manuscript, and they are well analyzed in the chapters. The aim of these chapters is to engage in discussions and debates on the concept of the African identity and home in new lands. The creation, definition, and substantiation of the African identity in diasporic spaces form a large corpus of the migrant and diasporic discourse. The chosen memoirists constantly negotiate the ambiguous meaning of home, the crisis of "being," and the politics of belongingness in their creative works of art. Major thematic engagements of migrant writings are centered on the depiction of what it means to "be African outside Africa." They primarily present the sense of loss, confusion, struggle to adapt, and race issues, among other things. They establish their affiliation with Africa by revealing the issues that triggered their mass departure, making commentaries on the shortcomings and issues of crippling growth and development in their homes.

Chapter 6 builds on the foundation of the previous chapter to assess the memoirs of Cherno Njie and A. B. Assensoh. Memoirs written by Africans discuss the concept of African identity, and the selected memoirs discuss African identities, belongingness, and the conception of home in diasporic spaces. The chapter also examines the conception of Afropolitanism as a form of hybridity that accommodates African and global identities. It is an evaluative appraisal of Assensoh and Njie's memoirs and how they depict home and the new diaspora, covering multiculturalism, migration, pan-Africanism, and globalization.

This chapter uses the concept of "home," as defined by Homi Bhabha, to evaluate the notion of home in Cherno Njie's *Sweat Is Invisible in the Rain* and A. B. Assensoh's *A Matter of Sharing* and *Migrant Stories*. It argues that memoirists seek to frame the idea of African identities around universalism. The memoirs are used to determine the configuration of identity and sense of self in diasporic spaces and argue that their ideas offer a collage of Afropolitanism, multiculturalism, and pan-Africanism to define a new kind of identity for a new African Diaspora. These concepts map the emergence of a global identity, not just an African identity, and this chapter interrogates the plausibility of these concepts and how they complicate the study of race and identity.

Globalization has rendered the idea of pan-Africanism insufficient to define African identity, which must interact with other identities without abandoning the specific properties of being African. More importantly, the chapter asserts that Africans in Africa and the diaspora must find a way to adapt to the new environment and its values, cultural mores, socioeconomic systems, and challenges. It appraises the synthesis of universalism, pan-Africanism, Afropolitanism, and cosmopolitanism, merging them into the notion of "glocalisation" that embraces both an African and global identity. Merging the tenets of universalism with particularism can help us understand a new generation of Africans who are global citizens.

Chapter 7, titled "Contrasting Experiences of Old and New Homes," explores how Africans who migrate to the United States usually experience culture shock—their experiences have been shaped by different attitudes toward communitarianism, the concept of womanhood, and the politics of postcolonial Africa. Chapter 7 reviews the experiences in Babatunde's *Kelebogile I Am Grateful*, Michael Afolayan's *Fate of Our Mothers*, and Cherno Njie's *Sweat Is Invisible in the Rain*. Common experiences between these writers show that African experiences are marked by family and communal systems, colonialism in Africa, the understanding of motherhood and womanhood, oral traditions, postcolonial realities, and African humanism. These writers must adjust to the new realities of their new homes, which requires coping mechanisms for enduring culture shock. The West prioritizes individualism and other values that are in opposition to the essence of the authors' African experiences. Another difference between their old and new homes is the reliance on supernatural forces in Africa versus the embrace of science and pragmatism in the United States. The authors all comment on differences in political stability, respect for the rule of law, and human rights.

Finally, chapter 8 examines how memoirs by Africans in the diaspora are influenced by slavery—these works are part of an essential genre in African American literature. Freedom narratives are the stories of Africans in the diaspora describing their encounters with slavery, freedom, segregation, and forceful migration. Olaudah Equiano and Frederick Douglass described the journeys made by slaves taken from their African homelands to the United States. This chapter traces the genealogy of immigrant stories from Equiano and Douglass to Booker T. Washington, Richard Wright, and many others. It also looks at the ideologies and theories that influenced the lives of slave descendants, chronicling the efforts of Blacks in the United States to end social and racial injustice.

Black movements in the United States pushed the agenda of pan-Africanism and agitated for the independence of colonized African countries, which is why chapter 1 explores the contributions of the Harlem Renaissance and pioneers such as Philip Randolph, Langston Hughes, and Claude McKay. The chapter also examines the theoretical dimension of freedom narratives by explicating the problem of identity and the admiration for one's color and cultural heritage; it evaluates W. E. B. Du Bois's idea of "double consciousness" and the ideology of Négritude as propounded by Aimé Césaire and Léopold Sédar Senghor.

Freedom narratives and immigrant stories adopted new forms during the civil rights period, which saw radical demands for equality from civil rights activists. Writers and activists, such as Maya Angelou and James Baldwin, wrote about the predicaments of African Americans. Their views of Black struggles in America are examined in this chapter. Slave and freedom narratives started with oral and written accounts from slaves who escaped the shackles of their masters, and conditions in the United States suggest that racism is not dead.

Overall, this book attempts to go beyond mere theoretical explications of diasporic concepts, investigating the theoretical and conceptual underpinnings embodied in the memoirs written by contemporary immigrants in the new African Diaspora. I evaluate the lived experiences of memoirists whose works have been used as case studies and representations of the dichotomy between home and abroad. Their work is the synthesis of the experiences and realities of African migrants before and after migration. This book hopes to contribute to and trigger conversations on growing literature on the African Diaspora, the Atlantic world, and Black studies. It is hoped that this unique genre will create a new wave of interest, fueling intellectual curiosity among scholars who are fascinated with pan-African scholarship.

Chapter 2

CULTURE AND CULTURAL POLITICS IN CHERNO NJIE'S *SWEAT IS INVISIBLE IN THE RAIN*

INTRODUCTION

Literature is indisputably a compass for appraising and representing societal trends, phases, ideologies, migratory patterns, and other general practices. It is a platform for the proliferation of dogmas and the depiction of the psycho-social realities in a given milieu. Therefore, any African literature functions as an index of its enabling society. Societal occurrences act as prototypes for literary engagements. Francois Lionett describes literature as "a discursive practice that encodes and transmits as well as creates ideology, is a mediating force in society: it structures our sense of the world since narrative stylistic conventions and plot resolutions serve to either sanction and perpetuate cultural myths, or to create new mythologies that allow the writer and the reader to engage in constructive rewriting of their social contexts."[1]

As a signifier of societal trends, contemporary literature privileges migrant writing and its attendant themes because the migration question is dominant in recent global discourses. As King et al. rightly state, many migrant writings are replete with "migritudinal" tendencies. Diasporic writers reflect on the "worrisome living conditions in their home country and the unwelcoming atmosphere in their host country, in their works. They consciously and consistently strive to maintain affiliations with their home country. These writers channel their creative energy towards portrayal of the realities in their natal home as they strive to give expression to their interest in the affairs of their home country from diasporic spaces."[2]

The literature of the African Diaspora represents the experiences of migrants by fictionalizing them. Edward Said argues that the crux of migrant writings is the inherent pain of alienation when he asserts, "While it is true that literature and history contain heroic, romantic, glorious, even

Fig. 2.1 – Cherno Njie

triumphant episodes in an exile's life, these are no more than efforts to overcome the crippling sorrow of estrangement . . ."³ Migrant works of art are sated with themes of nostalgia, homelessness, in-betweeness, alienation, racism, despondency, identity crises, and many more. Salman Rushdie captures the diasporic experience when he maintains that ". . . exiles or emigrants or expatriates, are haunted by some sense of loss, some urge to reclaim, to look back, even at the risk of being mutated into pillars of salt."[4] Also, Paul Zeleza, in his diachronic survey of the growth of African literature, avers that the postindependence African intelligentsia had a trinity of dreams for "purity, parity and personhood." African intellectuals are adamant about reinforcing African authenticity, history, and humanity.[5] Zeleza's claim emphasizes the dogged insistence on promoting African culture, identity, and humanity that is relevant and widely discussed in contemporary African literature.

As a mode of writing, the memoir, which can be categorized as a form of (auto)biography or a form of fiction with dashes of believability and truth, has, in recent times, gained a lot of attention. The autobiography/biography bifurcation and the interpenetration of the two forms have been noted by critics like James Olney[6] and John Eakin.[7] Autobiographers become biographers when they focus on parents, siblings, and other significant persons in their lives; conversely, one who injects personal details into the narrative of another's life ends up producing an autobiography. To adapt James Olney's idea of the open-endedness of autobiography, an autobiography half emerges in the act of living and writing about others. One can write one's own life story obliquely by writing the life of another, a status Paul John Eakin calls crypto-autobiography. Commenting on her own life and work, Caroline Bretell says, "As a book by a daughter about a mother who was a writer, this text involves a blending of voice, by extension, a blurring of genres . . . it is both a biography and an autobiography, not only because it weaves my words with those of my mother but also because the lives of a mother and daughter are inextricably intertwined."[8]

This is a natural thing because people do not live in isolation. The lives of people in society interpenetrate, and individuals define themselves in terms of mutual inter-influencing between their lives and those of the people they have around them. Life is given significance by the social milieu and the culture in which it is found. According to Remy Oriaku, a memoir "as a form of narrative in writing about a person's life, can be put to several uses. These include [to preserve] the subject's life in the public's consciousness, document his/her record of public service and accomplishments, repair of a reputation that is impugned, especially after death, and set him/her up as a model for future generations."[9] Not every person gets to live a life so eventful and prominent enough to sustain the writing of a full-length memoir, so the usual subjects of memoirs tend to be persons whose lives are considered significant enough to arouse public interest.

Over the years, a new crop of writers and thinkers have engaged in discussions and debates on the concept of culture and cultural politics in a diaspora.

These writers focus on the worrisome living conditions in their countries as well as the experience of not belonging in their host country. Consciously and consistently, they work to retain their ties to their homeland. In the scope of this research study, it is pertinent to give a brief analysis and explanation of the term "cultural politics." This study is going to draw its insights from the definition and postulations of the term cultural politics stated by Stephanie Newell, which "refers to the way that culture—including people's attitudes, opinions, beliefs, and perspectives, as well as media and art—*shapes* society and political opinion, and gives rise to social, economic, and legal realities."[10]

The tenets of culture and cultural politics are related and presented in various forms and manners in the memoir in this study. *Sweat Is Invisible in the Rain* by Cherno Njie[11] is a narrative of an African childhood, the author's life in the American space, and his essential quest to topple a dictator in his natal home, The Gambia. In the memoir, it is pertinent to note that Njie discusses some aspects of culture that informed or contributed to his upbringing, from his life as a child in The Gambia to his adulthood in another country. This consciousness later contributes to his political dealings in his country, which are shown in the narrative. These tenets of cultural politics will be analyzed in different formats.

Notably, there are some issues to be discussed from this memoir, including the contemporary issues in The Gambia and the social landscape of the society. This study will also highlight the varying politics across the African continent after the demise of colonialism and the role of diasporic communities and their position in global affairs. In the same vein, the propagation of the media and arts and how they shape society and political opinions, giving rise to some realities in the country, are also central to this study.

FREEDOM AND CULTURE: TENETS OF SOCIETAL CULTURE IN *SWEAT IS INVISIBLE IN THE RAIN*

The world today has several cultural variations, each with its own set of traditions and systems that include the whole range of human activities in both private and public life. Basically, these societal cultures are commonly associated with nationally oriented groups that create questions about how freedom is attached or dependent on the presence of these societal cultures.

In his introduction to the book, Njie discusses how it is necessary to sustain a distinct societal culture and how responsive people should be to those cultures. The objective is to show the value that freedom of choice has on certain cultural preconditions, and that the issues of belonging to a culture must be incorporated into the daily dealings in that society. As illustrated in the memoir, Njie starts each chapter with a proverb or saying in Wolof, which is interpreted in English. The sayings are not to be read on the surface, but their underlying meaning should be attached to the chapter being read. The proverbs give the reader an idea of what Njie wants to be deduced or inferred from the chapters.

This method of writing is a postmodern way of introducing readers, especially those who are not of the author's culture, to the deep-rooted meanings inherent in the culture and how they reflect the problems in society. For instance, the preface of the memoir starts with an opening proverb: "When the goat chases away a thief from the compound, the dog should be ashamed." The connotation of this proverb showcases the ills of The Gambian society in which competent individuals are being forced to move out while the incompetent ones take over. However, the author injects the migrant tendency—the push and pull factors, the complexities of home, and the role of diasporas—to correct these ills. In citing or stating the problems of the country and how he is involved in it, he states that:

> An attempted coup in The Gambia staged on the grounds of the State House in Banjul failed. A number of the plotters died at the State House, while I, waiting apart from the assault, and a few of the others involved separately escaped to Senegal after having been informed by one of the survivors of the failed attempt. From Dakar I flew to the United States, stopping in Baltimore, as I tried to make my way back to the quiet neighborhood in Austin, Texas, where I live. I was arrested, however, when I got to Maryland.[12]

In relation, the author shows the importance of tackling these issues by stating he felt a responsibility to The Gambia, a sense of civic duty as a successful Gambian of the diaspora, and that many individuals had grappled with the thought of removing the sitting president. These are the thoughts and the conflicts in the text that expose his cultural role in his society. It is not surprising that at the end of the preface, Njie attaches a cultural tenet to his actions by saying, "Call it patriotic if you will, even as I sit apart a great many miles of water and earth from West Africa."[13]

The term culture has been used to cover only the aspect of the societal culture in the text, as it is, according to Will Kymlicka, "a culture which provides its members with meaningful ways of life across the full range of human activities, including social, educational, religious and economic life, encompassing both public and private spheres."[14] However, these cultures tend to be based on territories but with some elements of diversity and multicultural tendencies, which the author explores through his life in the USA. As discussed above, they are replete with cultural tenets ranging from the nostalgic memories of an African childhood, the symbols and relationship of culture to real life, the caste system and nexus between Njie's African childhood and adult life in the USA, and the complexities and politics of home, exile, and alienation.

The chapter "Close Quarters" narrates Njie's memories as a child in The Gambia and how he assimilated these cultural values. This chapter emphasizes that societal cultures involve "not just shared memories or values, but also common institutions and practices."[15] They are shared and incorporated into social life, which is "embodied in social life or practices covering most areas of human activity."[16] And in the modern world, for a culture to be embodied in social life means it "must be institutionally embodied—in schools, media, economy, government, etc."[17] Njie highlights how he learned different lessons from his father and mother, who complemented each other and how they were embedded in Wolof traditions, which denotes complex networks of meanings. As he states that his mother borrows extensively from the Wolof traditions to understand certain concepts, even though such meanings tend to be complex in nature. This innovative and inventive device by the author's mother is rather a show of universalist tendency that shapes the memoirist's idea of traditions.

These words that signify different cultural meanings and concepts are deeply related to the world, showing a layer of universal meaning. Also, the narrator states that some proverbs and folktales from the Wolof society were told by his mother. This shows the didactic nature of the tales that contributes to the moral perspectives of the narrator and a sort of initiate to the community as a member. These elements of culture help shape who one becomes as one grows older and understands the workings of society.

Another element of culture in the text is the value of cultural membership and its toleration and limits. Over the years, it has been argued that individuals can endorse certain group-differentiated rights for ethnic groups and community minorities. This principle hinges on the community demands for external protection, which reduces the minority's vulnerability to the larger society. Thus, liberalism and tolerance are closely related both socially and historically. This system is generally humane, tolerant of group differences, and remarkably stable. It is also important to note that societal culture must be protected from decay and that survival is not guaranteed. The interactions between people in society and how valuable they are depend on the societal culture that people have access to that allows a range of meaningful options.

This is evident in the text as Njie describes the caste system in the Wolof society. As noted in the text, these caste systems have their symbolic functions, are made up of three different groups in the society, and they serve as the custodian of the cultural heritage. Njie states that they tell stories, keep histories, and serve as diplomats. Despite their differences in class, the three groups maintain a tripod for the community's cultural values and relate to individual assessment, compared to the significance of castes and meanings, which are also dominant cultural symbols presented by Njie to signify how Wolofs think of one another in various circumstances. However, the examples of the cultural systems are "made up of three general groups within the Wolof: the nobility (jambur), the artisans (nyenyo), and the lowest caste, the servants and bondsmen (jam). The griots are of the nyenyo, which also includes the tega (smiths), ude (leatherworkers), and laobe (carvers); the griots are artisans of a different sort. They tell stories, keep the histories, and, in the past, acted as advisers, diplomats, emissaries, and confidants, especially for the jambur."[18]

Furthermore, there is a tolerance perspective on the values, cultural ideas, and practices from the standpoint of that culture. This practice eliminates cultural prejudice and the use of one's own cultural norms to judge another culture. This notion of cultural relativism and the belief that cultures can coexist in peace are regarded as an attempt to eschew ethnocentrism and encourage hybridization. The idea of contact and adaptation to each other's ways resulted in the emergence of a new cultural reality embedded in multiculturalism and transculturalism. Multiculturalism is an ideology that embraces cultural diversity within a given geographical setting. It is a concept that aims to address issues of the coexistence of multiple cultures as co-equal, nonhierarchical, and nonhegemonic. The multicultural model is different from the assimilationist model, which requires minorities to forsake their traditions, substituting them for the culture of the dominant population. However, there is a model of acceptance and recognition of different cultural lives by Njie based on his recognition of Lebanese, Japanese, and Senegalese families, as he recollected his childhood memories in Banjul.

These different nationalities were involved in the economy of The Gambia, and they prospered at their own level by also contributing to the development of the society. It is then important to state that the narrator did not record or remember any act of hostility to these members in the new land as they tend to thrive economically and culturally, a vivid example of cultural success in the memoir. As an illustration, the author notes a striking semblance in the Banjul of his childhood and of the one of today, which he aptly describes and presents as new formations on contact zones. The spatial dimension and features of Banjul of his childhood and of the present, therefore, paint a multicultural background with different nationalities striving positively in the multicultural city. In presenting one of the beneficiaries of the spatial setting, Njie observes that:

> The Banjul of my childhood, as it is today, had few manufacturing industries. The center of commerce was Wellington Street, a hub of the retail trade and of warehousing of imported goods that shipped to neighboring countries, particularly Senegal. There was a groundnut processing plant at Saro, just outside the city limits. Another source of employment apart from the government and the civil service was a bottling plant at Fitzgerald Street owned by a Lebanese-Gambian family. Indians operated a textile mill.[19]

Thus, contact zones allow geographically and historically separated people to come into contact with one another, frequently associate with one another, and establish relationships, even though they are associated with coercion, inequality, and conflicts. These contacts between the colonized and colonizers are seen in terms of co-presence and interaction. In this multicultural and transcultural world, one must have an intimate relationship with human products, and the politics of belonging must be adhered to.

In another dimension and by showcasing the African communal life over individualism, the narrator also notes a sort of multicultural tendency, which is another cultural tenet in the text. It is noteworthy that the author narrates his family structure, which is worked out in the typical African community. There is the placement or putting filiation over affiliation, where people who are not related by blood are treated as if they are family and they all share common values. This is evident in the text as the narrator notes that people who were not part of his family lived with them, and there was no distinction among them. They all stayed in the same compound, and the community of people was where the "family revolved."

This sense of accommodation, tolerance, and lack of disparity among people in the community is what Njie showcases in the definition of the typical African community and what can be adopted universally by placing communalism over individualism as it is common in the Western world. A proper reference from the memoir and the part that captured it is where he describes the community, attachment, and living conditions of different family members who all coinhabit the same compound despite differences in filial relations and no distinctions made. The vivid description of the level of cohabitation in the compound, which comprises different families, suggests the communal nature of his family.[20]

The preaching of diversity and interconnectedness of family lineage and the transcending of religious biases as a mode of cultural template is also discussed by Njie in the text. This is a basic element of transculturalism as it implies transcendence, a person or group's ability to go through and beyond these psychological inhibitions or limitations. It also implies the ability to transcend social boundaries, the limits that society sets for both its citizens and "Others." These include taboos, dos and don'ts, and so-called traditions.

A major component of social borders is spiritual, the mode of worship, the dress code for men and women, what is considered sacred, profane, or sacrilegious, and the relationship between and among various religions. This is stated in a relevant manner as he notes that "the compound was quite small, and was the home of so many."[21] This form of open-mindedness transcends in the narration to the nodes of religion where there is toleration and diversity, which is duly narrated in the sense of solidarity that accommodates and homes the Muslims, Christians, and even Yorubas all under the roof of the Wolof Gambias. More interestingly, the motif of the universality of music brought by the Yorubas is employed by Njie in his narration to show the interactive and transformative space in The Gambia, as such music binds the children together as they look forward to it because of its beauty.[22]

The example of the interconnectedness of family lineage to bring out the cultural example of the ties that bind is also replete in the memoir. There is the fear that "group differentiated rights will undermine the sense of shared civic identity that holds a liberal society together."[23] This method serves as a source of unity that can lead to the coming together of smaller groups or families. In a way, this can make accommodations necessary for a functioning communal life and a proper way to develop a shared civic identity.[24] In the memoir, there is a coming together of different families from different backgrounds and a form of celebration of the households. It is pertinent to note that the author involves or tells the readers about a family that is of a different culture. Even though there are differences in the family traditions, the compound celebration of households represents the ties that bind by unifying the Aku family with the Njie family coupled with the American families of the Socks and Georges in the New Street irrespective of the size and class.[25]

ANOTHER SAVANNAH: THE POLITICS OF HOME, DIASPORA, AND CULTURAL ADAPTATION

It is essential to discuss the politics of home, nostalgia, and the complexities of living abroad with regard to the tenets of culture in the text. This is vividly abundant in the chapter titled "Another Savannah," where Njie narrates the period he was in America and what made him leave. This is one of the ways contemporary writers talk about the complexities attached to culture and different modes of adaptation in this globalized world. Thus, this aspect will focus on the concept of home, nostalgia, migration tendency, and ways of adapting to a new culture in new lands.

Furthermore, it is noteworthy to state why people migrate, both push and pull factors, as narrated by the author. In modern times, Africans in the diaspora appear to be motivated by other factors that drive them to leave their homelands. These factors are different from those of the old times—colonialism and slavery—and some of them have been generally identified as growing unemployment or underemployment, stagnation or decrease in earnings for those employed, job insecurity, increasing poverty, inadequate education, and increasing marginalization and exclusion. In an integrated global economy and with the rising disparities between rich and developing countries, increased migration is unavoidable. The high level of development attained by industrialized countries with higher per-capita income attracts migrants. To the author, the pull factor is uneven education and the need to know another world. This is evident in the memoir as Njie writes about how he left his job as a banker in The Gambia to pursue an undergraduate degree at Texas in his mid-twenties, fueled by his desire to explore another location outside Africa. The love and attachment for New Street did not hinder him as well as the connections to his family, which are deeply rooted in attachment as well.[26]

After a border crossing, physiological and sociocultural estrangement sets in because of change in space shaped by distinct norms and ideologies present in the new space. The conscious attempt by the ego to absorb these differences and adapt to the new culture leads to hybridity and syncretism, and often personality disorder and disillusionment. As revealed in the words of Ralph and Staeheli, "Individual migrants often fail to meet normative expectations of behavior, language, appearance, dress, eating habits, and countless other materialities and context-dependent etiquettes, and are in consequence perceived and discursively constructed as a group as being different to dominant others."[27] This estrangement and feeling of alienation results in the necessary identity formation and adaptation that precedes migration. This is evident when Njie notes he felt a moment of loneliness when he moved to the new world but was later instructed by other people on how to survive the culture shock as he missed his home and developed nostalgic feelings. To combat this, he embraced the idea of solidarity by meeting and attending a community of other Africans, such as "four or five other Gambians, as well as Senegalese, Nigerian, Malian, and Zimbabwean students; it was a tightly knit community which effectively contributes in navigating his new space."[28]

Also, the complexities of home are discussed or showcased in the memoir, where the narrator states that individuals should make anywhere home. In this postcolonial world, home is a disputed site where opposing discourses of race, gender, class, and nation meet and merge. It is not a private sphere but a space where the private coexists with the public. The concept of home poses a complex relationship between subject and space due to the rapid growth of globalization. Home is, then, a location of many points in a space, which makes it a multidimensional concept. Therefore, humans should be able to adapt and face multiple cultural forms. They should define and redefine themselves every day and celebrate transgressed identity in areas where cultural identities collide. In the text, the author describes how he fell in love with Texas, which is a tenet of a cosmopolitan, and had given up hope of going back home.[29]

The formation of diasporic communities is also an important element of culture discussed in the memoir. It is a sort of pan-African tendency and a way of building African networks in new lands. As described by various researchers, diaspora is an undertheorized concept, particularly in a society where identity politics and ethnicity are frequently emphasized. There are various ethnicities, nationalities, races, and religions that claim diasporic identity around the world.

Khachig Toloyan expresses the view that the term "diaspora" used "provisionally to indicate our belief that the term that once described Jewish, Greek, and Armenian dispersion now shares meanings with a larger semantic domain that includes words like immigrant, expatriate, refugee, guestworker, exile community, overseas community, or ethnic community."[30] This explanation of the origin, current meaning, and usage of the word "diaspora" tries to put it into context, where the narrator involves himself with other African students and they move with purpose by engaging in a protest to fight inequality. As shown in the text, the diversity of the network of the diasporic community is essential through the formation of a community of student bodies from The Gambia and other African countries.

Njie also describes the diversity of the diasporic community's network when he arrived at the University of Texas at Austin and met other students from different parts of Africa. The contacts created a long-lasting community, so enriching that he did not miss his natal home, Gambia, despite being the only Gambian on campus. In other words, home is not where you are from but what you make of where you are, which is the idea and ideal sense of belonging that Njie preaches in his memoir, which he navigates by joining in social life and meeting other nationalities that seek to open new opportunities for him in numerous capacities.[31] Also, to describe how the community moved with purpose by engaging in protests across the African states and the community in the USA, especially the Black Americans shows how to overcome the culture gap, engage in solidarity, and make way for a better African nation. The author notes there were joint efforts from Americans and Africans in the struggle for self-determination and freedom for Africa, which he finds easy to fit in with seamlessly.[32]

Njie incorporates these Afropolitan ideals into his memoir. The lived experiences of the narrator are cosmopolitan and exhibit intense erudition. In describing the Afropolitan, Taiye Selasi posits that we are "at a law firm/Chem. lab/Jazz lounge near you . . . matching our parents in number of degrees, and/or achieving things our people in the grand sense of it only dreamed of."[33] The narrator is primarily a cultural hybrid. Selasi goes further to describe the cultural hybrid thus: "Some of us are ethnic mixes, e.g., Ghanaian Canadian, Nigerian Swiss . . . American accent, European affect, African ethos. Most of us are multilingual."[34] Their affiliation to two or more cultures reflects in their lifestyle. It is not surprising that the narrator can predictably speak more than one language.

Similarly, the narrator displays an aptitude for cultural intermingling and interplay both inside and outside the continent. Afropolitans, as primary proponents of interracial mingling and inclusion, desire to be understood beyond the boundaries of statehood; that is, being affiliated to a country should rarely be the foundation for understanding people. This is evident in the narrator's success in the USA, where he works at a housing ministry and uses this experience to understand basic cultural expressions and later cultural entrepreneurship. These workings are reflected in the memoir through the spatial symbol of the neighborhoods and later in cities as a form of a cultural community and a perfect example of the ideals of cultural expression.[35]

A PHASE OF CULTURAL POLITICS: POLITICS AND CULTURAL POLITICS IN *SWEAT IS INVISIBLE IN THE RAIN*

The Gambia, as it is popularly known, is a former British colony with a population of over two million people, the majority of whom are Muslims. In 1965, The Gambia gained independence from the United Kingdom, with

Dawda Kairaba Jawara serving as the country's first president. The independence of Gambia is often attributed to the resistance of The Gambia's elite to continue to be governed by a foreign government. According to Sulayman S. Nyang, "The first reason why the British colonial office decided in 1964 to grant independence to The Gambia was the general feeling that The Gambian elites were not too keen about a federation with Senegal and, for this reason, nothing short of independence was acceptable to them."[36]

This is hardly unexpected given that before its independence in the late twentieth century, The Gambia had a loose confederation with Senegal. Though Senegal was colonized by the French and The Gambia colonized by the British, they are two nations largely inseparable in geography. However, the independence of Gambia and many other countries was an attempt aimed at the dissolution of the British Empire. As much as The Gambia is an independent state, there are postcolonial links between the nation and Britain.[37] So, just like its West African Anglophone neighbors, the politics, constitution, governance, and general social mood of post-independence Gambia showed a certain "commitment to stay within the British Orbit."[38]

The state of affairs in Senegambia is well revised in the study by H. J. Van Mook, Max Grassli, Henri Monfrini, and Hendrik Weisfelt titled *Report on the Alternatives for Association between the Gambia and Senegal*. There is also a scholarly devotion to understanding The Gambia's politics and history before independence in D. P. Gamble's unpublished manuscript titled *Bibliography of the Gambia*. The reference of this research is to lay a foundation for the colonial marriage of Senegal and Gambia between imperial rivals (Britain and France). It is also to indicate the tone set in the post-independence Gambia and how it relates diplomatically with the rest of the world, especially the West. The post-independent rule of President Jawara is attributed to a reasonable proportion of peace. There was political stability in The Gambia and this, at the time, dictated its diplomatic dealings, one of which was The Gambia's backing of Nigeria in the Nigerian Civil War (also known as the Nigerian-Biafran war).

As noted by the author, Jawara propagated the element of cultural politics and manipulated the media, and the power is evident by enforcing the power of the military, which dominates all in an undemocratic manner.[39] Two important points emerge in this brilliant assessment by Nyang. He points to the Wolof as a minority ethnic group, which shows that The Gambia is made up of several ethnic groups. The ethnic composition of The Gambia is always a point referred to in its polity and by the fact that in the early years of its independence, the nation did what it had to in order to protect its stability at all costs.

President Jawara ruled for twenty-two years before he was overthrown in a coup orchestrated by Yahya Jammeh and four other Gambian National Army officers on July 22, 1994. The coup, which was seen as a great turn in the political history of The Gambia, ousted Jawara and his People's Progressive Party government. According to Arnold Hughes, the coup "brought to an end one of the most open political systems in Sub-Saharan Africa."[40] Like in Nigeria, when Kaduna Nzeogwu toppled the civilian government, the justification was that the government became corrupt and unnecessarily tribalistic. In the case of The Gambia, Jammeh's justification of the coup was that it was "an anti-corruption effort aimed at a stagnant elite."[41] Jammeh and his government "received extensive support from young marginalized people and other sectors of society who felt that Jawara overstayed his welcome."[42]

From being a military leader, Jammeh contested as a civilian and won the elections. According to Hutlin et al., after the elections, "Jammeh quickly developed a persona as a classic African 'Strongman' with a paternalistic, patriarchal and devoutly Islamic identity; democratic trappings aside, his record was that of a bullying autocrat, a brutal demagogue, and he embraced the title dictator."[43] Literature on the presidency or dictatorship of Yahya Jammeh reveals the turn of a supposed savior of democracy to a well-established and well-known dictator.

Aboulaye Saine carefully analyzes that there was an "overt consolidation of a police state" in The Gambia.[44] The police state in the country bordered on several denials of and trampling on human rights. This abuse of power influenced by the cultural attitude and minds of the people and their leader coupled with the president negates the freedom of expression in The Gambia, where the rights of journalists were trampled on. This sort of intimidation is clearly stated in the text:

> In 2002 a formerly proposed National Media Commission bill was passed in The Gambian National Assembly. The legislation had been dropped in 1999 because of very natural concerns about press freedom and the right of expression in a country where journalists, both foreign and Gambian, were being daily intimidated by the regime . . . Probably, it was some combination of the two—and evidence of the ever-growing and increasingly absolute power of the Jammeh regime.[45]

In the twenty-two years of President Jammeh, his politics and that of Gambia highlighted many issues. Some of them were Jammeh's open declaration against the LGBTQ community, his shutting out of the diaspora, and many more. In considering the politics of Gambia, cultural politics cannot be relegated. The use of cultural schemes to determine the sociopolitical dynamics was eminent in Jammeh's Gambia. One cultural attitude to be considered is religion. As stated earlier, 90 percent of the Gambian population are Muslims, with Christians and traditional believers making up the remaining 10 percent.[46] The high population of Muslims influenced President Jammeh's decision in 2015 to declare the country a Muslim state. According to him, "In line with the country's religious identity and values, I proclaim Gambia as an Islamic state. . . . As Muslims are the majority of the country, The Gambia cannot afford to continue the colonial legacy."[47]

There is an undeniable syncretism between religion and culture. According to Alieu Sanneh, "Culture and religion reinforce and strengthen one another in the formation of an ideal society. The dilemma faced by people of the new Islamic State of The Gambia is the struggle to protect the unique cultural identity, which holds moderate Islamic beliefs, amidst massive pressure from the politicians and other Islamist groups to transform the country into an Islamic state."[48] Also, there were concerns about the interest of the minority Christians and traditional believers. This declaration affected the way The Gambia is perceived. Human-rights groups, such as Amnesty International and Human Rights Watch, suggested that the declaration of The Gambia as an Islamic state could well be "a politically motivated strategy of using Islam to justify arbitrary detention and killings of opponents to President Jammeh's regime."[49]

It is imperative to point out that despite the declaration of The Gambia as an Islamic state, there is religious tolerance, but one does not expect less since 90 percent of the population are Muslims, and the 10 percent left are shared between people of the Christian faith and indigenous beliefs. Declaring the country an Islamic state is a stylish stifling of the opinions and identities of people with different faiths. As evident in the memoir, the idea of cultural politics in relation to religion is to make the country ignorant and intolerant, which is not communalistic but a notion of separatism. This is illustrated in the text:

> The move was in keeping with Jammeh's campaign to cast the country as an Islamic republic and to exploit ignorance and intolerance as an opportunity to gain, or hold on to, political support, in spite of the history in The Gambia both of religious tolerance and the separation of religion and the state. It was behavior that was, again, out of place in The Gambia, or so it seemed at least. The new laws, for the most part lifted from legislation passed in Uganda and already condemned

by the international community, created new and rather ridiculous language for managing the so-called criminality of LGBT persons.[50]

Declaring The Gambia an Islamic state and the fact that it is a nation that comprises a large number of Islamic adherents may well have affected the stance of the Gambian government and the citizens to look down on and despise any idea of homosexuality. LGBTQ advocacy is now a political movement throughout the world. It has become a movement to seek fair treatment of homosexuals all over the world. However, in certain parts of the world, especially in the Arab and African countries, such ideas or movements are not entertained, largely due to the influence of colonial policies.

For scholars, governments, and Africans at large, the idea of homosexuality is un-African. In some parts of Africa, the people believe that homosexuality degrades the core nature of Africanness. For them, it contravenes natural and biological laws. Homophobia, discrimination, and stigmatization are common. Legal barriers prevent LGBTQ persons from equal treatment in many countries in Africa (West Africa in particular), and many countries have laws and sanctions against homosexuals, with Nigeria and Gambia stipulating fourteen years in prison for confessed homosexuals. In nations where such restrictions do not exist, the people's social views typically accomplish the same results. Not so far from The Gambia, the Yoruba people of Nigeria, in their system of divination, strongly oppose homosexuality. In a canto of the system of divination, *Ofun Irete* opines that there is an allowance for cross-breeding that might be harmful in different capacities and instances. The elements of woman, man, palm oil, and the art of lovemaking are duly recited in the canto system by emphasizing non-complementarity in different forms. An excerpt goes thus: "If a man sleeps with a man, it will result into lumps, boils, and yaws. If a woman makes love to a fellow woman, it will result into murk, stinking odour, dirt and irritation."[51]

As highlighted in his memoir on the issue of homosexuality, Njie notes the denial of human rights and trampling on LGBTQ persons and how the international community reacted to it. The element of cultural politics comes into play with Jammeh as he uses the term "aggravated homosexuality"[52] and describes it as criminality. This infringes on the right of the people and lack of solidarity for a national minority, taking away their voice. In the text, Njie notes the optics of the cultural politics with regard to homosexuality as it is heartbreaking through the law of aggravated homosexuality on the LGBT Gambians.[53] The general feeling amongst most Africans is that homosexuality is a taboo or an abomination that should not be permitted in society. This attitude shapes the laws of the land and their enforcement.

So far, the analysis done is to state the general feeling among Africans that influenced discrimination against homosexuals in The Gambia, and this informed President Jammeh's declaration against the LGBTQ community. Jammeh made a much-referenced statement that, "We will fight these vermin called homosexuals . . . the same way we are fighting malaria-causing mosquitoes, if not more aggressively," and continued that, "As far as I am concerned, LGBT can only stand for Leprosy, Gonorrhoea, Bacteria and Tuberculosis; all of which are detrimental to human existence."[54] This is similar rhetoric to the idea of the Yoruba people of Nigeria. The attitude of the people and the laws made are influenced by their culture and the religions they practice.

Identity politics is an ever-growing aspect of political philosophy that cannot be jettisoned. The word "vermin" is the use of a cultural tool, language. The word transmits the idea that LGBTQ people are diseases that should be quarantined and cut at their very roots. It is important to point out that the use of "cockroach" for the Tutsi by Hutu extremists in Rwanda led to genocide. One cannot also even forget the use of "Yanmiri," a bastardization of "nye m mmri," which means "give me water," and is often used for an Igbo person. The sociolinguistic implications of words are heavy, and the use of "vermin" by Jammeh could set gay people up for lynching and jungle justice in a population that is highly religious. Significantly, Jammeh was the most outspoken opponent of the LGBTQ community in West Africa. He used the cultural and religious attitudes of the people to argue his case. He stated in his address that "Promoting homosexuality and imposing it on weaker or poorer nations is a declaration of war on both religions and human existence."[55] Jammeh knew the cultural attitude of the people and he appealed to it. And though he was not the only leader to clamp down on homosexuality, he was the most vocal.

The Gambia's politics are seriously marred by human rights abuses and not just restricted to the LGBTQ community. Under Jammeh's rule, there were severe human rights violations, including arbitrary imprisonment, forced disappearances, extrajudicial murders, and widespread abuses. Amnesty International remarked that:

> Gambia's history has been marred by serious human rights violations, especially since President Yahya Jammeh led a military coup in July 1994, overthrew Dawda Jawara's government, and declared himself Head of State before winning elections two years later. During this 21-year period, the space for expression of dissent has been severely limited. Amnesty International has documented systematic

human rights violations during President Jammeh's regime including enforced disappearances, torture, restrictions on freedom of expression, arbitrary arrests and detention.[56]

Amnesty's remark and assessment of Jammeh's rule are not a fabrication but a reality. People of all ranks in the country faced human-rights abuses. President Jammeh's authoritarian rule is now a part of Gambia's history that is largely seen as a dark period. His human-rights violations did not exclude his political rivals and the press. The human-rights group again describes the situation succinctly as it is a form of violation of human rights. The Amnesty report is just a few of many cases of intimidation, arrests, and detention of political opponents. Jammeh, like every other dictator, created an atmosphere of fear.

Additionally, the intimidation of the press was also one of the many political weapons in Jammeh's arsenal. In a democratic government, the press is absolutely important. In fact, much has been written about the importance of freedom of the press. In the United States of America, the CNN-Trump media war demonstrated both the beauty of press freedom and the shortcomings within that society. Aboubacar Abdullah Senghore argues that:

> Press freedom is a prerequisite for the establishment of a functioning democratic system of government and fundamental human rights. Embodied in the principle of freedom of expression, press freedom is a concern and principle of international and national human rights law and a basic norm of civilised behaviour. It is viewed by many as a fundamental necessity for democratic governance. Thus, governments are expected to permit the press, and particularly the private press, to function responsibly without undue obstruction. Press freedom is not only an indispensable pillar of democracy, but it is also important for the long-term sustainability of social and economic development.[57]

Senghore concludes that the freedom of the press is as important to a democratic government as the three arms of government. There is also the general consensus that the press is a measure of checks and balances in a civil democracy. However, it would be intellectually dishonest to say that The Gambian press enjoyed any freedom under President Jammeh. Senghore, in his paper "Press Freedom and Democratic Governance in The Gambia: A Rights-Based Approach," highlights the human-rights angle of the restriction and intimidation of the press. He argues that press freedom is a fundamental human right, and politicians should see freedom of speech as a political privilege. He insists that:

> In the period after independence, particularly during the last two and a half decades, the private press in The Gambia has been very vocal about human rights violations and bad governance, but this has not happened without a heavy price both in terms of human and considerable material losses. Media houses, writing and publishing equipment, including a printing press, occasionally were burnt. Private radio stations closed down, and journalists were physically assaulted and in some cases murdered.[58]

These cases of human rights abuse, outright dictatorship, and the unfair treatment of the diaspora led to Jammeh's ousting in 2016, and he subsequently relinquished power in 2017. The politics of Gambia is largely affected by the twenty-two-year rule of Jammeh, and it cannot be overlooked. It is then important for the President Adama Barrow-led government to mend fences between the ethnic groups. It is also a task to reorientate the people to embrace peaceful coexistence with people of different ethnic and religious backgrounds. Their ideas of politics are undeniably shaped by sociocultural experience, but they should not dictate how they see one another. The idea of "vermin," as created by Jammeh, should be ejected from people's minds. Economic hardship should be taken care of because with economic empowerment, the people's rights to freedom and to vote for good leaders cannot be bought. There is no country that is not shaped by cultural politics, which ultimately influence its decision-making; however, this should not be at the detriment of democracy and the rights of others.

ANOTHER PHASE OF CULTURAL POLITICS: THE ROLE OF MIGRANTS IN THE DEVELOPMENT AND PEACEMAKING IN NATAL HOME

It is equally important to examine diasporic activities in countries of origin, host nations, and transnationally. Analyzing memoirs seeks to provide a deeper knowledge of diasporas' roles in the dynamics of war and peace in their home countries. The focus is on studying diaspora activities, especially relating to the dynamics of peace and development. In recent political debates, the concept of diaspora has resurfaced. People who identify as refugees are considered exiled populations with a stake in the fate of their country, as seen in Njie's involvement in toppling a sitting president so that peace and development can reign in his home country:

> I felt required to act concretely upon what I felt was a responsibility to The Gambia, upon a sense of civic duty as a successful Gambian of the diaspora. The noisy crashing of calamity across the Atlantic held, however, a deadening power over me. I experienced in the months after Jammeh's victory in 2011 an odd sort of paralysis, a folding up within myself characteristic of a despair that is the consequence of an endless string of frustrations on the one hand, and a sense of urgency on the other—the urgency to stem the loss of yet another generation to the despair of a life lived through Jammeh's tyranny. The prospect for change in The Gambia was increasingly bleak.[59]

Liisa Laakso and Petri Hautaniemi state that the way diasporans are involved in conflicts is a call for a transformative trend in transnationalism. They observe that these diasporans are "motivated by their personal experiences and facilitated by broader globalization processes, diasporas play an important role in the various stages of civil war, as well as in peacebuilding and development activities. Indeed, diasporas have become global forces which shape the interaction and interdependencies between countries, regions and continents."[60]

A further example of the diaspora as a force to reckon with in the international community is observed by Njie during the NADD coalition on Jammeh's misconduct to tackle and put an end to the horrid show for the baseless and inhumane arrests and executions in The Gambia.[61] Academics and policymakers have raised concerns about the significance of diasporas in domestic disputes and political instability. In the aftermath of the 9/11 incident, there is an increased understanding that individuals, and not just nations, may endanger global security. There are concerns regarding the likelihood that the diaspora may pose a threat to local and international security by bringing disputes into their host communities. Thus, in Western countries, discussions about immigration and security have gotten more entwined. It is not surprising that Njie was also reprimanded and jailed in the USA by the intelligence from The Gambia: "Word had begun to get out, to put it simply, that there was a Gambian ready to bankroll a coup in The Gambia. It was not untrue—I was quite ready to provide funds for a meaningful effort to oust Jammeh. I did not find that characterization very tasteful, however, but I discovered that was the nature of the shadowy world into which I was making naive forays."[62]

Transnational diaspora networking activities are considered resources for survival, welfare, and development. In memoirs, in particular, there has been a new awareness that nations in crisis or under bad leadership most often rely on aid from the diaspora. This notion is cited and evident in the memoir as the author notes the amount of work and monetary support for the cause of the nation, which is to topple the president. In the memoir, there is a bulging tap networking the diasporic community of the Gambian society as they seem to oust the sitting regime.

It is important to state an aspect of cultural politics in the diaspora as they employ different methods to propagate their wishes as well. They are formed in a team of professionals, and they also gather the best set of individuals who know the society properly or are aware of the main regime to attack. They employ the press to voice out their purpose too, which is a way the media promotes the social realities of the country. It should also be emphasized that when migrants leave their homeland and cross boundaries, culture shock is unavoidable, especially when the migrants' expectations are something different from what they initially envisaged. Somehow, they are psychologically willing and prepared to adjust, but the culture shock that they experience as returnees to their homeland is different. Because they were part of the homeland culture before migrating to the diaspora, they believe they know and understand the culture so well, but things are no longer the same by the time they return. Their spaces have been occupied, so returnees come back to their homeland faced with the question of survival. Those who are at home also get complacent or worried about their arrival.

For the returnees to survive, their agency must be aggressive and comparatively superior to that of the stay-at-homes. Very much like integration, returnees must go through a reintegration process, and how they reintegrate will depend upon their aggressiveness and agency. This subversion of theory is evident in the text as the narrator seems to learn from individuals who are much aware of the military workings and situations in The Gambia and thus put resources together to showcase the role of this migrant in the development of their country.

Unlike the neoclassical approach to returning migrants that a returnee's migratory experience will be considered an individual failure in relation to the diasporas' migratory goals abroad, the return-aggression approach contends that a returnee's migratory experience will be considered a success only when there is an exhibition of superior agency and advantage over the stay-at-home. The success or failure of returnees is measured by relating the returnees' ability to reclaim all that once belonged to them before leaving the homeland. This approach is quite similar but still different from the structuralist approach, which argues that the success or failure of a returnee is gauged in relation to the "reality" of the homeland with the hopes of the returnee. For the structuralists, the returnees' intention to return to the homeland forms their hopes in the diaspora, while the return-aggression approach argues that whatever the intents of returnees are to return home, their survival depends greatly on the level of their agency and display of superior ability.

Nevertheless, it is instructive to say that the return-aggression approach differs from the social-capital-network theory as it argues that returnees' success is beyond possession of or access to resources alone. Though he was jailed for it, the narrator's aggression was effective because it ousted the sitting president. The return aggression would be classified as a success in the eyes of Gambians, which further substantiates the roles of the diasporic community as contributing effectively to the land and helping in national matters, especially the one concerned with peacemaking and ensuring the betterment of the country. As stated in the memoir to affirm this theory and notion, and as said by another Gambian:

> The opportunity was lost when he was not opposed from the beginning, probably sometime in his first term as president of the country. In the year after my release from prison, I traveled to my native country. Jammeh was no longer there. I was speaking with another Gambian, a prominent businessman, who lived through the Jammeh years. He thanked me for the action we took in 2014 and said to me then, as almost a sort of apology, "The signs were there, we should have acted sooner."[63]

THE REPRESENTATION OF TRADITION AND MODERNITY IN EMMANUEL BABATUNDE'S *KELEBOGILE*

INTRODUCTION

Tradition communicates cultural norms and beliefs from one generation to the next, including customs, rites of passage, practices, rules, and doctrines. Together, these elements shape a group's principles and social behavior. Mani Joshi has observed that values, beliefs, ways of life, aesthetic and symbolic standards, and societal forms constitute a tradition that maintains continuity with the past.[1] Communities have traditions to establish and uphold different classes and levels of social offices, methods of governance and politics, systems of military intervention, and practices for trade and commerce as well as for religious roles and fiscal operations.

Humans require social activities to function, which creates a need for rules, practices, customs, and traditions. Tradition forms the foundation for the ideological and philosophical structures of a group of people—traditions and customs serve as a defining yardstick for social behavior. These practices endure as sets of values, habits, knowledge systems, and cultural expressions transmitted from previous generations to their successors.

Traditional societies have social classes, divisions, suburbs, systems of farming, and methods for surviving and organizing knowledge, such as oral literature and other cultural developments. Traditional communities have developed aesthetic and social structures along with systems for justice, governance, and administration. Nelson Graburn has opined that tradition encompasses processes and cultural materials passed down over time. A dance, for example, is a property of tradition that transmits a performance type to the next generation.

Tradition and modernity are part of the social and cultural transformations that occur from one historical phase to the next. Modernity has

Fig. 3.1 – Emmanuel Babatunde, courtesy of Michael Efionayi.

influenced the process of social and cultural change that led societies from the preliterate era to the industrial age, and tradition is commonly considered to be its opposite. There is tradition in modernity, and there is an equally modern presence in tradition; cultural features are forms or materials of tradition that have been maintained, preserved, and taught to groups of people in a social group or community. Symbols, stories, myths, rituals, and practices that ascribe identity and personality to a group of people, marking them out as a distinct social group, are known as aspects of tradition.

A society thrives on the social and cultural materials embedded in its tradition. Skills, utensils, goods, aesthetics, and beauty products that have existed for centuries have been transmitted, either orally or through performances, as part of a community's traditions. Tradition can be viewed as a reservoir of strength to draw from, the basis of a historically defined identity, and a source of safety, specialness, or differentiation.[2] The conceptualization of tradition as a reservoir implies that it is a pool of information—either sacred or secular—about the nature, origin, identity, practices, and religious and spiritual motifs of a group of people. Tradition draws from the life experiences and wisdom of sages, ancestral heritage, ancient skills and writings, mystic insights, and esoteric knowledge to create a new order of life.

It is important to define the concept of tradition so that the concept of modernity can be explored clearly, which allows its representations in memoirs to be adequately discussed. As a concept, modernity refers to the expressions of values that change society's social and cultural structure. It is often a replacement of traditional modes, practices, beliefs, knowledge systems, and structures. Modernity is seen in the organization of capitalism, empirical reasoning, ideological traits, industrialization, and secularization in the West, which contrasts with existing epochs and civilizations of the past. Modernity stems etymologically from the word "modern," which means new, originally used in history to separate the Christian era from the Pagan era.[3]

As a term, modernity accentuates the relatively new label applied to the advent of modernization and the modern era. It is the consciousness of a new historical phase, removed from the receding primeval period. For this discussion, modernity is essentially the introduction of values, customs, and culture from Europe introduced into the African space. Modernity replicates itself in concepts such as urbanization, industrialization, capitalism, rationalization, independence, and individuality as new structures and systems for civilization. As Babatunde demonstrates in his memoir, modernity brings a paradoxical benefit to humans.

In his research, Madsen explores modernity as social, cultural, and intellectual conditions that fix the distinct within Western society.[4] In this instance, modernity means the appropriation of new, Western ideologies, values, practices, and culture or the replacement of traditional ones. Modernity as a concept implies a discontinuity from an epochal or historical past, signifying an idea or progression that is essentially different from traditional ways. The terms "modern" and "modernity" occupy a central position within the discourse of Eurocentrism, positioning Europe as a central axis around which the rest of the world revolves.

Modernity is used to distinguish a new period with a different social order—that period's knowledge, culture, and power overthrow the old social order and systems. According to Eisenstadt, "Theories of modernization identified the core characteristics of modern society as the decomposition of older 'closed' institutional frameworks and the development of new structural, institutional, and cultural features and formations and the growing potential for social mobilization."[5]

Modernity is gradually swallowing many forms and aspects of tradition and culture—especially African traditions—because modernity has introduced new science, knowledge, innovations, culture, and values that change the norms and customs of traditional societies. Superstition, which is a component of tradition that privileges belief in concepts and ideologies, is regarded as archaic and stifling in the modern era. Modernity has swept through the idyllic organization of tradition and its attendant structures, disparaging superstition and preferring the rationalism of science and technology; it has introduced urbanization as a replacement for traditional settings, and villages have given way to cities.

Modernity prioritizes empiricism and contemporary theories about the existence of God, humans, and the world in general. In contrast, tradition revels in mysticism and prioritizes animism and dependence on a spiritual figure for the creation of humans and the cosmos. Through science, modernity weighs facts and scientific processes as plausible explanations. Modernity is also the term given to hedonism, self-gratification, and radical emancipation, pushing African tradition and culture from the center to the periphery. Youth are embracing modernity, and they want nothing to do with the family traditions of their ancestors.

The properties and materials of tradition in Babatunde's work—the elements such as songs, taboos, proverbs, practices, ceremonies, festivals, belief systems, artwork, values, norms, and customs—can be examined as social and cultural products and processes of preliterate people. A careful analysis of Babatunde's writing can explore the representations of tradition and modernity to understand how tradition has been contextualized in the work and how modernity has been symbolically placed.

As aspects of modernity, science and technology undermine the certainty and world order of tradition—the foundations of traditional belief systems and knowledge have been undermined by modernity's knowledge systems. The traditional concept of an *abiku*, or a child who dies in infancy, is part of a belief system that science may dismiss as irrelevant to biological processes. The concept of *abiku* is neither superstition nor irrelevant; it is a Yoruba belief concerning children who continually torment their mothers by dying in infancy and returning again and again to cause distress. The traditional belief explaining the existence of *abiku* holds that these children have spiritual powers and that they must be given names to subdue those powers, stop them from tormenting their mothers, and compel them to stay alive.

Another tradition among the Yoruba people is to keep a pregnant woman hidden for a few months to prevent miscarriage or harm from befalling the mother and her baby. The advent of medical technology and new practices to care for pregnant women through science and technology have discouraged the taboos and beliefs that were formerly propagated by tradition. Herbs and concoctions such as "Ose dudu," "Ideyun," and "Madarikan" are used in traditional society to provide physical and spiritual protection for mothers and children. Another tradition of the Yoruba people is the collection of the placenta for burial. A father is not allowed to witness his baby's birth, but it is his duty to bury the placenta afterward. Modernity, represented in the work of Babatunde, places the father right in the delivery room. Not only does he witness the birth process, but he also takes classes to prepare for the delivery.

Names and Identity

Names are symbols of identity, telling the history of our birth and bearing a symbolic translation of the tradition from which a person originates. A central tenet of Yoruba tradition is to name their children as torchbearers of their ancestry, connecting them with their progenitors. Traditionally, a Yoruba child is given a name specific to the circumstances of his or her birth, historical period, and family profession. Babatunde emphasizes the rationale behind naming children—these names carry messages encapsulating a parent's abiding wish for the child's future, signaling the enormous potential that the child can achieve or aspire to.[6] In the African space, identity is carved out of the names we bear; they are not mere labels as modernity would use them. The Yoruba tradition considers the maxim "ile la n wo ka to so omo li oruko" before naming children, meaning that the name should reflect the atmosphere and beliefs of the home or family. Names are more than a person's identity; they are the prayers and wishes parents make for their children to symbolize their love for the child.

Names are traditionally believed to have a metaphysical significance—it is thought that knowledge of a person's true name can be used to affect their life, positively or negatively. The process of naming is significant to the Yoruba people; only a child's parents and family members are imbued with that power and responsibility. The traditional motives for naming a child in the Yoruba tradition are to keep the family's hope, faith, and aspirations alive and to serve as a constant reminder of the link to their ancestors and heritage. Names keep an individual's identity alive and maintain the attachment to the roots that are an index of that person's being. The preference for foreign English names, which do not express the values or customs of African traditions, reflects modernity.

Western culture, values, and manners—seen in deviations from naming traditions and rituals—are also reflected in the attitudes of Africans who adopt foreign names to appear sophisticated and to accommodate foreigners. Their baptismal names and Christian names make no contribution to their essence and identity as Africans; they are merely sources of modernity in Babatunde's presentation of foreign contrivances.

Life after Death and Reincarnation

Traditional beliefs, such as that of life after death and the reincarnation of the dead, are woven into the fabric of African communities. Africans believe that the dead can replicate themselves in younger generations through a process of rebirth. The modern discovery of Deoxyribonucleic Acid (DNA) has always been known by traditional Africans, explained by the reincarnation process.[7] In the African knowledge system, reincarnation is not a myth—it is the process of transmitting genes and human traits as metaphysical materials and essences. The transmission of the dead's metaphysical essence into living descendants influences people to behave like their deceased ancestors. The belief in life after death encourages Africans to live a life of value, knowing that they will live again on another plane. Babatunde notes that the Yoruba perceived the womb as a sacred passage from the realm of the ancestors to the world of the living.[8]

Belief in life after death is different from the belief in heaven and the existence of a supreme being who oversees human affairs. African beliefs are entrenched in their culture of speaking and interacting with ancestors who are alive in another space that is different from earth. These beliefs also include ideas of predestination, destiny, and fate, where the future is determined by events from the past—the present not only foreshadows what is to come but it also references what has happened. Belief in destiny and predestination is silently explored by Babatunde; the ancestors watch over and control human destiny, steering their path to success.[9] Several African communities believe that humans are predestined to assume specific roles in life, and traditions are followed dutifully to ensure that their destiny comes to pass.

Purification Rites

Traditional purification rites are another representation of tradition in Babatunde's work. Three stages are recognized in the purification process: separation, seclusion, and reentrance into modern society after having been fortified by purification in the old ablutions of traditional culture.[10] Purification rites are a process of self-discovery and a psychological shift, repositioning the individual in relation to life's different dimensions. The traditional purification rite equips the individual with new strength and skills to lead a balanced life in the present day. There are several traditional rites, like the rite of passage in African communities, that redeem and reconnect the soul with African roots, mores, values, and customs. The purification rite cleanses the soul, removing the miasmal cloud of modernity that corrupts a mind that would otherwise be rooted in African tradition and culture.

Purification rites are steeped in African lore and the traditions of repositioning and rediscovering the African spirit and identity. The ritualistic elements in these rites penetrate the soul in distress, realigning it toward self-redefinition. Physical separation from the outside world, seclusion in the ancestral grove, and reemergence in modern society purify the psyche to lead a life that is infused with tradition.

Home as the Structure of Tradition

The home is a vast classroom in which one negotiates spaces filled with different facets of meaning, learning the ins and outs of Yoruba and Batswana cultures.[11] Tradition thrives in the home, which is the original structure for the transmission of culture, customs, values, and norms for the family and society. The home is one of the pillars of tradition, and Babatunde describes it as a vast classroom where values, rules, etiquette, and customs are built up, brick by brick and layer upon layer, establishing the traditional home as the keystone of a larger community where values are taught and passed to new generations. In the traditional sense, the home involves everyone related by blood and by kinship. In modern society, the home has diminished to encompass only the family unit of a father, mother, and their children.

In the African tradition, especially among the Yoruba people, home is the space for kinship and relations to thrive. It is the structure for appraising value, orienting customs, and configuring the culture of extended and nuclear family members. Tradition creates the home, organizing the distribution of duties and responsibilities for every member of the household. The home enables the structural calibration of traditions and customs within society.

Family as the Axis for Tradition

A major theme in Babatunde's work is the central place and importance of family. In the Yoruba tradition, family is all those who are related by birth, joined by marriage, and sustained through duties and responsibilities. Family members are not validated individually; they are identified through their contributions to their families and communities. Every man's success is celebrated as the community's success, and the community's resources—from its values, morals, and customs to its educational efforts—are invested in individuals to advance the community.

Babatunde's memoir traces his success as an investment made by his family and community. In Africa, especially in Yoruba communities, family is highly revered as one of the basic segments of tradition and culture. Through the establishment of family, the entire community is developed and transformed. This is reflected in the proverb stating that "it takes a village to raise a child,"[12] which applies to all African cultures. A community or village is only realized through the creation and maintenance of the family. Tradition is sustained through the family, and the family relies on tradition to thrive.

Commitment is the thread that binds the fabric of humanity into families, and tradition ensures that the fabric remains intact. Tradition strengthens the belief in the fundamental strength of communities and families, enabling them to thrive. Babatunde's work shows the belief in family and the unification of all family members as a core basis of Yoruba tradition. Families include all the aged, young, wealthy, poor, able-bodied, and incapacitated relations who contribute moral support and monetary investment to the greater good. Yoruba tradition keeps the family grounded through duties and responsibilities. Tradition encourages sacrifice for the advancement of the family; when a member of the family accomplishes something great, the whole family celebrates together for their role in that success. During times of pain and loss, no person stands alone. Every member of the community is affected, and they stand together to mourn the loss or lean on each other for support.

In Babatunde's memoir, Ayinla's father assumes the role of father for his dead brother's children, sending them to school and providing emotional support. Babatunde's work presents the family as tradition and tradition as family, showing that the two rely on each other for survival. Families are central to almost all African culture, shown in the "Ubuntu" ideology of the Sotho-Tswana people. The central philosophy of Ubuntu emphasizes community: "I am because you are." Babatunde notes that the Sotho-Tswana, like the Yoruba people in Southwestern Nigeria, believe family is sacred.[13] This sacredness ensures that the family becomes the base for love, humanity, tolerance, civility, and spirituality. African tradition places family at the core of spirituality and sacrificial living, and African traditions maintain the family. Family units are the foundation for upholding values and driving social change at the community level. The family integrates cultural and traditional values such as religious institutions, religious materials, and worship with ancestral veneration.

Tradition privileges and places great value on family and healthy human relationships, including the relationships between extended family members and the community in general. Family and community become a shield that protects against loneliness and fends off alienation. The family grants strength to individuals, providing stability and support to its members during times of hardship. Tradition offers stability through the structure of the family and the support from the community.

Language as the Bedrock of Tradition

Language is the foundation for encoding and transmitting tradition from one generation to the next. Babatunde emphasizes the importance of African languages through the various linguistic elements and symbols explored in his work. Tradition is encoded in language, and it is taught as an important pillar of African culture. The Yoruba language, with its different variants and dialects, is taught and spoken to children in tradition-oriented families and communities as an essential culture that must not be lost in the face of modern sophistication and civilization. The ability to communicate in a native language is essential for familiarity with African traditions and customs. Babatunde describes Reverend Setiloane's attempt to keep his family connected to their culture through their tradition of speaking the Sotho-Tswana language, even when they were in Europe. Their refusal to lose their African heritage and language shows how tradition can sustain Africans in the diaspora. Linguistic materials and forms are not merely the retainers of tradition and values; they are also a base for cultural implantation.

Modernity has implanted foreign languages in the African space that displaced the learning and speaking of African languages. Babatunde's work shows how elite Africans discourage their children from speaking the local language at home. European languages, manners, and values are cherished by a new group of African youths—they seek the urban language of upward mobility in the new African states.

Ceremonies and Remembrances of Ancestors

Babatunde describes the annual remembrance ceremonies organized in memory of deceased ancestors. This tradition, remembering the sacrifices of the dead, involves the ritualistic killing of a sheep to symbolize the replacement of human blood with that of an animal.[14] Remembrance ceremonies remind the living of the contributions made by the dead; as Babatunde observes, it is in remembrance of the dead that the living are named after them. These ceremonies are a tradition that has been established and continued for generations. The names of ancestors are remembered as testaments to their valor, contributions, bravery, and accomplishments. Prayers offered in graveyards to dead ancestors are a common tradition in most African communities—it is believed that ancestors have been imbued with powers to hear these prayers and grant wishes to their descendants. Like the Yoruba, the Sotho-Tswana tradition of remembering and praying for the dead maintains the presence of the dead among the living. The dead are not distant; they are memorialized as sacred and deified people.

Witchcraft and Witch-Catchers

The Atinga cult and the witch-catchers in Babatunde's memoir are part of a tradition that has a metaphysical, mystic, and cultural foundation in the Yoruba philosophy and worldview. In Yoruba cosmology, witchcraft is associated with malevolence, destruction, unhappiness, and evil. Witches are hunted by the Atinga cult to protect society from their dark powers. Male members of the cult identified witches as women who possessed malicious, metaphysical powers used to terrorize the community. In the traditional African space, the witch is a social and cultural phenomenon. Some females are assumed to have malevolent spiritual power that is used to harm the community and threaten its survival—these witches are women with evil powers who use their power to bring society to its knees.[15]

Babatunde's work explores core beliefs of the Yoruba people that are connected by their interpretations of the mother figure, which is a highly revered tradition among the Yoruba people. The mother is the force that keeps life flowing, ensuring a group's longevity and serving as the vital organ in society that gives and ensures continuity of life. Witchcraft cults are a metaphysical phenomenon that applies feminine power to stop this process. In the Yoruba cosmology, witchcraft follows a tradition that maintains a female cult system for spiritual manipulation and the subjugation of both sexes. The mother and the witch are both female life forces that are powerful structures within tradition and society.

Babatunde's exploration of the Yoruba belief system and values discusses the metaphysical powers of witches. As a female cult, these witches are powerful and can sometimes be too much to handle; they are an aspect of the Yoruba worldview that is highly feared and revered by different people. Babatunde contrasts tradition and modernity to show how tradition is unraveling under the influence of colonial powers. Witches and witchcraft were part of the Yoruba world order before the introduction of witch-hunters known as the Atinga. The witches and their craft embody an aspect of the Yoruba tradition, while the Atinga cult symbolizes modernity's encroachment—Babatunde has juxtaposed the existence of a diverse worldview with the modern introduction of a witch-hunting, all-male cult.

Marriage and Childbearing as a Yoruba Cultural Tradition

The Yoruba people believe in procreation as part of a fundamental life force, regarded as part of a man's wealth. In any Yoruba community, a man's physical, social, and metaphysical wealth is lacking if he fails to have children of his own that continue his lineage. Babatunde observes that fathering children is a component of identity that reconstructs a man's role. This new identity carries the "baba" prefix attached to the child's name—a Yoruba man's identity and status as a father is only recognized when his first child is born, and he carries that new identity with his first-born child's name.

Babatunde briefly explores the Yoruba tradition of christening male children on the seventh day and female children on the eighth day. This practice has endured for centuries to become a tradition that celebrates a new life, identity, and status. The system ensures the tradition of celebrating new identities; fatherhood and motherhood are consistently woven into the minds and philosophy of the Yoruba.

The significance of the Yoruba phrase "Iya ni wura, baba ni digi" (mother is gold and father is a mirror) comes from the idea that a mother's job is nourishment and preservation, beginning from the time when a baby develops inside her body. "Iya ni wura" likens the mother to a precious metal linking the community through her role as sustainer, caregiver, teacher, and shield for the child. Motherhood is almost revered as a religion, which ensures the continuity of the Yoruba people. The second part of the phrase, "baba ni digi," describes the reflection of the father in the life of his children. Babatunde observes this system at work when describing the important role of motherhood as the wheel that turns society. Tradition also refers to the mother as a sacred deity, "orisa bi iya ko si" (there is no deity like a mother). Babatunde also discusses how marriage and a firstborn child signify maturity and stability in Yoruba society; the institution of marriage among the Yoruba people follows a deep-rooted tradition ensuring that both partners understand and uphold their roles and responsibilities at home and in the community.

The memoir unpacks Yoruba tradition among the substrand of the Ketu people, emphasizing the mother figure as a symbol of divine power, creativity, and regeneration through the biological tradition of the monthly flow. Traditionally, the christening of a baby takes place in the home of its father. Babies receive names that signify the challenges that parents have overcome, and these symbolic identities are believed to affect the outcome of the child's life. Names also indicate a child's status as a warrior, chief, or member of a royal family. Names can reflect the events surrounding birth, carrying memories of festive periods, famines, drought, or war.

Among the Yoruba people, male children are traditionally christened on the seventh day, when every member of the family comes together to celebrate the new addition to the family. The introduction of Christianity and the arrival of the Catholic Church introduced the ritual of baptism, which Babatunde presents as modernity's influence, and the selection of biblical names for babies. At this stage, tradition and modernity coexist without conflict. The memoir also hints that polygamy is the traditional way of the people.

Ifá Divination as System of Knowledge

Ifá divination is an important representation of tradition among the Yoruba people—it is their oldest, most respected religion and knowledge system. Ifá divination follows a system of geomancy that works with the Ifá literary corpus, Odu Ifá, the codification of the culture, belief systems, myths, and legends of the Yoruba people. Babatunde explores how this reveals the mysticism of witchcraft and the source of their power.

The Odu Ifá embodies the traditional beliefs of the Yoruba people, including medicinal practices, religious observances, and explorations of metaphysical space. Orunmila, the divinity that is second in command to the highest god of the Yoruba, is associated with Ifá and known for wisdom. Babatunde discusses the myths and legends of the Yoruba people as part of a tradition that incorporates valor, power, and metaphysical and philosophical features. Healers and priests who work with Ifá are known as Babalawo.

Babatunde explores other Yoruba cults, including the Gelede—their dance, where men dress as women, has metaphysical connotations. By appearing in feminine garb, their metaphysical intervention pleads with witches to apply their powers for the good of the community. This activity validates the power of the female cult and its significance in the community. The Gelede cult illustrates Yoruba belief in the power of the female figure, viewed as physically weak but spiritually powerful.

Fortune Telling

Fortune telling is a system established by the Yoruba to predict what will happen in the present and the near future to determine the fate, destiny, outcome, or result of an event or action. Babatunde examines this aspect of tradition as an instrument for retrieving information from collective memory. Fortune telling is the first of three strategies applied to solve any problem afflicting a Yoruba community. It is based on data from experience retrieved through the expertise of the traditional Babalawo authority. This system of knowledge gives a feeling of "certainty." When it is unsuccessful, methods escalate to the next level of placation.[16]

The system of searching for answers and looking into the future requires a special leader to extract answers from the archive of collective memory and resources. The traditional system is different from modern empirical methods of science and technology. However, it works for the people who believe the Babalawo or priest who has been charged with the responsibility of telling fortunes.

Yoruba Divinities and Traditional Religion

Babatunde discusses and explores the traditional pantheon of Yoruba gods and their festivals in his memoir. The egungun festival is an annual tradition where the community celebrates the return of their ancestors and asks for blessings. The Gagalo festival, which celebrates human superiority over other living things, is a tradition that maintains the relationship between the Yoruba community and their pantheon of divinities. These festivals are celebrated annually by the followers of these traditional religions, along with others who do not share their beliefs. Modernity has brought Christmas and other Christian events to replace traditional festivals; these liturgical celebrations have gradually become important to new converts.

Esu is one of the most revered divinities of the Yoruba gods, known for his mischief and tricks. He is the divinity trusted by Olodumare, the highest Yoruba god, bearing Olodumare's ase (seal) and the authority to act as his emissary. Orunmila was the second in command to Olodumare, who is also known as Ifá. This divinity is the god of fate, reflecting the omniscience of the Supreme Being.[17] These divinities have been given the power to grant the requests of humans and celestial bodies. Esu, Ifá, and Orunmila are representatives of the Yoruba gods and divinities worshipped with specific ritual materials.

Oriki/Praise Songs

Songs and poems, known as Oriki, chronicle the history of a specific family or lineage. These oral narratives of the Yoruba people are committed to memory and passed from one generation to the next. Poems contain different praise names and titles recounting the ancestral activities of a family, stating their accomplishments as warriors, hunters, or royalty. Babatunde describes how this tradition is maintained by tutoring new wives who learn a family's poems and songs as part of an orientation program. The poems are more than memorized songs; they follow patterns and use mnemonic devices to aid their recollection. Oriki praise names are sung to placate angry men and crying babies or to calm strained nerves and raise morale when the situation calls for it. Yoruba tradition gives oriki to children as part of their naming rituals, and these praise names are tied to the core of the child's being. They can also be sung to children as lullabies to stop them from crying or put them to sleep.

Songs and poems in African traditional folk culture praise good behavior and discourage bad attitudes or actions. The court poetry tradition of the African people uses this approach in its diverse oral renditions of court poems and songs for the veneration of monarchs and titled individuals. Such songs and poems can describe the physical features of a person, their position in the community, or their strength, bravery, or material possessions. The memoir includes the following poem:

> Ìyá-àgbà Folásadé,
> Òpéléngé pupa;
> Ó subú l'àwò, àwo ò fó
> Ó subù l'odó, odó fàya.[18]

This example shows how the Yoruba tradition is rich in songs and praises that discuss physical attributes, behavior, and demeanor in their praise of a person. Babatunde explores this custom of appreciating valor, courage, bravado, good manners, and prowess in Yoruba communities.

Songs, praise poems, and panegyrics are composed with the Yoruba philosophy of praising the good, lampooning the undesirable, and correcting the ugly. Songs and poems exist for different reasons, ceremonies, and festivals, used for veneration, celebration, mourning, satire, and sarcasm. Yoruba tradition values good character and behavior, believing that there is no beauty to be compared to good breeding and disposition. Customs and traditions encourage good character, which is mentioned in proverbs and idioms such as "eni to ba mo'nu ro ni m'ope da" (a grateful heart is a reflective one). Every aspect of Yoruba songs and poems acknowledges the tradition of passing information and messages through lyrical notes and rhythm for the seasoned ears of the elders and the developing lips of the youth.

Female Training and Circumcision (Ikola-abe)

Another tradition of the Yoruba people is to circumcise female children. The practice is known as "ikola-abe," and it signifies the transition into womanhood and marriageability. Customs maintained by the community train girls to learn the skills needed as wives and mothers. This training is founded on traditions that represent the belief system, customs, and culture of the Yoruba. The training of a girl who has been engaged to marry is managed by the eldest woman in the household. These lessons involve cooking, modesty, and home management, developing skills through games and competitions.

Babatunde describes one of these games, played to determine which lady has the most pleasant voice, called "olohun-iyo." It is based on the tradition of training women to have pleasant and sonorous voices for singing lullabies, songs, poems, and dirges performed for babies, husbands, and aged or deceased members of the family. The "olohun-iyo," literally translated as "voice-of-salt," tests and trains a woman's ability to remember songs, praise poems, stories, and history that she will share with her female children. These lessons test the memory, knowledge, intelligence, and listening skills of these young ladies to become better wives and mothers.

Yoruba tradition includes cooking competitions to determine the training and readiness of young women. The participants are expected to have mastered appropriate condiments and seasonings for different meals, along with their proper portions. Indigenous condiments and seasonings are used for both the training and the competition—the goal is to teach life-sustaining home maintenance skills to help women cope with difficulties such as drought, scarcity, and famine. This training is applied in their new homes, which makes women invaluable as sources of history, support, and succor for their families. Yoruba training ends with the recitation and performance of a family's oriki.

Home Life and Household Management

Babatunde's memoir describes the traditions of the Yoruba people in organizing their homes and running their households. When a man marries more than one wife, unwritten rules and customs hold that the first wife becomes the senior. Polygamy was prevalent in the Yoruba tradition, and any man who kept a single wife was said to be under the spell of that woman. Divorce or separation is not a modern innovation; Yoruba tradition allows a woman to return to her parents if her husband abuses her. In such cases, the parents would have to return the dowry paid by the man.

Modernity, as represented by Babatunde, has introduced separation and divorce without involvement from either the wife's family or the husband's family. Divorce or separation is rarely encouraged in Yoruba tradition, and families on both sides would normally call for a reconciliation between husband and wife. Emissaries are traditionally deployed to plead the case of an erring husband; members of his family represent his interest in the wife's house, acting to settle the dispute. Tradition normally dictates that the emissaries are men from the husband's and wife's families—women are normally absent from these meetings, and the emissaries are entertained after settling the issue between the couple. The wife receives a verdict from the meeting after the elders of the house have reached a decision. If the matter proves difficult to resolve, the woman is subjected to coercion, and the man is advised to refrain from abusive behavior. In Babatunde's memoir, the mother of the protagonist initiates a separation that is a modern break from conservative traditions.

Modernity introduced female freedom into a male-dominated society, liberating them from the oppression of rigid customs and traditions. One such tradition was the view that a woman's responsibility was to care for her husband and children; tradition holds that a man should not be seen in the kitchen trying to cook or wash dishes. Among the Yoruba, the man is the head of the family who dictates his wishes as lord of the house.

Yoruba tradition does allow any member of a family to be left destitute, which means that wives are inherited by other members of their deceased husbands' families. When a groom's family pays a bride's dowry, Yoruba tradition involves every male member of the prospective husband's family—they all make contributions to pay the dowry, and when a woman's husband dies prematurely, she is inherited by another member of the dead man's family. This tradition keeps widows and their children fed and protected after losing the head of their household. However, this practice has been replaced by Christianity and colonialism, the forces of modernity.

Yoruba tradition demands that every man must contribute to the welfare of his extended family—each member of a family is responsible for the others. The "agnatic" succession pattern of Yoruba tradition ensures that any male child born to a family will be considered senior to any woman who marries into the family after the birth.[19] Babatunde stresses that this tradition can be seen playing out when distant family members visit and stay with their uncles. They enjoy an education funded by other members of their family, seizing the opportunity to receive schooling for free.

Modernity has altered these traditions, and people put their own interests, or that of their immediate family, ahead of the extended family. The modern mindset leaves everyone fending for themselves, with no obligation or duty to other members of their extended family. Babatunde notes that the family had previously been the most sacred institution in the African tradition and the base for all communal development and progress.

Proverbs and Idioms as Carriers of Values and Customs

Proverbs and idioms symbolize philosophy, values, customs, and traditions within strings of words; their epithets reveal how a group organizes its thinking. Babatunde's memoir mixes Yoruba tradition with the modernity introduced by colonialism as it merges old and new worldviews. "Obe ahun la fi í pa ahun," which means "a hangman's noose is also used to execute him," codifies a Yoruba system of thought. These proverbs present customs and traditions that emphasize values, knowledge, and good behavior.

When words are insufficient for a difficult situation or problem, the Yoruba people go to the reservoir of tradition to extract proverbs that are appropriate. Proverbs unravel what ordinary words could not begin to grasp, and they reflect tradition by compressing values and customs into bits to be swallowed as healing capsules for the soul. These idioms are especially important when ordinary words cannot capture the speaker's intent. The philosophical basis of Yoruba proverbs and idioms rests on the principles of their belief system.

The proverb, "eni kan ki i so pe awa de," emphasizes the principle of collectivity and communality. The idiom "united we stand but divided we fall" is close to the Yoruba proverb "Ka rin ja po, yiye ni i yeni," essentially translating the Yoruba worldview—it describes the principle of collective strength and the power of collective aspirations, preferring communal strength and collectivity over the radical individualism of modernity. The proverb "Aiwopo ejo ni i f'iku pa won" (the snakes' failure to move as a group makes them easily killed) summarizes Yoruba's thoughts on the dangers of individuality and solitary living. These proverbs, as explored by Babatunde, teach the importance of doing things together, working in concert, and looking after one another.[20]

The Engrossment with Material Possession

Babatunde's work shows that the obsession with profit and wealth has been one of modernity's greatest impacts on human life. The modern aspiration to acquire wealth at any cost has replaced more sedate African traditions of diligence and contentment. African values and customs have eroded under the pressure of modern culture, manners, values, and customs. African youth have dismissed tradition as primitive and uncivilized, preferring to live as Black-skinned white men in their ancestral lands.[21] Among the new elite group of Africans, it is a sign of modernity to reject the idea of speaking the mother tongue within the home. African tradition trains children in domestic activities and chores, such as cooking, cleaning, and caring for the young and old, but this has been replaced—to the detriment of the younger generation—by hired help that performs cleaning and other domestic chores.

The absorption of foreign lifestyles, practices, and values is applauded by African elites. Their preoccupation with rising to prominence quickly, cutting corners and buying their accomplishments is presented by Babatunde as modernity that is in direct opposition to African values and tradition. African parents are traditionally the primary caregivers and protectors of their children, training and disciplining their wards through close monitoring and supervision. Modernity has encouraged parents to abandon their children to stewards and hired help so they can pursue wealth and acquire material possessions.

Modernity has made material possessions more important than immediate family members, and children are left to their own devices, preyed upon by irresponsible adults and teenagers. In the African tradition, the home is a place of responsibility and care maintained by the father and the mother working together. Modernity's preoccupation with personal advancement instead of communal progress has culminated in greed and selfishness among African youth and the emerging class of educated Africans. Modernity, as a new form of innovation, imports foreign cultures and values that displace African traditions. This is seen in the pursuit of material wealth with little or no care for humanity or cultural values.

The introduction of modernity has overturned African philosophical traditions, inherited practices, and beliefs that were passed down through generations for centuries. Babatunde's work shows how modernity has increased the desire for material wealth, emphasizing the importance of amassing riches as quickly as possible and abandoning African values, customs, and traditions in the process. His memoir explores the modern city of Ibadan and the vices that modernity has brought. Imeko city displays traditions, values, customs, and practices that focus on the African community, and the new, modern cities of Lagos and Ibadan have lost their cultural attachments to roots and ancestry. Modernity has driven a scramble for material possessions, leading to exploitation and unhealthy competition while eroding the African spirit of contentment and honest work.

Ebo (Sacrifice)

"Ebo" propitiation materials are offered to divinities in the Yoruba community when seeking the favor of a deity. It is an aspect of Yoruba tradition that indigenous Christians and other religions adopt when they discuss misfortunes such as the sudden demise of an influential young person. When a person dies prematurely, Yoruba people commonly believe that it was caused by witches or wizards in the community or the family. Ebo is more than a sacrifice; it is a system for making offerings to the gods, and the sacrifice is consumed to grant the wish or request of the supplicant.

Babatunde's work acknowledges the traditional ebo system of seeking assistance from the metaphysical powers and abilities of the pantheon of Yoruba ancestors, divinities, and deities. Ebo offerings are placed at a crossroads or strategic junctions of roads, which Yoruba people believe are seats of power. From those locations, the deities who watch over their affairs can take up the request and act accordingly. Babatunde situates this aspect of Yoruba cosmology in the modern era. The belief in the efficacy of ebo is linked with modernity's expectations for instant action and immediate answers. It carries heavy significance in the southwestern part of Nigeria, where Babatunde was raised.

Traditional Medicine and System of Healing

In the older African community, herbs and traditionally prepared medicines were used to combat ailments and diseases. Some medicines were used as ointments on the body, and others were ingested or eaten as part of meals prepared for such purposes. Traditional medicines protected pregnant women and their babies from miscarriages and infections. Similar concoctions were developed to protect against spiritual and metaphysical attacks from witches, wizards, and other malevolent forces. Babatunde describes how these mixtures operated on a magical principle where similar items produced similar effects.[22] These traditional medicines have become less common because modernity created alternative options for medical supplies and treatments in hospitals.

The Belief in the Supernatural World

Traditional societies believe in supernatural powers and worlds that can only be visited by humans who possess such powers. The Yoruba people believe that "ehinkule lota wa, ile l'aseni n gbe," which is Babatunde's explanation for the belief in spiritual and metaphysical powers. The Yoruba knowledge system, aided by tradition, includes a metaphysical world of witches, wizards, and other entities with extraterrestrial abilities and metaphysical powers.

Because magical attacks cannot normally penetrate a home without assistance from an insider, a family is safe when everyone is united and protective of one another. The Yoruba believe in the existence of "orun," "aye," and "agbede meji aye ati orun." This belief in heaven, earth, and the space between worlds—occupied by half-humans, spirits, and other spiritual bodies—is part of the African tradition.

Medical Practices

Babatunde's memoir reflects tradition and modernity in different phases of its narrative development. The modern materials and innovations of Britain and France, the colonizing countries, directly oppose the traditions of Africa's indigenous people. One such area of disagreement is medicine, where Western approaches disagree with traditional wisdom concerning the care and nourishment of pregnant women. Babatunde explains the traditional taboos for pregnant women, preventing them from eating certain food types, such as meat, milk, and fish, to avoid giving birth to deformed and feeble babies. Women are traditionally confined within the home to protect them from witches and evil forces. However, modern Western medical practices encourage women to take walks and exercise outside so they can be fit and strong for their delivery. When it is time for the mother to give birth, traditional methods are employed, and an indigenous midwife delivers the baby.

Modernity, through the influence of modern medicine, also introduced bed rest for heavily pregnant women. Babatunde's memoir explores how tradition gave way to modernity in adopting this new medical practice—the traditional midwife represents indigenous traditions, and the modern nurse replaces those traditions. The traditional midwife, known as "Iya Abiye," shows that indigenous people have their ways of healing and caring for sick people through herbs, traditional knowledge, and skills that were practiced before the introduction of Western medicine and medical practices.

Songs and Poems

Traditional songs and poems encapsulate the value system, codes, conduct, customs, culture, and thought system of the Yoruba people. Songs are not merely for entertainment; they are mediums for conveying culture and traditions, which Babatunde explores in his memoir. Songs and poems are performed to venerate village and country life or sung to impart wisdom and the history of the land, law, and cultural values, which are duly presented in the memoir by mentioning the contributions along class lines of the poor and the rich, which should be done in moderation and humility as tomorrow is unknown:

> Mangoro to so lagbala Oba
> Olowo ni o n ka a
> Talika ko gbodo ka a.
> Aye ko le dun-dun; Ka gbagbe ola o.[23]

Songs and poems are cultural materials that transmit tradition from one generation to the next.

Collective Responsibility

The traditional Yoruba family value is that of collective responsibility.[24] Everyone in the extended family must play a role to advance the family and act in the interests of other community members. Individualism is discouraged—all hands must work together, and wealth must be shared to guarantee the safety, protection, and stability of a lineage. Babatunde reiterates this essential part of tradition as something inconsistent with the doctrine of the Catholic faith and modernity in general. Reciprocity was the traditional foundation for communal strength and progress, pulling resources together to advance the entire community. He opines that the greatest resources for the survival of families and communities are the reciprocal relationships inherent in the tradition of the family as the base for a dynamic community.[25]

African tradition relies on reciprocity for basic growth and development—collective efforts clear lands for farming, contribute resources to pay bride prices, accommodate extended family members, and even pay for education. In Babatunde's work, the collective reciprocal love and communal responsibilities shared among people of the same nationality and origin are efforts to maintain traditions. African tradition emphasizes the dignity and honor in collectivity, unlike modern lifestyles that value individualism. Traditional beliefs encourage sharing and caring for every member of the community, exalting selflessness, collective duties, and shared responsibilities. It is a foundational principle of every African community to be accommodating to all.

Christian Values and Ways

Christianity is a major component of modernity, and its values have transformed the culture and traditions of Africa's indigenous people. Catholicism has introduced several aspects of modernity into the lives of Africans, opposing the worship of many Yoruba deities. The Christianity that was introduced through colonialism became a focal point for modern innovation, merging modernity with church doctrine. The teachings of Christianity taught people to see African traditions and values as evil and unsophisticated, ending the practice of ancestor worship and the festivals, ceremonies, and rituals that involve African deities. The introduction of Christianity and its modernizing influence has discouraged Africans from taking pride in their culture, teaching them to prefer imported values and European culture. Babatunde presents the Batswana people as resistant to the modernity brought by Christianity, preferring the wealth embedded in their African values and traditions.

Religion, in the guise of Christianity, became the means for a new group of elites to shift the cultural focus from African values and traditions to the materialistic drive of modernity. Churches are now obsessed with the acquisition of wealth, and pastors pander to the dictates of the rich and powerful. Religious activities in the nation currently lack a spiritual base—the church has failed to teach the value of accountability, hard work, and discipline, making it exude the same crude materialism found elsewhere in society.[26]

Festivals

Tradition has put ceremonies in place to celebrate and keep memories and values alive within African customs and culture. Some festivals have strict rules for participation, which can involve gender inclusion or exclusivity. The Egungun festival remembers deified ancestors and celebrates the return of their spirits,[27] maintaining Yoruba tradition by linking the living and the departed—loved ones are never truly gone but transformed into celestial beings. Representations of the Egungun festival symbolize an aspect of Yoruba tradition by showing festivals that have been organized to celebrate the memories of the dead and encourage the living to aspire to lives and legacies that would honor their ancestors. In addition to maintaining the traditions of reincarnation and ancestral worship as mementos of the Yoruba gods and divinities, these festivals allow people to request blessings for their businesses, households, children, and properties. The festival is celebrated by all, even after the introduction of foreign religions.

Festivals act as salves for communal wounds, allowing people who had been quarreling to join in the celebration, forgetting the past and their grievances with one another. Traditional festivals maintain African culture, customs, values, artwork, spirituality, and identities. The memories of the dead are celebrated so that their good works remain in the community's collective memory.

Modern Buildings and Structures

Contemporary buildings, stores, and structures are burgeoning signs of modernity that disrupted the fluidity of traditional rural life. Boarding school, which schedules and orders lives according to strict requirements, is another introduction of modernity. Babatunde's memoir presents the preference for city life and its associated contraptions as the influence of modernity. Although the rural, agrarian lifestyle of people in traditional African villages is removed from modern contaminants and pollution, young elites prefer to steal money through political appointments and build modern houses that detract from society. The obsession with modern houses and apartments, and the willingness to obtain them through dishonest tactics, are shown as modernity's influence on the newly independent African state.

Celibacy

Celibacy is an aspect of modernity that Christianity and the Catholic church introduced to Africa. Celibacy is one of modernity's major features that opposes the Yoruba worldview. Priests in the Catholic church are celibate; they do not follow Yoruba traditions that stress the importance of procreation and the continuation of a family line. This imported European concept, introduced through colonialism and at odds with Yoruba tradition, becomes a commodity used to acquire positions in the church and society under the modern value system. Celibacy is explored by Babatunde in his memoir at great length—this requirement introduced by the Catholic Church has rendered priests genetically moribund.

Facial Marks

In Yoruba culture, tribal marks are traditionally made on the face or body for several purposes. Some children receive facial markings as part of a family tradition; these marks set them apart from other families and symbolize the child's identity. Some incisions are made for protection from evil, and *abiku*s are marked to stop their cycle of death and torment. These Yoruba traditions are explored through discussions of physical features and marks.

Radical Individualism and Communal Kinship

Yoruba tradition views kinship as an essential ingredient for the community's growth. Communal relations are one of the core aspects of Yoruba culture and tradition, strengthening the relationship between family members. However, Babatunde's memoir shows that the life of a Catholic priest focuses on individuality, which is a modern feature introduced by Christianity. The close-knit kinship discussed by Babatunde shows the traditional Yoruba family system and discusses their philosophy around organizing the community. Their worldview, which believes in expansion and productivity, relies on procreation and expects every male member of the community to uphold their responsibility to take a wife and produce children. Celibacy, as the driving principle of the Catholic priesthood, is a modern value that creates friction and conflicts.

Representation of Tradition as Idyllic

The traditional values in Babatunde's work are transparency, honesty, hard work, and dignity. Preliterate people enjoyed an idyllic life in traditional society, maintaining their own system of education, morals, and philosophy. The memoir provides an idyllic example of tradition when it describes the tales told after the evening meal, by moonlight, in every household. Children gathered to receive life lessons embellished with these folktales, and Babatunde notes that the stories taught virtues that were cherished by the community.[28] These collections of cultural and traditional materials used folktales, songs, poems, and riddles to teach and educate children about history, values, thought systems, knowledge systems, and religious views. Babatunde uses these traditions to showcase the idyllic and serene system of Yoruba societies and communities, which are further explored through interpersonal relationships and the accommodation of strangers.

Modernity has brought many changes to the idyllic ways of preliterate society. Babatunde describes this serene, simplistic way of living as preferable to the commotion and pollution of the city. A city is a place where vices are boldly displayed in a bid to move up the social ladder.

Patriarchal System of Dominance

Babatunde's memoir frequently notes how African traditions and customs have maintained a domineering male society, especially among the Yoruba. These traditions enforce rules, values, customs, and practices that validate the supremacy of the male gender while viewing the female gender as "the other." Systems of administration and community governance, and the family structure itself, places a male figure at the center of every important process. The memoir explores Yoruba tradition as one that marginalizes the female gender, keeping males at the center of the community while females revolve round them. The author's portrayal of Imeko city and the Sotho-Tswana culture shows women at the mercy of male-dominated societies. Tradition, as represented in Babatunde's work, is patriarchal and male-centered.

Representation of Modernity in Freedom and Feministic Ideas

Modernity is represented by the "been-tos" in Babatunde's memoir. These people have been to Europe and spent a considerable amount of time experiencing its values and opportunities. They fail to apply their experience and education in African countries. Instead, they display a preference for city life filled with modern conveniences.

Female freedom and rebellious attempts to gain freedom are represented as modernity in Babatunde's work. Feminism and feministic tendencies are encouraged by modernity, leading women to rebel against traditions and customs, showing defiance in an attempt to wrest control and power from a male-dominated society. The memoir explores the modern concept of equality as the grand principle of feminism. In the memoir, the fluidity of gender roles creates an egalitarian society enabled by modernity.

African tradition has created social roles for males and females in society, holding the male gender superior to the female gender, but the modern marriage of Ayinla and Kelebogile shows the decomposition of these sociologically constructed gender roles. In the modern marriage system, men and women are equal, disbanding traditional polygamous structures through the church and Western monogamy.

In the memoir, Ayinla becomes an embodiment of the modern system of monogamy. In the egalitarian structure of his household, he provides for the family and acts as the caregiver when his wife is absent. Kelebogile is a symbol of female freedom and rebellion from the traditionally constructed image of the African woman. Babatunde explores her confluence of tradition and modernity through her educational achievements and the success of her marriage—she is depicted as a strong and successful woman in the memoir. Kelebogile calibrates African traditions and values in synthesis with modernity, achieving a positive fusion of energy.

Representation of Modernity as a Liberating Force

Babatunde's memoir illustrates how modernity can be a liberating force for otherwise illiterate people, freeing them from outdated aspects of tradition that stifle their abilities and add little to their quality of life. Catholicism is shown as the foremost avenue for liberation from ignorance, achieved through the introduction of Western education.[29] Aduni reminds everyone that white people brought opportunities to improve the status of women and make them competitive. New opportunities to excel were shown in the ability of women to provide for their children and send them to new schools that taught skills of survival for the modern world, which had changed in the aftermath of the Second World War.[30]

Modernity offered the power for women to liberate themselves from patriarchal dominance, breaking from the African tradition that had made them subordinate to their male counterparts. For women, modernity was more than a few innovations; it was an eye-opening call for freedom. Modernity awoke feminist ideas in women and offered academic excellence for their children. In Babatunde's memoir, Catholicism was one form of modernity that represented an instrument of liberation, giving freedom to African women. They were no longer at the periphery of society. Instead, they took a new place of power as a fulcrum to enable the prosperity of their households and communities.

Alienation in Modernity

Babatunde's work discusses how modernity can lead to alienation from origins and ancestral roots. Modernity eroded the communal living of the African tradition to promote a spirit of alienation and distance from the values and customs of the African space. Elite African groups and youths who had visited other parts of the world, especially Europe, had to reacquaint themselves and their children with their roots and origins. Alienation from values and customs—which translates into the essence of not being in Africa but instead carrying its consciousness in a new identity—is modernity's major impact on the alienated African. Social scientists, psychologists, and anthropologists who have studied the process of social and cultural transformation agree that alienation is a symptom of modernity. The African who is alienated from traditions and culture is also unable to claim an identity from borrowed or acquired Western values.

Purity and Cleanliness

Modernity and tradition intersect in Babatunde's memoir; traditional features and modern inventions wrap around each other in an intricate design that embellishes the author's work. Purity and cleanliness are shown as elements of both Yoruba tradition and modernity: Yoruba tradition stresses the importance of purity in character and service, while modernity espouses the same values through the Catholic seminary. Both tradition and modernity stress the need for purity in all activities. The concept of "Omoluabi" is one of the principal intersections of tradition and modernity in Babatunde's work, showing the purity of character valued by both. Yoruba tradition encourages Africans to be pure in honor and character, and the teachings of the Catholic church urge priests and parishioners to remain pure through confession.

Gendered and Patriarchal System

Yoruba society and its traditions are centered on men and highly gendered, like the modern practices of the Catholic Church. Women are at the periphery in the church and at home; structures within tradition and modernity limit female power. The highly gendered structures of tradition, with rules and stringent customs for women, are similar to that of the Catholic Church. The priest becomes a male figure of dominance, and all must submit to the one acknowledged as "father." In the African tradition, the father is the man whose authority is sacrosanct in the community and at home. Tradition and Catholic modernity are gendered and patriarchal.

Duality of Existence

From the exploration of tradition and modernity in the memoir, Babatunde reveals similar philosophical views in Yoruba tradition and modern projections of Plato's ideas. A foundation of Yoruba tradition is the belief in the duality of human existence, both at the celestial level and on the earthly stage—"Orun" was the abode of divinities, deified ancestors, and the Yoruba high god. Both Plato's dualistic world and the Yoruba dual levels of existence prove that tradition is rarely the absence of epistemological inclination. Instead, it is the beginning of modern ideas, philosophies, and epistemologies.

There are also contradictions and areas of divergence between tradition and modernity, such as the Yoruba belief system's differing ideas about eternity and heaven. Modern ideas about the nature of man also contradict the Yoruba worldview regarding the innate personality of humans. The modern view, drawn from the philosophical writings of scholars, states that human nature is malevolent; the Yoruba view is that humanity is intrinsically good.

The ideas of Western scholars tend to conflict with African and Yoruba worldviews and traditions. Modern ideas advanced by Sigmund Freud were inherently different from Yoruba customs and traditions—the concept of Oedipus and Electra complexes upturns the tradition and customs of the

Yoruba related to sexual attraction and copulation between members of the same family. The Yoruba tradition forbids any sexual attachment to either the father or the mother, although Freud's theory seems to espouse it. The ideas and philosophies represented as modern are in sharp contrast to the traditions of the Yoruba people. Celibacy, as a requirement to serve as a priest in church, is challenged by Yoruba traditions of procreation and the continuation of a family's lineage.

Projection of Tradition in Modernity

Modernity is not always a departure from tradition; it can expand traditions into a larger perspective that enhances preliterate knowledge, thought systems, values, culture, and customs. Babatunde demonstrates the eruption of traditional views and knowledge systems in combination with modern knowledge systems about science and technology. The Ifá system of knowledge, which works on binary permutations and the manipulation of divination beads and seeds, is a system of geomancy that applies to computer science and mathematics. The coding, writing, and programming systems of computer science are reminiscent of the Ifá cipher and the marks made on its divination tray.

Projection of Modernity in Tradition

Babatunde's work shows the projection of modernity within Yoruba tradition, explored as a foreshadowing of the future during the preliterate era. Tradition is not the mere continuation of archaic thought systems, values, customs, and knowledge. It is the careful study and examination of the world based on experience and practice. Modern ideas had begun to develop even in traditional customs and knowledge systems.

Pan-African ideas and ideology developed from the auspices of traditional values embedded in African beliefs about family and communal relations. This projection of modernity developed from tradition as one of the core principles of the African people—to unite and create "one nation" of people who believe in the same system of "family." The conceptualization of pan-Africanism is that of a modern ideology espoused by intellectuals in the nineteenth century, but close examination shows that the main idea behind traditional African values and belief systems has been woven into communal responsibilities and family development. Pan-African ideas and philosophy are not much different from knowledge systems in traditional African communities, although they have more refined labels and definitions. The "Ubuntu" ideology of the Sotho-Tswana people and the communal cooperation of the Yoruba resemble modern pan-African constellations of ideas. Pan-Africanism has risen from the ashes of African traditions and values, seen in the communal strength of the Yoruba tradition and the Ubuntu family-oriented Sotho-Tswana tradition.

CONCLUSION

This chapter has explored representations of tradition and modernity in the work of Emmanuel Babatunde. "Tradition" refers to cultural materials, values, customs, beliefs, practices, and rituals that are recorded in the memoir. "Modernity," explored in this chapter, engages foreign practices, values, cultures, manners, and thought systems introduced into the African space, supplanting tradition and taking a prominent place in the lives of African elites and youths. Babatunde's memoir displays the nuanced interaction and fusion of African traditions and European modernity; an exploration of African traditions represented in the work can examine how these values, knowledge systems, beliefs, practices, and customs encompass the ingrained African tradition and the confluence of values seen in the memoir's male Yoruba protagonist and the female Motswana protagonist.

Modernity became a fixture in the African milieu through colonialism and missionary work. Celibacy, as a way of life in the European Catholic church, became an aspect of modernity that conflicted with African traditions of procreation and multiplication through marriage and childbearing. Babatunde's exploration of celibate priesthood and his eventual married life engages the influence and representation of both tradition and modernity. Although tradition is gradually succumbing to the pressures of modernization and civilization, it remains at the center of any African identity. Traditions are what make an African true to his origins. Modernity will continue to spread, but its influence on the African space cannot overshadow African traditions. Tradition and modernity are two sides of the same coin, and they are needed to negotiate the intellectual landscape of African space.

Chapter 4

DERIVING MEANING

Nuances of Language, Nodes of Orality, and Sense of Communitarianism in Michael Afolayan's *Fate of Our Mothers*

When talking about language in Africa, the discourse is riddled with the influence of colonialism. Colonialism inflicts damage on the cultures of Africa. Language is a dominant criterion of a culture. No matter how mild the encounter between two cultures, it tends to produce favorable and unfavorable results. Therefore, whether it is episodic or epochal, colonialism brought about changes in African society. The impact of colonialism on communication and language cannot be overstated. The history of African societies shows that Africans were essentially oral before cultural encounters with the West. That is, in Africa, there are several oral traditions that ensure that everything is done within the scope of orality. These oral systems were sustained so much that language and its orality are intrinsically tied to meaning.

It is important to note the influence of cultural encounters between Western cultures and African cultures, and point out how the question of language affected intellectual discourse during and after colonialism. Language discourse in the early years after colonialism centered on metalanguage—that is, can an intellectual discourse be truly African if it is done in a Western language? The humanities, most especially, were contented to be inauthentic for adopting the language of the oppressors. The question of the importance of language and the adoption of a foreign one rests on the idea that indigenous African languages are not capable of intellectual engagement.

There is a politics of language that brings about the inequality of languages. It is impossible to examine the role and status of languages in a multilingual situation without confronting the reality of power and dominance. As applied to English, "the overwhelming and towering status of English has been characterized in terms of dominance, power, hegemony, and linguistic imperialism."[1] According to Amuseghan Adejimola, "Factors, such as number

Fig. 4.1 – Michael Afolayan, courtesy of Michael Efionayi.

of speakers, socioeconomic status of speakers, legal status and domains of use are often regarded as possible indicators of dominance. English enjoys dominance mostly in the former British colonies because of its elite status, political influence, higher socioeconomic opportunities and its neutrality, though the colonial impostors were in minority when it was introduced."[2]

Examples in Africa include Swahili in Tanzania, Akan in Ghana, Hausa in Nigeria, and Zulu in South Africa. Dominance may be associated with a minority of speakers if that minority also has a higher socioeconomic status.[3] The point here is that colonialism brought about the dominance of the

English language, which has made the utility of English the universal and acceptable linguistic paradigm. This also has affected the meta-intellectual discourse of language in many fields.

To corroborate Bamgbose's position, it is pertinent to note the dominance of English, which has relegated the relevance of indigenous African languages. For Alamin Mazrui, the ideas and machinations of colonial education have greatly affected the linguistic configuration that has thus elevated European languages over African languages even in official capacities.[4]

The adoption of the English language as the mode of communication and education has made the linguistic debate in Africa very difficult. There is a common assumption that African educational systems would benefit more from the use of indigenous languages. The underlying idea is that language has its intrinsic resourcefulness, and the use of indigenous language will help Africans grasp ideas directly.

In relation to this is the text under study—*Fate of Our Mothers*—that is riddled with variations of languages that contribute to its meaning. It is important to note that the essence of language is its meaning, and it should be translatable to the readers so that they can derive the thematic concepts in such a text. This has, however, been explicated in the memoir, which is a compilation of memories from childhood to adulthood, the age of reason. The book starts off with accounts of the learning process of a child in the family system and how they steer into the nomenclature of society. Also, the narrator drifts into the struggles and energies of the parents raising him, and he delves into the actions and the inactions of some important personalities in the society that helped him to develop from a flat character to a round one. It is pertinent to note that the narrator also tells the context of the government and official situations that helped him to adjust and learn about the lessons in society from his days of humble beginnings to his days of maturity.

One interesting thing about the memoir is the language it employs. The author weaves the stories of his life in a rich and exciting manner. This is exciting due to the way he carefully balances the Yoruba cultural mosaic of the different ways of life and deftly translates some Yoruba into the English language, which makes it readable, fascinating, and endearing to the readers. This skill is worth analyzing for language critics, and how he merges it with some figures of speech in the literary world is commendable. With these efforts, the text can bridge the gap between the category of world literature and the language patterns that have contributed to the overall derivation of meaning by readers of the memoir. It is important to state that even though language is the most important element in searching for meaning in a text, some other factors have contributed to the realization of meaning. This is what Afolayan has expertly done in the memoir by making use of orality, sociocultural tendencies, and the basic difference between individualism and communitarianism in his narration to help the readers to understand the main reason he is writing the memoir. These other concepts will be engaged in this chapter as subheadings that contribute to the understanding of the meaning in the text by considering how Afolayan combines Yoruba and English in the memoir. Other language and literary theories that are relevant to the analysis of the text will also be discussed.

NUANCES OF LANGUAGE IN THE TEXT

In a linguistic context, a text can be regarded as the basic unit of meaning in language. There are components that contribute to the understanding of language in a particular text: the context of the situation and the register. These aspects, both internal and external, are not separated from the way a reader responds unconsciously to chapters in a text. However, the language critic examines these aspects; they are expected to make judgments based on the language patterns in a text, which are the grammar, vocabulary, and other concerns between the language and relevant features of the narrator's social and ideological environment. Invariably, language critics have identified these to fall within the domain of linguistics and contribute to the structure of the text, which makes it more understandable to the readers.

These language patterns of the text under study are germane to the derivation of the meaning of the text, which Afolayan has carried out quite well. The context of situation, which is the extralinguistic factor that has set the bearing and tone of the text, is what makes the language of the text noteworthy. It can be seen in the memoir that there are some factors that affect certain linguistic choices that the writer wields and thereby influence the overall effect of the writing. The significance is that it contributes to the medium and purpose of the way the writer is communicating and the kind of audience Afolayan is writing for. For instance, the memoir starts off with a dedication to different names, from Mama Agba to Venita Hammond, followed by two concrete poems, and ends with an adapted quote on mothers. Afolayan strategically places this at the beginning of the text, before the reading of the stages of memories, to make the readers know the people who surround him and whom he appreciates.

Also, the concrete poems are significant. The first one is a kind of praise concrete poem, and the second poem offers salutation to the people around him before he starts writing. The significance of these is the invocation of a sort of visual and mental imagery that the readers can connect with and tag along with his stories. It can also be said that the narrator has morals as paying homage through his poem and ending with prayers counts as a sociological situational context. The writer also adopts intertextuality by bringing on prayers from another book to substantiate his own. These techniques and the language he uses are endearing to the reader and will make the reader want to sit back and follow his stories. The language also serves as a form of offering credibility and believability to his coming stories in the rest of the book.

In relation to this, the writer's personality can be sensed through the language Afolayan employs in the text, and he thus helps the readers to derive the meaning as well. The language in the text helps to create a tone and social setting for the readers by focusing on the form, content, medium, genre, and interactional norms in the text. For instance, in the preface of the text, the writer starts off with a proverb that helps to categorize the genre of the text, which is a memoir and a narration of stories. Through words such as "write," "history," "landscape," and "mythical,"[5] it can be deciphered that the genre of the text is a narration of different and personal stories. This is a careful method by Afolayan that has contributed to one of the concerns of the text.

Also, through the preface, the author's narrative viewpoint can be determined and how he attributes the stories to the collective responsibility of the whole people in his community: "*Fate of Our Mothers* is not my story; it is a careful weaving together of our collective tales in the words endowed me within my privileged space and from the eyes of my privileged self. Were it to be my story, I would have had to embellish it, build strength to it, fortify it with the good news of life, and be deafened to the parts that deflate my personal ego."[6] Through this quote, it is important to state that even though the author narrates in the first person, he has adopted a sort of quasi-omniscient point of view by narrating the stories from his mouth through the mouth of other characters who have made the stories in the text possible. This is another mode that has contributed to the nuances of language in the text.

Additionally, the field and mode in which the text is functioning and how it contributes to the purpose are important. In a way, the writer weaves the subject matter and the methods and functions of the text together to show his creative influence and power of language. Through the language of the text, the reader can decipher that he has documented the stories to show his beginnings and what he has passed through, coupled with what shaped his development into becoming what he is now. It is not surprising that in the forty-six chapters of the text, he goes from writing about his life in the village and how he moved to the city to writing about his parents and teachers.

This, however, opens the theme of personal reflection for the readers and creates the field of the memoir.

To accentuate this, the function of this text, which connects with the theme of the text, has been channeled by the language adopted by the writer in the text. It is visible that the language in the memoir is a written one, but it can be categorized as a "pretense" spoken and an extempore node of writing embellished with the flashback technique. In all the chapters, the language is narrative and descriptive in nature. We can see the heavy use of adjectives showing a vivid description of places and names that are relevant to the author in the text. For example, in the way he describes a character, Baba Agba, he notes, "Baba Agba, our father, who often simply called Baba was noticeable in the village, as he sat in his armchair, always surrounded by some of his eleven children."[7]

Also, in describing the city of Ibadan, the author notes the fascinating landscapes and alluring items that beautify the city, such as vehicles, electric poles, and even cables.[8] These are totems that are distinctive about the Ibadan city and aptly appreciated by the author. The overt use of adjectives and vivid descriptions by the writer shows his style of writing and a sort of mental imagery to the readers. Also, Afolayan writes as if he is chanting, with more of a spoken narration in his compilation of stories. He uses language so hauntingly that even after the readers are done with the text, they can still recite some parts of the book. It thus creates so many functions in the minds of the readers, and they are all persuasive and didactic in so many ways, ultimately creating a sense of mental communication between the reader and the narrator.

Another mode of language adopted by Afolayan in his memoir is the appropriate use of tenor, the tone of the book. It is noteworthy that Afolayan adopts a consistent tone that is associated with the chapter and its subject matter. It is a sort of interactive role between the writer and the situation or person he is describing. That is why when he narrates the death of Baba Agba, the language and mood are somber and show pain. In the chapter describing his move to a new town, the language and diction are expectant and happy. These differences in tenor resonate in varied ways according to the situation of each chapter. Thus, it can be assumed that the tone is a set of relevant social relations and contexts. In other words, the text does not have a permanent or temporary tone in the text, and the readers are attached to it in a way as well.

Consequently, it can be assumed that the field, tone, and mode of communication of the text have an intricate relationship with the collective situations in the text in any context. These nodes of language, which are the context of situation, have helped the readers to understand the themes and the situations that are narrated better. These nodes also help readers to negotiate the relationship between the themes and situations presented. Thus, Afolayan has finessed his memoir, and he has given it a universal understanding to different sets of readers.

With the complexities of language problems in Africa, different writers across all genres of literature in Africa have devised ways in which they write that satisfy their local nuances and, at the same time, let their writing be of universal significance to all readers. *Fate of Our Mothers* depicts a collection of memories from Afolayan's childhood days in an African village with a rustic setting. It has tenets and traces of his first language in the stories, coupled with descriptions of how these linguistic patterns affect the structure of the text, which is mainly written in the English language. It is expedient to note that the use of the mother tongue in the text on different occasions is at the appropriate time and context. The reflection of different local styles in this text will be critically examined.

One of the glaring features of indigenous language in the text is the use of chants, praise poems, and the call and response form. These are part of the oral literature of most African countries, as they serve to be part of different tribes and are used in different situations on people. The writer of this memoir has used praise poetry, chants, and call and response to further explain what the characters discussed and how significant they are at the time of narrating. Also, these oral renditions are used to analyze or show the importance of a situation and how important it is to the main character or the society at large. For instance, in the narration of "The river shall flow but not blood," where the writer discusses the marriage ceremony of Ebe, the whole community chants some poems to accompany her in receiving blessings from families. These chants are carried out in a courtyard by families, and the language of the chants is recited in such a way that it can be committed to memory because it is in the form of an interesting story based on the spatial qualities that draw the interests of a child. The chants employ the features of the river, sky, and denizens to perform didactic functions.[9] These beautiful lines portray characters that are interesting and situations that are tall tales in nature, which make reciters commit them to memory and thereby transfer them from generation to generation.

In addition, songs are used for different situations. They are used in terms of kinship, where drummers use their talking drums to chant and the people tag along. These words are easy to recite, and they have interesting actions that can make the readers remember them vividly: "The evil machination that you have been scheming since last year, without sleeping and without dosing off, have fallen right into our hands. We challenge you to swear if this were not true, we challenge you to swear! The petition you wrote last year for which you neither slept nor dosed off has fallen into our hands. We challenge you to swear if this were not true. We challenge you to swear!"[10] It can be seen that these lines also have a form of repetition of words and some situations to make them more understandable and ring in the minds of the listeners and readers, which is a unique aspect of the praise poems in the Yoruba language.

To corroborate this and to show the universality of poems and songs in different languages to capture situations, the writer also gives the example of repetitive songs in the memoir, which are captivating and can be committed to memory easily. For example, in the narration of "Days of reckoning," when the writer remembers his school days during holiday periods, the repetition of words is seen. This gives musicality to the language, making it alluring for children. In the text, the writer presents the repetition of phrases of "holiday is coming"[11] to effect happiness in the mind of the child.

Another style of language used in the text is the translation of native proverbs and idioms. The text is filled with so many proverbs and wise sayings that are situated in the Yoruba culture, but what is interesting is the way Afolayan has handled these sayings and proverbs to capture the situation he is discussing without losing their deep, underlying meanings. The way he translates each situation into English is noteworthy as it is still intelligible to readers who are non-Yoruba. In the text, the examples of these loosely translated instances are replete, even though they are sung in Yoruba. The translation into English by Afolayan has not made the language lose its entire meaning, but they have allowed readers who are non-Yoruba to have a feeling of the situation and, at the same time, understand it perfectly well. For instance, the recount of when it rains:

> The rain is falling
> The sun is shinning
> Two old folks are fighting up there in the sky;
> Who will settle their dispute.[12]

In the Yoruba meaning, we all know it is talking about the clouds gathering together before it rains, not that two people are floating in the sky fighting it out. But the writer has narrated it to make it more intelligible and help readers who are unfamiliar with the Yoruba language understand that it is the context of the rain. Another example is the salamander animal, which is a reptile that children hate, and it shows the children's alertness to such an animal by reinforcing their strength through the song that notes that "Before you become a snake I will turn into a needle, my blood is bitter than the taste of the bitter leaf."[13] This situation is really not talking about turning into a needle but stating that the person is smarter than the reptile and would kill it even before it ran away. The writer portrays the needle as an object of destruction to the reptile.

Another instance is the narration of the girls doing the cheerleading parade. The translations of the cheers into English show that the word "chicken" suggests the superiority of the girls to other girls, and not literally hens to hens. Also, there are some words that have more effective rendition when they are not translated into the English language. Afolayan, therefore, has explained and translated these words perfectly in the book, and the context in which they are used is portrayed appropriately. Examples of such words are "opomulero," "oorun ojo-kanri," "ogunso," "Olu-orun," and sayings like "eni ojo pa ti Sango o pa, ko maa dupe." These words and sayings are translated expertly, but some lose their meanings during translation, which the writer has explained well. However, there are other examples from the text to support this variation of language in translating from one language to another.

The different variations in the Yoruba language are another aspect of language that the writer notes in his memoir. Just as the English language has different accents peculiar to different regions or countries, the Yoruba language has this too. This is well espoused in the text and has a relation or connection with the way the memoir is discussed. The author starts his stories with a certain variation of the Yoruba language that is peculiar to his village, where he is growing up and what his parents say to him. As the memoir is a compilation of stories of different episodes of childhood memories, the noticeable variation of other Yoruba accents is detected when the writer recounts when he traveled to the town of Shaki in "The Place of the Wander Boy."

It is important to state that society determines the variation of linguistic patterns and sayings in it. The writer notes that in Shaki, a town that is part of Yorubaland, even though it contains renegade sons of Ogun in Yoruba history, the people have their own version of the Yoruba language. The author notes this when he enquires from Brother Akinola, who was his guide during the sojourn: "I see! I said to him. So, is 'sha' then the same as 'sa,' which means to run away, and 'ki' as in 'kiri' stands for 'to roam about the place?' I asked. You got it right!"[14] It can be noted that there is a difference in the phonology of the Yoruba language, especially in the consonantal explosion, which is different from one Yoruba society to another. This basic difference that the writer has noted can contribute to the understanding of the phonotactics of the Yoruba language.

The bilingual mode of writing is another nuance of language in the text. The author does not only depend on cultural speech styles and English alone but also mixes pidgin English into the narration. Pidgin English is a form of language that is mangled in nature but remains intelligible despite the lack of coherent syntactic patterns that are found in the standard form of the English language. Pidgin English is sometimes used between speakers who are not of the same tribe when one of them lacks the ability to speak the standard version of English. In the writer's narration, when he visits the city of Ibadan, he notes that the pidgin English there has different tonal markers. This is shown in the text, as some of the words like "okay" and "wait" have different spellings, and words like "mineral" have another representation and meaning, but at the same time, they are intelligible to both speakers. For example, "oke, mek una weit, oga; a go fit git beta minira, sa"[15] is translated as, "Okay, Sir, let me get another cold drink for you."

It is evident that there are differences in word formations and sentence pairings in the pidgin language and the standard English language as well. Another example is "eh broad, dat moto no be for una; if e be ya own, una for don catch am . . . broad, ya bus don de come. Make una enter am kwik, a go carry ya potmonto put for back. Hia, take dis packet of a-si-pro wey fit mek una bodi de kampe when una don reach for Ibadan. God seif una o."[16]

Another node of language in the text is the process of naming in Yoruba. This process of naming is captivating, especially in Yoruba land. There are objects and things in English that are named due to the way the objects are shaped or seen because naming is based on visual representations of the objects. Also, there are names for characters and towns as well that serve as a convenient mode of calling them. For instance, in the text, the author notes how an object such as the neck of the gramophone is directly translated to "snake neck" even though it is called "his master's voice." It is called the former because it looks like a snake and the structure on the neck of the object. To capture this, the writer says, "I learnt that they stood for 'his master's voice.' Villagers called these record players *Olorun ejo*, meaning 'snake neck.' This was because the part that played on the record looked like the neck of a snake."[17]

ORALITY AND SOCIOCULTURAL IDENTITIES IN THE TEXT

The African literary space has been a site of and for orality, giving people a voice and the capacity to record and preserve their beliefs, worldviews, and everyday experiences. This means that in Africa, orality, which is the oldest medium of interaction, has served as the vehicle for literary expressions. Orality is at the foundation of all poetic and dramatic expressions, including African prose fiction. As a result, orality has continued to influence African literature in general, especially African prose fiction. Walter Ong agrees that the orality form preceded literacy. He stressed the importance of orality before literacy was hailed. He opines that, "You cannot without serious and disabling distortion describe a primary phenomenon by starting with a subsequent secondary phenomenon and paring away the differences."[18]

Orality is the fundamental feature of African literature, with writing as the secondary phenomenon. In places where the people have not developed writing skills, orality is generally their means of thoughts and vocal expressions. However, orality should not be mistaken for oral tradition. Oral tradition may be defined as a body of beliefs, behavior, practices, and customs lived and valued by a culture; a defined action or behavior pattern in society or among a group of people. Africans have a rich and dynamic oral tradition that is usually used to transmit values from one generation to the next.

Through oral traditions, we know about older African religious and moral practices, rituals, and all forms of cultural expectations. According to Eileen Julien, "For centuries the oral traditions of Africa, in Amharic, Bambara, Hausa, Lingala, Poulaar, Swahili, Twi, Wolof, Xhosa, Yoruba, Zulu, and hundreds of other indigenous languages, have thrived in the form of proverbs, tales, epics, riddles, and poetry—religious, ceremonial, political, occasional, personal."[19] In African prose fiction, there are lots of traditional proverbs, festivals, witty and pithy sayings, festivals, and folklores to demonstrate the richness of African oral traditions. Modern written African literature also tap into established oral traditions to create a hybrid.

Thus, Afolayan has adopted the conscious use of orality in his work, bringing out the elements of the Yoruba culture mostly to point out or display the fact that the African culture existed in its own form before the advent of colonialism. He has mastered the Yoruba culture and adequately translated it into English in a form that can be categorized as world literature. This node of orality has contributed meaning to the overall text. And with these accommodations of orality, the sociocultural identities pertaining to the African literary space will be critically examined.

One of the salient sociocultural identities that can be recognized from this memoir is utilitarianism. This text is functional in nature; it is more socialized than the ones based on individual psychology, which means our stories are community-oriented and serve the purpose of the community. This is absolutely portrayed by the writer of the text, as he exclaimed that it is a story based on the community and not his individual experiences. With this, most of the stories narrated in the different chapters where elders were involved always reveal a didactic effect. This is espoused in the text as the author uses folktales to substantiate this. The narration of folktales in the text serves to teach a lesson. For instance, one of the characters in the memoir, Baba Agba, loves to tell tales that are aimed at teaching morals to kids, including the narrator. In one of his tales, he taught the listener the lessons of humility and talking when the time is right by investing and creating a didactic tale of a mythical character.[20]

These tales are always effective, and they can be retold in any situation. The Yoruba always add or refine the stories just to suit the instance in which they are telling them. That is why it is not surprising that the character of Baba Agba tells another tale again in the text just to serve another purpose. Baba Agba teaches another lesson of cooperation when the kids are playing football to preach the idea of unity.[21] It is pertinent to note that these folktales serve as moments for the ethical and cultural development of the community. The stories are ways of civilizing the people to acculturate and enculturate, and they serve as the conscience of the people.

Another cultural identity in the text is the way it draws from the worldview of the heritage of the Yoruba people. This memoir narrates the different cultural views of the Yoruba people. For instance, there are stories about the marriage system, religious life, home, and fashion. Also, the cosmology of the Yoruba is evident in the memoir. The relationships of the different worlds—living, dead, and unborn—are discussed in the text. The relationships are related to it in terms of the dead. In the Yoruba cosmology, death is the beginning of another spiritual existence, and birth into this world is also the end of one's stage of existence, which is the concept of time and space. In the text, the author talks about the transition of the world of the dead.

In addition, another signifier of sociocultural identity is the language used in the text. Our language is also a signifier. It is noted that even when we write our stories, most writers do not use standard English; they employ the use of African English, what Adelugba termed "Yorubanglish." This example of Yorubanglish by Adelugba is espoused by Afolayan in the memoir. He highlights instances of different characters who coin words by joining suffixes to Yoruba words just to sound educated because, most times, language determines the class in which an individual is placed in society. For instance, the character of Ogadi repeats Yoruba words by adding suffixes from English to coin words that can only be intelligible to an individual familiar with the sociolinguistic words in Yoruba and that are not understandable to users of standard English. This is shown thus:

Some of us were either too young or villagers were too ignorant to recognise that Ogadi was only repeating Yoruba words. He was making them to sound like English words or in some cases he was just uttering gibberish sounds altogether. This is because when something was attractive to a Yoruba person, it was common to say about that thing, "*O fanimora*." For Ogadi to say he translated it into English by simply adding "ous" to "fanimora" left so much to be desired, but nobody knew any better. He used many of these words so often that my friend and I called him "Baba Igilajuba . . ." People would say he spoke "*Baba nla Oyinbo*."[22]

The English tainted with "Africanity" is often used by Afolayan, and that is why there are a lot of African proverbs, axioms, and oratorical structures in the memoir. Some other texts even have pidgin English embedded in them, which is not missing in this text either. Therefore, language serves as the revelation of our stories. Afolayan has espoused this perfectly well in the memoir. Similarly, the memoir can also be adjudged to be a defense of the African culture, as it is a quintessential weapon to defend the Yoruba culture in what it entails and in its tenets. Most writers write bearing in mind that it is a view to affirm their faith in the culture and how it can bring goodwill and the like. Afolayan also espouses African mystical life in the memoir through a careful reading of it. In the text, there are different ways in which the writer mentions the gods of the land and their functions in society. This is a way of de-westernizing the memoir genre in Africa and making it more peculiarly situated in the Yoruba context, which the author has greatly done in his stories.

As much as Afolayan has talked about some cultures of the Yoruba in a good light and defends them as well, he has also highlighted some parts of the Yoruba traditions that he did not like while narrating his stories. For instance, the writer denounces and detests the custom of circumcision. Discussing this tradition in his memoir brings a balance to the story without over-romanticizing the Yoruba culture in condemning the practice of circumcision, which the author calls a cultural aberration. The result of this harmful practice, even though he understands it as a tradition, is always painful and sometimes leads to death as the author "heard of stories of girls who never survived the experience."[23]

Having analyzed the correlation between language, orality, and meaning, another perspective that cannot be ignored is the essence of orality, language, and meaning in the African family system. The African family system is believed to be essentially polygamous. However, many practices have changed due to Western encounter, modernization, and urbanization. Modern ideas of monogamy, inheritances, and joint incomes are becoming very popular. As a result, the traditional and cultural norms and values that defined rural communities have all been altered. One of the cultural norms of a traditional African family is the use of oral tools to teach history, moral lessons, and educate family members on the socialization of a certain culture. In the traditional Yoruba family system, for example, the use of poetry connects descendants with their ancestors. Panegyrics are recited to praise the traits of the ancestors seen in their descendants. For example, Ijala is "one of the various type of oral poetry of the Yoruba-speaking people, a buoyant and resilient people who have a zest for enjoying life while at the same time attaching great importance to hard work as the only guarantee of economic well-being."[24] The takeaway from this is that the African family system fulfills itself in its orality. It is not just a vain orality but an orality that comes with purpose, meaning, and wealth of words.

Oral tradition in the African family system is more significant when examined from historical and philosophical perspectives. The African family system benefits from what is known as "Tales by the Moonlight." Orality in the traditional African family system assumes roles for family members. As a result of the commitment of the events of the family to memory, some members are often regarded as family historians. Also, due to the ability of a member of a family to discern knowledge and his native wisdom, the member is considered the family sage. When matters arise, these members are summoned or approached to make historical references to the past. This is done orally and not by reference to written documents. Their oral prowess has made them custodians of family history and ancient systems.

Orality in the African family system is often achieved by the use of folklore, songs, and poetry. Arguably, African orality focuses more on its folkloric nature. Folklore to Africans is essentially an anthropological process. In defining the relationship of folklore with linguistic presentation on the understanding of tales and proverbs, which are traditions the memoirist expresses, William Bascom notes that "folklore, however, falls squarely within the fourth field, cultural anthropology, which is concerned with the study of the customs, traditions, and institutions of living peoples."[25] Bascom lucidly explicates the relation between linguistics and orality. The nature of orality amongst Africans, especially in their family system, serves the purpose of passing down customs and traditions. The source of authority, norms, and behaviors is rooted in orality. Without orality, African families lose their history, customs, and traditions.

YORUBA FAMILY LIFE AND ITS COMMUNITARIAN NATURE

There is a notion that Africans are essentially communitarian or communalistic in nature. Contrary to Western culture, the African way of life is based on communitarian values. Personhood in Africa is achieved by the assumption that the destinies of its people are interwoven. That is, the existence of the one depends on the affirmation of the existence of the other. That is why aphorisms such as "I am, because we are; and since we are, therefore I am"[26] and "it takes a village to raise a child"[27] are considered truisms. According to D. A. Masolo, his idea of communitarianism is the "antithesis of individualism, but its manifestations in intellectual traditions around the world reveal important regional modifications."[28]

The idea of communitarianism, according to Masolo, borders on geographical and racial characteristics. That is, communitarianism in Africa differs from communitarianism in the West. However, what cannot be removed from the idea of communitarianism is the idea of community and togetherness because communitarianism preaches the importance of the whole instead of the part. Western ideology since Rene Descartes's *cogito ergo sum* (I think, therefore I exist) has focused on the principles of individualism. The principles of individualism and solipsism in the West have brought about capitalism and liberalism. However, the concept of unity, togetherness, and a shared destiny is the foundation on which African societies are laid. Africans believe in the principle of "We," rather than "I," as obtainable in the West. African society has moved from merely existing to the consciousness that their existence is tied to that of others.

Therefore, it is not surprising that the narrator in the memoir depicts communal life, the act of helping strangers rather than only family, and also portrays the concept of home as dynamic. The majority of Africans believe in communalism rather than individuality, as is the case in the West. This concept of communal affiliation is related to humanism, in which the other person is as important as you are, and not just in filial relationships but affiliations generally. This is an acculturation and enculturation process and a fundamental principle that helps in the acceptance of diverse cultures. The beginning of the text shows the narrator dwelling on the presentation of characters that are of a family and their actions, but the narrator tilts toward the embrace of the community and how long-lasting relationships can be built.

In the stories by the writer, there is the idea of communal life and helping other tribes. For instance, during wartime, as narrated by the writer, some people who were not Yoruba were protected even in the face of execution, and they were regarded as family members rather than visitors or refugees. This is a step toward humanism and the essence of living a fulfilled life. In the text, the memoir notes, "the case throughout the Yoruba communities, all those from the east who lived in our house during the war were all protected, and not a single one was killed. Sometimes if some military people visited the village, asking if there were "rebels" working on our farms, we would tell them they had all returned to their villages."[29] In emphasizing this model of communitarianism, the memoir presents the character of Mama Agba as she hides individuals in the face of attacks, which is a model Afolayan seeks to promote.

Also, the concept of home as everywhere is espoused in the text. The idea that home is fixated, or someone's natal abode, is subverted and challenged in Afolayan's memoir; this is part of the communitarian tenets that Africans imbibe. In the memoir, we see the acceptance and protection of a migrant Igbo worker in the village of the narrator. He was protected from those who can be regarded as tribal conscious and welcomed into the community, which serves as his own home. This is shown in the text through the character of Brother Gbagbo as an anti-communitarian who does not espouse the ideals of unity and inter-relationship as he tries to threaten to turn a migrant Igbo worker in to a soldier in time of adversity. However, a saying of the community counters this notion, which is that "a friend from outside is better than an enemy from within."[30]

The concept of multiculturalism is another way of preaching community growth in an ideal African society, which Afolayan has revealed in the memoir. Through a close reading of the memoir, there is a sense in which it can be argued that multiculturalism preaches tolerance and diversity. As a matter of fact, the idea presented in the memoir successfully preaches love and solidarity between people of different religions and beliefs while promoting equal treatment of individuals in society and making them more relatable. In the text, the housing together of the different religions in Oke-Awo is seen as peaceful and worthy of emulation as "Muslims, Christians and traditional worshippers had always lived together harmoniously in Oke-Awo without any complaints and consume food together during different festivities concerning one religion or the other without hassle."[31]

It can be deciphered from this extract that there is love, a sort of interconnectedness, and the resonation of the plural pronoun "we"—instead of the singular pronoun "I"—which shows solidarity and enrichment among diverse people in a community. This is the ideal of a communitarian world that Afolayan has displayed through his memoir. Yoruba family life exhibits the idea of communitarianism. In fact, the Yoruba believe that only four eyes give birth to a child, but it takes two hundred eyes to raise the child. This notion is riddled throughout the text as the whole community has a role to play in the life of the main character, which is the narrator as well.

CONCLUSION

This chapter discusses the search for meaning in the memoir *Fate of Our Mothers*, by Michael Afolayan, through the lens of language—that is, first and second language. The components of the context of language, linguistic patterns, and the social setting are analyzed as well. The sociocultural identities that are replete in African literary documents are also examined in the sense of how they have contributed to the understanding of the text by different readers. Also, the text has debunked the culture of orality with the intention to project literacy as its cultural superior—and necessary successor—possessing all that is lacking in the former. However, it is important to note that cultures of primary orality need to be encouraged to see reality using the descriptions with which they are familiar, rather than being made to gaze unthinkingly at a letter-induced private reality.

This work has attempted to demonstrate the effects of individualism and communitarianism in the strive toward a good human society. The text notes that individualism, on the one hand, holds negative implications for a good community, while communitarianism, on the other hand, fosters a great human community. This conclusion is arrived at through the analysis of the tenets of both theories, as they are well-espoused by the author in the text. A community means a communion in unity. It is the unification of a society's diverse and separate parts, which can be found in every civilization. Therefore, as indicated in the conclusion, a thriving human society symbolizes a sociopolitical arrangement that unifies these different elements of the society into a mutual and cooperative whole, where the talented productivities of those who are well off and the fittest are made to benefit the weak and the worst-off of society, with the intent of ensuring everybody's happiness and flourishing.

Chapter 5

THE DENSITY OF CULTURES
A. B. Assensoh's *Journeys*

INTRODUCTION

A journey, in itself, takes the frame of a trip from a specific geographical location (or space) to another. In the course of a journey, there are different experiences and divergent encounters, which may be eventful, notable, or inconsequential. In totality, journeys are sometimes metaphorical and symbolic, just as a movement from one place to the other is sometimes imperative for growth and expansion. A. B. Assensoh's journeys, couched in a published memoir, are like travelogues but with interesting twists and detours, which include a text within a text that is almost like having a hypertext and hyperlink of people, race, ethnicity, places (sites of interaction and education), emotions, death, memories, remembrances, immortalization of friends, and expansion of knowledge on foreign lands. The memoir is multilayered, requiring a deft detangling of ideas, the purpose of the first journey, the brief African political space and culture, with the introduction of such modernity as serial monogamy, culture shock, copyright laws, and healthcare policies to the appreciation of cultural values in China and to the unwelcoming nature of American society. In sum, the memoir is a hypertext of people, experiences, discourses, trips, pictorial illustrations, and achievements in the wake. The topical issues are some of the effects of Assensoh's journeys, which will be discussed and explored in this chapter. This chapter will also explore the many journeys in the memoir and the intention behind the migration to each place, as well as the numerous ways in which the journeys have impacted Assensoh, who is the center of the discourse.

Migrant Stories: A Memoir of Living and Survival in the West and Asia is written by A. B. Assensoh as a sequel to his first memoir, *A Matter of Sharing*. This second memoir reflects and refracts the life, struggles, pain, journeys,

Fig. 5.1 – A. B. Assensoh, courtesy of Michael Efionayi.

and sojourns in the West and Asia. Assensoh's memoir codifies the journeys of his struggles as a journalist in Ghana, who is being hunted for his writings about the military regime and its undemocratic rule. Assensoh's memoir, like others written by scholars like him, is filled with a template of academic excellence, intellectual discourses, and educational issues that are confronting Africa. This dissection will delve into the migrant's stories, as the title of the memoir frames and detangles the meaning(s) of his journeys, coupled with the essence of the different shades of experiences gathered and sometimes absorbed by the author. More importantly, it will look at how Assensoh has presented cultures in three locations, from Ghana to China and back to the United States of America, in a bid to effectively showcase how a culture, no matter how big or small, may be an embodiment of everything good at the global level.

SECTION A: AFRICANITY AT HOME

African memoir writers in the diaspora are committed to events at home despite being far away from home. Ayo Kehinde observes that "Africa, and specifically the neo-colonial betrayal of the emancipatory promises of independence, becomes a recurring these directly or indirectly dominating the works of these writers who have been driven into exile by agonies of disillusionment."[1] This shows that African fiction and nonfiction writers' abandonment of home cannot be detached from the sociopolitical and economic situation in their different countries. African fiction writers in the diaspora have been classified as "New African Diasporas." Assensoh's first portrayal of culture is of Africa, and he can be considered an African migrant whose memoir writings have been "glocalisingly" appraised. This part of the memoir has been able to survey the sources of postcolonial African conditions and how the major topics like polygamy, family tension, modernity, and identity have been able to present African portraiture in line with cultural, social, and political realism in the global sphere.

The African Political Landscape

My return from Africa to Europe in the early 1970s and, later, to the United States of America has a story of its own. However, since I am now writing about my experiences in Europe, Asia and America, I have decided not to delve into the details of the story I have in mind. What I however, recall for relevance is that I left my native Ghana in a hurry to escape the wrath and clutches of Ghana's military dictatorship led by General Ignatius Kutu Acheampong.[2]

This is the beginning of Assensoh's journeys to the West and Asia; however, this shows the political current and situation in Ghana, where the author of the memoir was a journalist in an editorial position that was eventually shut down by a stroke of a decree: banned! The memoir depicts tension in the country due to the numerous coups and counter-coups, especially the one that finally toppled the democratically elected president and shocked Assensoh that such an act could be successful. Assensoh could only take flight because the regime and military dictator had shown that nothing was beyond his reach and especially the media, which happened to have been stifled by his dictatorial rule.

Assensoh started out as a journalist before his journeys to the West and Asia, where he became not only an accomplished historian but also a legal guru (with a postgraduate law qualification). The political turbulence in Liberia is also explored by Assensoh in his memoir as part of his wide-ranging journalistic research and experiences. Assensoh says, "I always recall, with deep sorrow, the distasteful public execution of Foreign Minister C. Cecil Dennis, Jr., a graduate of historic Lincoln University in Pennsylvania as well as a Georgetown University School of Law–educated lawyer; he was one of fourteen Liberian cabinet members and ruling True Whig Party leaders and functionaries, all of whom were condemned in kangaroo courts and sentenced to be publicly executed in 1980 by Samuel K. Doe's military regime, the People's Redemption Council (PRC)."[3]

In the first chapter of the memoir, Assensoh begins to narrate the main reason behind his flight to Europe, which is why he titled the chapter "Far Away from Home." The chapter chronicles the challenges the journalist/historian faced in his home country, Ghana. The political atmosphere and space were turbulent and repressive of the media. He said that the self-promoted general, who would later be kicked out of office in a palace coup d'état and subsequently executed, had, on January 13, 1972, unseated the elected Progress Party Government of Professor Kofi Abrefa (K. A.) Busia, who was educated at the University of Oxford, where he also became a don in his exile years. The coup was an antidemocratic act that made Acheampong unpopular in the eyes of believers in democracy.[4] This act of unseating the elected government made Assensoh, as a journalist, critique the antidemocratic act. Assensoh reveals that his editorial work against the Acheampong government caused him to be arrested and detained for over two weeks, together with his business manager, Mr. Ofori. The regime was also against the freedom of the media; hence, the National Redemption Council (NRC) regime banned *The Ashanti Pioneer* newspaper through a military decree. After this entire saga, it was obvious that the regime was after Assensoh, and so there was a need to take flight from such an oppressive dictator.

Assensoh's first journey portrayed and captured the African milieu and political landscape, especially Ghana, which was being ruled by a dictator. The memoir is, first of all, taken on a rollercoaster of escaping and seeking refuge and asylum from the hands of the dictator. Assensoh was granted a visa to escape the clutches of the military junta: "This diplomat granted me a visa, which designated me as a self-employable writer and a journalist, with which I returned to London, the former colonial capital of the United Kingdom. With that type of visa, I could establish my own newspaper or magazine and, also write for and get paid by such established news publications as *West Africa Magazine, Africa Confidential, Africa Magazine, New African*, etc."[5] This remains one of the lowest experiences of the memoir's author, who rose like a phoenix from the ashes. The escape from Ghana to London is the beginning of his long sojourn in the West, having studied Journalism much earlier.

His first job in the *West Africa* magazine was secured through the recommendation of Mr. Kaye Whiteman, who recruited him as a freelance journalist with a contract to write about some specific political issues in the West Africa sub-region.[6] Assensoh's partial exile in the West became a launchpad for him to continue his journalistic work outside his home country but with the opportunity to record political moves and countermoves in other West African countries. One of these political sagas, as recorded by the memoirist, was, interestingly, at that time in London:

> I remember being sent on an assignment to research ritual murders in Liberia, a story that I felt very much committed to; my published articles in African Confidential and other places enraged the ruling True Whig Party leaders in Liberia to the point that Mr. Jonathan Refell, the former popular Liberian Radio/Tv announcer, as the Minister Counsellor for Information at the Liberian Embassy in London, was instructed to avoid me by the Liberian Ministry of Information.[7]

Assensoh's voyages and work were places of pleasure and pain, constantly bringing him close to people and putting him in danger. His journey was a site of the intersection of many political issues, legal matters, cultural contexts, and ideologies. Assensoh's arrival in the United Kingdom set his intellectual ball rolling at a much-accelerated speed. Assensoh slowly but steadily rose to pursue his career in London while also juggling a part-time job at an ice-cream company to support his child (who was British) and girlfriend. At this point, Assensoh accepted several freelance journalism jobs while also studying law. He wrote several articles for renowned pan-African journals and magazines, including *To the Point International Magazine*, which was published in Antwerp, Belgium, by South African–born Dutch journalists. During this period also, he began to make public declarations through lectures and broadcasts that General Acheampong was not a Ghanaian by birth because his middle name was Kuti.[8] In London, Assensoh proved to be a scholar and a researcher tackling several issues from his home country and in different parts of the world. He started writing and doing some editorial work, whereby his claim about the true identity of the Ghanaian military head of state raised opposition and threats to his life. These threats to Assensoh's life made him flee to Sweden as a political exile.

Assensoh's journeys seemed to be spurred by the threat to his life as he became a thorn in the flesh of the Ghanaian military regime. However, Assensoh's exile in Sweden becomes another point of elevation in his career as a journalist and writer. Assensoh notes that when visas were made available, he chose to move from London to Stockholm, Sweden, where he eventually received political asylum with full benefits. He could also have gone to

Germany: "I was, indeed, able to bring my Ghanaian girlfriend, with whom I had my first son (Philip). A second son, Sam, was born in Sweden, but my relationship with their mother did not survive the pressures of my political climate, and the rest is history."[9]

Though filled with a lot of exciting experiences, Assensoh's were also turbulent due to political pressures. The journey to Sweden was both sweet and sour; Assensoh recalls memories of meeting good friends and several dignitaries: "While in Sweden, I had the opportunity to meet then Tanzanian President Julius K. Nyerere, who was in Sweden as the guest of then Prime Minister Olof Palme, whom I had met at one of the banks in Stockholm. His office made it possible for me to attend a dinner reception in honor of Dr. Nyerere, who was in Sweden to march with Mr. Palme in a May Day parade honoring Swedish trade unionists and workers."[10]

The journey to Sweden was exciting because of the relationships and friends Assensoh made. However, during his stay in Sweden, Assensoh decided to acquire more knowledge at an American University, but he decided against going down the journalism road, as he expressed in his memoir: "When I recalled the brutalities Journalists suffered from military regimes in Africa, including my own arrest and detention under Acheampong's NRC regime back in Ghana in the early 1970s, I chose to avoid doing any more studies in Journalism. Instead, I decided to earn degrees in History, political science and English Language. Therefore, when I came to the United States, I decided to enter a Louisiana-based university to begin my studies with a lot of patience."[11] Because of several flights from the political enemies Assensoh had gathered during his journalistic days in Ghana, he decides to make a detour from a career in journalism to history, political science, and English. This part of the memoir reveals how journalists and the media are targets of political and military juntas, especially since they have to call out these people on their undemocratic and dictatorial decrees.

Assensoh eventually moved to the United States of America, where he enrolled in one of Louisiana's historically black colleges and universities (HBCU) (Dillard University in New Orleans). After so many years of studying and writing, Assensoh moved up the academic ladder by becoming a professor of history. Assensoh expresses that after almost a decade at Indiana University, "I competed for and was appointed to the Bernstein Chair, an Endowed Professorship at University of Maryland at Eastern Shore (UMES), and spent a year in that position."[12] Assensoh's journey back to the United States marks his growth in the academic world and as a distinguished professor who served in different capacities in many universities. Assensoh's journeys are testaments to his strong will and determination to survive and live despite the many challenges and obstacles on his way. It is not surprising that part of the title of his memoir is "A Memoir of Living and Survival."

Assensoh, indeed, survives the many obstacles in his path to success even though it was not completely obstacle-riddled. The memoir deflects a little from the life of the author, who shares his pain and loss in its second chapter. The author takes a metaphoric journey to the lives of close friends, family, and colleagues who lost their lives.

Faces, Places, and Celebrations: The Hyper-textual Space and Intersection of Personalities

In the second chapter of the memoir, Assensoh takes us through people (faces), spaces (places), and celebrations. The memoir moves from the point of view of the author as he tries to engrave its meanderings onto the readers' minds. The subtitle, "Memory Lanes: Lasting Memories of Chance and Professional Meetings in Indiana: When Deaths of Loved Ones and Professional Colleagues Become Worthwhile Celebration," has a pull that captures the entire chapter in a few sentences. Life has no smooth sail, and this chapter of the memoir depicts that wise dictum. These deaths of loved ones are a testament that life is fleeting and the impact one makes is the true essence and legacy of one's existence. The deaths of these five people serve as indices of the meaning of life and the transient matrix of humanity.

Assensoh agrees by interestingly pointing out that "their deaths taught me that no matter how long you live, life is just too short. But during their time on this earth, each of them blessed my life and the lives of many around them in America, Africa, Europe, Asia and beyond. That is one of the reasons that it is fitting to memorialize them in my own memoirs."[13] This chapter takes the achievements of these people who have lived exemplary lives that are worthy to live on in the heart of the writer and others. It is a text within a larger text, as the memoir relays the stories, achievements, and experiences of the author and takes on the project of linking the lives of these different people into the making of the author.

The death of Mrs. Bridget Kyerematen-Darko—whose hard work for Ghanaian artisans and craftsmen, to whom she had contributed immensely—was felt by Assensoh and his wife. As he wrote, "Sister Bridget's life and death remind us of the 'candle in the wind' axiomatic depiction of the short but meaningful life of the late Princess Diana of the United Kingdom. The circumstances of her passing do remind us of the mournful poem, 'Death the Leveller,' by James Shirley, Britain's mournful poet, whose poetic opening words do memorialize her well."[14]

It is obvious that the death of the subject really affected the author of the memoir, as he memorializes her as a close person or even friend. The pain is palpable as he writes about her life, achievements, and death with strong emotions and words. Assensoh divides the second chapter of this memoir into several parts to account for the death and achievements and immortalize his friends and family member who have passed on. The deaths of Ralph Uwechue and Kwadwo Asenso-Okyere were recorded as a tragic loss to the West African subregion, as the two men from Nigeria and Ghana, respectively, had been intellectuals from these countries. Assensoh shifts focus from the personal pain of losing these two to the national pain and void that will be felt by their absence. He observes that as two brotherly nations in West Africa, Ghana and Nigeria's intellectual realm was badly shaken because of the irreplaceable loss that the subregion suffered when death laid its icy hands on a former seasoned Nigerian ambassador Ralph Uwechue and Professor Kwadwo Asenso-Okyere, the former vice-chancellor of the University of Ghana.[15]

Assensoh narrates the achievement and contribution of Dr. Samuel DuBois Cook, a former university president who carved a niche for himself as a highly regarded American political scientist and a true scholar. He was a well-known educator, author, teacher, administrator, civil-cum-public servant and civil-rights activist.[16] The memoirist sings the praises and achievements of this man with a reverent disposition. The memoir links the lives of five people whose lives, achievements, and death have impacted the author and humanity positively in their various career paths. Assensoh provides pictures of some of his friends, colleagues, families, and associates in the memoir as a graphical illustration of their importance and contributions. This memoir is, indeed, a fusion of different faces, places and achievements, as it silently explores the brevity of life and the certain promise of mortality of human life. Assensoh makes a literary allusion to Shirley's poem, "Death the Leveller." This is a clever intersection of his intellectual forage into the world of literary works as a student of English. To Assensoh, the poem codifies the death of his friends. Amidst the celebration of the success and achievements of the author of the memoir, there is a moment of mourning the dead and celebrating their footprints on the sands of time.

The Intersection of Law, History, and Humanities in Assensoh's Migrant Stories

In Assensoh's memoir, there is the collusion and web of interdisciplinary discourses of law, history, and politics, which are the bedrock of his career as a historian, political scientist, and legal expert. Assensoh's journeys are filled with excerpts of his educational trips to different parts of the world. Assensoh reveals in his memoir that part of this publication includes some topical discussions in law: "issues with which I developed an interest after enrolling in the Master of Law (LLM) degree program of the School of Law of University of Oregon from 2014–2015. During my course of study, I was sponsored to visit Southwest Chinese University in the summer of 2015 to pursue studies in Environmental Law."[17]

The author's educational pursuit in America as a lawyer earned him the opportunity to travel to China as a student of law to gather sufficient knowledge of environmental law. From the memoir, it is obvious that Assensoh, a scholar in search of knowledge, when expanding the boundaries of academic and scholarly research, gets an opportunity to see the world while also getting an education in the cultures, laws, and history of these places.

Under the title "In Asia as a Fulbright-Hays Scholar (1986)," Assensoh's journeys to different parts of the world were explored to show that as a scholar from Africa, he had come a long way to achieve a lot intellectually and in international spaces, such as the award of the Fulbright-Hays scholarship. Assensoh affirms in the memoir that "the all-expense paid trip took our Fulbright faculty group to Japan, South Korea, Singapore, Malaysia, Hong Kong, China and also Indonesia, where we had our Fulbright residence on a local university campus, where we had Fulbright seminars, lectures and research."[18]

The memoir, *Migrant Stories: A Memoir of Living and Survival in the West and Asia*, is a story of the multiple journeys that Assensoh, a migrant from Africa, undertakes to the West and Asia. His migration from Africa, though involuntary, has made Assensoh intellectually and politically bigger in his sphere of influence and beyond.

Traditional Law and Education in Africa

In the memoir, Assensoh makes a case for traditional/indigenous education in Africa and Western education. Assensoh declares that colonialism played a variety of roles on the continent, including its unlimited involvement in the introduction of several aspects of education, including legal education.[19] Assensoh declares that before the introduction of colonialism or, more accurately, Western education, Africans already had a working system of education and justice. This system of education is controlled by the Elder. He says, "As amply demonstrated in former colonial African countries, there were in existence some indigenous (or traditional and customary) systems of education on the African continent in the late 1700s and early 1800s."[20]

This testimony to the ingenuity and invention of the African people and space called to the narrative of the historian and legal expert the necessity of documenting the richness and propensity of the African space and peoples. The indigenous education system is organized by the "elders" who have accumulated years of knowledge and wisdom and studied the tide of the waves of the world.

One of the aspects of tradition that Assensoh explored in the memoir is rites of passage. The transference of sociocultural norms, which included how to cope generally with the particular African environment without causing havoc or danger for others; how to use locally manufactured farm implements, including bows, arrows, spears, and dane guns, to do hunting for game or animals and birds used as meat; how to use fishing nets to fish and catch fish products; how to prepare indigenous meals generally and, above all, for the boys to learn how to construct buildings to serve as houses and the girls to learn how to cook and take care of midwifery duties and, in the end, how to cook to take care of future husbands, children and the home, in short, how to be homemakers.[21] These are some of the traditional education that Assensoh elucidates that the African continent has, which is comprehensive enough to guide the younger generations to lead a good life.

The elders are the custodians of the African traditions and culture, which also includes the training and education of the youth and children in the customs of the community. Assensoh opines that the rites of passage depended on what the elders felt that the younger generation needed to know in order to grow up to become worthy citizens of their societies.[22] There are stages and levels of rites of passage as they have to observe their strengths and level of knowledge before taking them to the next level. These rites of passage are numerous depending on the culture of each region and community. There are rites in transition from childhood to adulthood, a maiden to a woman, and so on. This is also reflected in death and burial arrangements.

Circumcision is another vestige of African traditions that Assensoh notes is carried out on both males and females. Assensoh noted that the first Kenyan president (Kenyatta) defended the century-old tradition of female circumcision of Kikuyu girls. Circumcision is almost a unifying experience for many African nations and communities, as many African communities carry out this tradition on both male and female children. The male children are circumcised differently from the female children in some communities. This tradition and mark of rites of passage is gradually dying out, according to Assensoh, and it is due to the influx of Western education and Christianity. He said that when Europeans arrived in Africa, they began to preach in their churches against female circumcision to make it unpopular.[23]

Assensoh further explored that many learned African customs and how to speak their dialects and languages well. African languages serve as the epicenter of the African tradition, which is simulated in different cultures and communities. The indoctrination and education of the African child start with the language and the linguistic nuances employed to teach them about their ancestors and ancestral ways. The wisdom of the sages and elders in the community is codified in the language of the community, and it is by understanding the language first that the child can then articulate the knowledge of the culture. Assensoh makes a case defending African education and tradition with the support of the scholar Ali Mazrui. Briefly, Assensoh explores one aspect of African traditions in his memoir: polygamy and the operation of a large family.

Polygamy and Family System

In the memoir, there is a brief introduction/glimpse of African marriage and family systems; polygamy and the large extended family systems are common in the preliterate African milieu. The author of the memoir alludes to the polygamous setting of his father and how large his family is:

> It is important to point out that my late father was a polygamist, who made sure that his wives lived in separate homes to avoid rival episodes. Back at Dunkwa-on-Offin, he lived in the big house, whereby the wife of the week went to live with and served him. It was, indeed, an orderly arrangement, but I swore that I would not emulate that lifestyle when I grew up, thus not to have more than one wife at a time. Of course, to be divorced and to have a new wife, which some people refer to as serial monogamy, is very much different from having more than one wife at the same time and living under a polygamous arrangement.[24]

The polygamous system of marriage leads to a large family as many wives mean the procreation of many children. Assensoh himself is a product of this type of marriage system. However, the author of this memoir declares that he would not be repeating history by being polygamous. There is a contrast between polygamy and serial monogamy; the framing of polygamy as a system that allows the union of more than one wife at a time is strongly a matter of structure compared to the new concept of serial monogamy. In essence, both systems of marriage are unique, with the same end results, as there is the possibility of having multiple wives and children at the end of these marriages. It is clearly a matter of framing and arrangement that makes polygamy an "unwanted" system of marriage and serial monogamy a better frame. From Assensoh's illustration of the marriage and family system, it is clear that he has a fairly large family of his own. This is a contrast between tradition and modernity, the juxtaposition of traditional polygamy and modern serial monogamy. There is evidence of tradition in modernity as reflected in the serial monogamy arrangement; in structure, serial monogamy is slightly different from polygamy, but in principle, it is the same, but with a new frame.

Modernity in Tension

Modernity is represented in Assensoh's memoir as Western education/colonialism with its attendant features. From the exploration of African indigenous education and tradition such as circumcision and the Western/European campaign against female circumcision, modernity shoots from the root of the matter. Modernity begins to sweep the African traditions and languages by introducing foreign languages and banning the use of African languages. The introduction of Western education in classrooms and foreign countries was strategies that were employed to cripple the reach and spread of African traditions and education.

Modernity offers Africans new horizons in intellectual awareness, the envisioning of space and world, different from what is available and the opportunity to explore and be explored. This exploration of new horizons, Assensoh opines, helps them to create the seeds of intellectual dependence on European scholarship. Modernity in the cloak of Western education also creates the capacity to transcend ancestral ways; the transience of ancestral knowledge, however, is anathema to the African continent. Assensoh says that it is a fact that the European or Western school systems—imposed during the colonial periods—have been among the main factors of social change on the continent. Therefore, what followed was what Europeans called formal education. In that guise, the colonial educational leaders brought to several places on the continent education officers to civilize the so-called "barbaric and un-Christian" Africans. In the end, such educators or (education officers) made sure that African indigenous ways, customs, and dialects (or even languages) were not allowed to be used in schools. They also made sure that the African children stayed away from their homes and local families for as much longer periods of time as possible in what they called boarding school.[25]

Assensoh goes further to say that for the African continent to truly rise to address the challenges facing the continent, there must be a conceptualization of sociocultural progress from the African perspective. He also states that the time has come for Africans to be Afrocentric and end the acculturation of Eurocentric ideas and customs. Pan-African ideologies and Afrocentric education with the view of overhauling the system with indigenous authenticity and identity development will change the landscape of African education. This stresses the need for African indigenous education and knowledge system to be included in the growth of the continent. The African legacies and knowledge system need to be reintroduced and embraced with vigor and fervency to inject the continent with the needed booster.

African knowledge system has been neglected due to the infiltration of colonialism and the suppression to keep the continent underdeveloped. Assensoh admonishes that African education—whether legally, traditionally, or otherwise—should transparently be seen to be meaningful to the continent and its citizenry, especially if it is structured to be purposeful, Afrocentric, and subjected to frequent reevaluation by experts who are familiar with African legal and secular education at all levels.[26]

SECTION B: THE CHINESE EXPERIENCE

The sophomore journey of the memoirist to China presents Assensoh as a diverse and essentialist multicultural individual. As the study of diversity is commonly envisioned, it can have its weakening or unequal features too, but Assensoh has ingrained these in his cultural lens and pot. His visit to China, which will be discussed in greater details, shows how he often learned about the different cultures in the region by actively engaging and participating in building bridges to merge the gap between his culture and that of the Chinese. In his narration, it is obvious that he noticed, described, and appreciated the festivals, foods, and culture of China to address the notion of diversity. As a result of his experience in the Asian nation, he can then be regarded as a pluralist who focuses on the differences in culture but tries to find equality in them. Likewise, he values the coexistence of people from different cultures and assumes cultures are equal and there is no form of bias.

The Journey to Asia: China

Assensoh's journey to China is filled with different encounters as a voyager-cum-researcher. The first aim of the historian turned lawyer's journey was to participate in research work on the Chinese law system. The historian narrated the circumstances preceding his trip to China in search of knowledge, where he was introduced to the Chinese laws on environment and society. Here, the memoirist begins to unravel the beauty of China and its spaces. As the most populous country and the third largest country, China represents a text of ideas, images, history, cuisine, and politics. The author narrates his encounter with the history of the nation, its legislative body and laws, leadership, and so on.

One of the narratives of the trip to China is the fascinating history of its political, cultural, and economic growth from a developing nation to one of the superpowers of the world. Assensoh notes that those with history backgrounds were fascinated to learn from Dr. Jie that China's environmental protection law was initially passed in 1989, and since that time, the country of over a billion people has become the world's second-largest economic power, which is also known to be the largest emitter of carbon.[27] The country has several languages or linguistic variations, as Assensoh puts it; however, these differences in customs and languages also harmonize the people. This trip to China was also a journey into the historical ambiance of the nation, which reveals the mystery behind the main symbol of the Chinese nation, the Dragon, a fantastical creature made up of seven animals. He said that legend has it that the dragon is supposed to bring the rain that Chinese farmers need to water their farm crops and other products. The Dragon, as we learned finally, is similar to the Chinese Great Wall, both of which are considered patriotic symbols.[28] In this part of the memoir, the author chronicles his journeys into the history, laws, principles, foundation, and space of China. One of the journeys into the heart of the history of the country reveals that Communist China, founded in 1949 by Chairman Mao, has a very rich and extensive history, which dates back several thousand years of rich civilization.[29]

The country has a rich culture that grew from the auspices of poverty to become one of the fastest-growing economies in the world through its strategic plans and leadership. Assensoh observes from the lecture that China is governed or ruled by emperors and that legal codes were in existence in traditional China, with the oldest surviving code being the Tang code introduced in the seventh century AD, and which was later developed by such dynasties as Song, Yuan, Ming, and Qing.[30] Assensoh moves from the history of the Chinese country to its law and leadership, which impresses the movement from the traditional imperial system of governance to the modern type that is constitutionally recognized. The family law implemented in the country to combat the issue of population explosion shows that the country implemented structures and measures to tackle issues of national concern and to be able to support the citizenry. In the journey to China, the author has been able to show the importance of this kind of venture and educational platform, whereby students from foreign countries could learn from the history of another country through a well-organized frame. Assensoh opines, "What I have gained from the SWUPL program was more beneficial intellectually, culturally, and socially. Hopefully, this chapter will enable anyone reading it to see an aspect of what they can gain by going on such an international educational exchange in China in future."[31]

The experience of a lifetime is gleaned from the memoir through the interaction of different parts of the world through education and exchange programs. The memoirist then swiftly moves to recount his expertise in the field of copyright law in the acquisition of African artworks. In this section of the memoir, Assensoh profoundly takes the reader through the importance of copyright legislation. He begins by emphasizing the importance of this aspect of law and the blatant infringement while comparing it to the history of the Germans with Jewish ancestry. Copyright law, Assensoh claims, grants authors proprietary rights in the works that they create.[32]

SECTION C: THE AMERICAN EXPERIENCE

This third part of Assensoh's narration focuses on the thought experiment on the workings of racism, superiority, and exploitation in America. As noted by David French, it can be deduced that racist tendencies and exploitative mood is prevalent in almost every part of the nation as most "Americans hate people of other races, and that hatred leaks out in various ways, including through comments and outright discriminatory acts."[33] In addition, the notion of white superiority is further espoused in French's article: "If you're black, by the simple law of averages you'll end up interacting with racists at some point in your daily life, and some of those bigots will make their views plain. . . . Those encounters will be shocking and infuriating—and they'll naturally make you suspicious that racial motivations may lurk behind other negative life events."[34] Overall, Assensoh showcases that these antimulticultural tendencies and encounters are startling and outrageous.

Racism

In the memoir, Assensoh takes serious discourses such as racism to write about his experiences as an African in Europe and other parts of the world. He narrates his first encounter with a white person, and it is shockingly an experience of a young child who had never seen nor encountered such a skin tone before. Assensoh avers that "the words above underscored my reaction when I first met a White man, a British education officer. Could that be because I was a racist? No, not so. However, it was my fear of the unknown causing me to panic, and, in the process, run away to seek either solace or safety in my mother's room."[35] Assensoh makes an argument for racism to include ignorance as one of the reasons for "racist" reaction, as the fear of the unknown makes people react and look at people whom they have never seen or known about. In one of his experiences in Sweden, he wrote, "My Swedish friends did tell me that basically, a Swede was not a racist at all. Instead, their reaction to foreigners during initial encounters reflected the fear of the unknown."[36]

In Assensoh's opinion/argument, one of the reasons for racism is fear of the unknown; the unknown represents a lot of ideas, such as humans from other countries, races, and people. He particularly recalls an incident that confirmed his conviction that racism is the affirmation and display of the ignorance of a particular people and the oblivion that some people exist who may not exactly look like they do:

> After the church service, about six to eight young Swedes, male and female, approached me. I wondered why. I did not have to wait long for my answer. Being their first encounter with a black man, they felt anxious to touch and rub my hands to see if the blackness would peel off to reveal another type of skin, possibly white skin. That did not happen. Then, curiously, one of the youngsters sought to know if I could talk at all. So she asked in Swedish: "Hur mar du?" ("How are you doing?") My response was that I was doing well, and I added, "Tack, bra," which in Swedish simply meant: "Fine, thank you." She turned to her mother and, pointing her finger at me say: "Mama, it talks." At that time, I was "it." There were some more incidents, but Mr. Arild Berglof of the Swedish Institute would always explain that it was due to either ignorance or the fear of the unknown, not blatant racism.[37]

This experience was an eye-opener to the author that racism is aided by ignorance of the existence of other people and race that generates an offensive aura toward the foreigner. This experience was followed by one that hit home more than the first because of the nature of the relationship. He recalls an incident where:

> A Swedish girlfriend and I dated for almost six months, but she was afraid to kiss me. She later realized that her mother had used a trick

to prevent her from being very close to me, a black man. "My mother said to me that if I kissed any black person, there would be spots in my face and on my neck for everyone to know what happened with a black man," she told me. When that did not happen in the aftermath of a passionate kiss, she burst into tears, and she wept bitterly like a baby, as she knew that her mother had lied to her![38]

Assensoh's girlfriend had been deliberately taught to be racist by her mother; this is a case of a transferred or brainwashed system of institutionalizing racism into children who do not have an idea of what to make of people of a different race or skin pigmentation. In this case, racism is a system of intended exclusion of a particular set of people.

Racism and racial experiences of Africans in the diaspora are often gruesome because of their identities. This was also weighed with the former president of Ghana, Kwame Nkrumah's experience in the United Kingdom. Racism is a serious discourse that Assensoh raises in his memoir to disintegrate the structure and demystify the arguments around it. He titles each segment on the discourse of racism as it has been affecting so many people, and Africans are not exempted. From his personal experience, he narrates how racism in America was disturbing and unpleasant. This memoir takes the issue of racism and identity in the diaspora as very important issues that Africans in the diaspora have to wade through. He writes:

> While in an outskirts of New York City in 1973, it was arranged for me and another black guy to have lunch at a local restaurant. We entered the place at about 12:06 p.m. and took seats; nobody bothered to seat us as expected. Unfortunately, we saw that several white customers came inside, but they hurriedly left, and they did not return. At the time, we had been served our meal, but a manager invited us outside and suggested that we could leave without paying for our half-eaten meal. "Sorry, we are losing customers because of your presence, and we can't have that" the female restaurant manager told me. "So, you want us to leave?" I asked in bewilderment. We obliged and left! A sad lesson in racism![39]

This is a different scenario from the experience in Sweden, which was due to ignorance and fear of the unknown. His experience in America is a major racist example of what Africans and other colored people experience in the West and Europe. He took an interest in Kwame Nkrumah's racial discrimination experience in the United Kingdom:

The late President Nkrumah's next experience in racial matters dawned on me when, as he put it, "So I at once set about looking for somewhere else to live. This was more difficult than it might sound, for accommodation was extremely scarce in London after the war. And of course, many landladies objected taking in colored lodgers [after the war]," (Kwame Nkrumah, 1957). After several tries, Nkrumah sensed that landladies were unwilling to give him a place to rent, not even at places with room vacancy announcements posted."[40]

The foregoing situation was the consequences of the structure of racism and the effects on colored people who have migrated from their home countries for different reasons such as forced exile, self-exile, education, and to seek greener pastures. These incidents were records of ten to twenty years of experience; however, Assensoh opines that the sad thing is that such things continue today, where Black people and other people of color are singled out for racist treatment at eating establishments. Consider, as an example, the recent incident at a Starbucks where the manager called the police on two law-abiding Black men. Not to mention the countless number of Black men and women who have lost their lives for driving while Black.[41]

These forms of oppression and racist attack on Blacks and people of color are still present with different forms of frames and structures to compartmentalize people of color in the West and Europe. Assensoh notes that American President Trump is working to combat the influx of immigrants, especially from Africa, into the United States of America as a form of subtle and sublimated racism. However, the situation still affects African Americans too because of their pigmentation, as many have been killed and maimed.

White Culture: Sexuality and Relationship

One of Assensoh's shocking experiences in the memoir reveals the conception of sexual relationships in the Western world. This is what he wrote about in chapter 3 as an African whose idea of relationships between adults puts the man's age as older than the woman's: "It was a bizarre situation for me to witness what should ordinarily have been part of textbook situations. I am referencing to a situation when a young black man in his early 20s, whom we will call Jeff reportedly fell in love with a white woman in her 50s."[42] This was a situation that the memoirist was witnessing for the first time, and he was in shock.

This memoir is a story of collective memories and journeys, referencing different spatial and temporal milieus, cultures, identities, ideas, discourses, and experiences. Assensoh's traditional notion of a romantic relationship between adults discredited the older woman having a relationship with a younger man. This shows that the author had a different background, culture, and orientation of what is obtainable in an adult relationship in the Western world. However, Assensoh had to adjust his orientation to embrace the Western idea of the age gap/difference in an adult relationship, which was totally different from his patriarchal notions. He observes that the relationship had no future because the woman had lied about her age to the man:

> However, what I found interesting was the reaction of Jeff, the young black lover, when he realized that Maree, the much older white woman (in her 50s) had lied to him. He went livid with anger. When they first met, the female "cougar" liked the black guy so much that she lied about her age. "I am just 47 years old," Maree told Jeff before they embarked on their sexual relationship. The truth would come out much later in Las Vegas, when Maree inadvertently let go her true age. Interestingly, Jeff had wondered about having children in future and questioned how this was to be possible with Maree. To allay his fears, she told him that she could be inseminated with his sperm.[43]

This is an aspect of modernity that Assensoh has observed and encountered in the West that has changed his orientation. He discovered from his voyage in the West that there were no rules against the relationship between the two people, one aged twenty-four and the other in her fifties, being involved in a romantic relationship.[44] This kind of relationship is unusual in what is available in the African setting, where the author of the memoir originates from. The parents of the man also did not support the relationship because of the age difference between the two people. This was a foreign and an almost strange experience for the author because of his cultural background.

The foregoing serves as one of the realities of living in the first world and experiencing the cultural differences between his home country and his diasporic home. He notes that the female "cougar" incident confirmed that in the United States of America, it is a regular occurrence for older women and older men to prey on the young. In fact, the father of the young Black man was directed to a "Cougar Sex" online program, which was a big surprise for the sheltered family.[45] Assensoh's journeys are like educational trips and voyages into the culture and traditions of the West and Asia. The modern cultural difference between the African man and the parents of the Black young man is a testament to the fact that there is so much difference in the articulation and composition of relationships and marriages in the West.

Exploitation of Africa

One of the themes explored by Assensoh in his memoir is the exploitation of the African countries by the colonizers, who disregarded the laws of human rights and of copyrights that protected intellectual materials such as artworks, art pieces, and artifacts. During the colonial era, many African countries were exploited by colonial leaders from the West and Europe. One of the ways the African continent had been ransacked and plundered by the former colonial leaders and countries is the nonexistence of copyright laws to protect intellectual properties and works. Assensoh observes that during the colonial period, there were no institutions and laws to protect African artworks, including carvings and paintings in many African countries. Instead, scholars have come to recognize traditional international laws, which often permitted victors in conflict to loot, plunder, and pillage the territory of the losing entity.[46] Assensoh notes the plundering of several expensive Benin artworks and carvings, such as paintings and busts, before the country's independence in 1960.[47]

Colonialism is a huge part of the African continent's history as it etched its trail on the minds and memories of the African people. Colonialism becomes more than a system of colonial rule and subjugation for the African countries; it is a framework for the exploitation of natural and human resources. The lack of copyright or any form of human-rights laws allows for the exploitation of the many unprotected African pieces. Assensoh claims that to make any laws to control the thievery and outright plunder of African art forms and carvings, which needed either copyrights or patents for their protection, was like the colonial leaders cutting off their noses to spite their faces.[48]

However, after independence from colonial rulers, many African countries had structures put in place to combat the issue of copyright infringements and other related problems of intellectual work thievery. He writes thus:

> However, not until Africa's decolonization processes in the various colonies, copyright laws were either foreign or alien to the indigenous populace. The main reason for such state of affairs was that the European colonial nations and their representatives made internal laws for governing the colonies. Yet, when they were benefitting from illicit trades and also stealing or plundering of artworks, they closed their eyes to the need for copyright laws, which would have made it a lot more difficult for the colonialists to take African art works with impunity and subsequently to ship them overseas to countries of their origin, including the United Kingdom, France, Portugal, Spain, Italy

and Germany, mainly countries which participated in the scramble for or partitioning of Africa.[49]

Meanwhile, Assensoh revises what notable scholars from the African continent have written about the stolen history and artworks that were claimed as part of the national treasures in museums across these former colonialist countries. He notes that, as maintained by this study, what made the removal of such art considered national treasures in the first place was the absence of any copyright or regulatory law that could have prevented the removal of the artwork.[50] The plundering of the national treasures in these African countries has sparked a lot of debates and essays by scholars and activists from the continents and other foreign activists who advocate for the return of these treasures back to their rightful countries and venues. Assensoh is concerned with the exploitation of the continent, which has contributed to the underdevelopment of the continent. For this nation to move from its current state toward a progressive position, the former colonial countries and leaders must contribute to the wealth that they have stolen and plundered during the colonial periods.

Assensoh observes that postcolonial African leaders and countries seemed to have awareness, with respect to the protection of intellectual property and other copyright interests, that surpassed colonial era Africans used selectively in such European governance.[51] The awareness of the law to protect African art forms transformed the landscape of the different art forms and properties. Due to the limited awareness of these African countries' knowledge about laws that protect intellectual properties and art forms, the Europeans and other colonial leaders took the advantage of the situation to plunder the continent. However, with the acquisition of independence, these countries have started implementing laws against the willful exploitation of the continent.

Although all the foregoing strategies, plots, and counterplots were aroused by the interest in protecting intellectual property internally, what resulted was the fact that African and other developing societies used their great numbers at the United Nations to wrestle power for themselves that they did not have before in the corridors of the International Monetary Funds and the World Bank.[52]

SECTION D: CHANGE AND CONTINUITY

After much analysis on the critical examination of the three cultures known and visited by the memoirist, it is pertinent to note that the urgent task of the typical average writer is to produce work or writing that will deconstruct the appalling image of Africa that has been propagated by the West. The West has ascribed the values of civilization to itself and has associated Africa with the primordial outlook coupled with the fact that they can make policies that can be of global standard and that are worthy of emulation. This reveals that the world requires not just a monopolized generation of assumptions but dialogue and interrelation, which will forge a greater level of understanding as people will be guided by knowledge. Over time, African postcolonial writers have established a tradition of reconstructing the African identity and nation, and counternarratives are salient tools they deploy in actualizing these ambitions.

Thus, African writings such as Assensoh's memoir are an expedient corrective tool for subverting the dichotomy and polarity between the West and "Others" that have been created by Eurocentric writers, scholars, and critics. It is important to note that Assensoh has illustrated this with the impactful and excellent policies created by a developing nation such as Ghana, which is worthy of emulation, and he explicates further that the United States, his second home, a developed nation and superpower, is not doing that. This part presents and characterizes Ghana as an epitome of a nation that is ready for development, and, more importantly, Assensoh is imbibing the spirit of transculturalism and multiculturalism, where every nation or culture, whether small or big, can gain from one another and see themselves as equals.

Ghana: An Epitome of a Progressive Nation

Assensoh, a historian-cum-legal expert, has taken an interest in the progressive turn of Ghana, his home country. In chapter 4 of the memoir, he says that the overarching aim of the discussion is Ghana's progress in terms of the country's health scheme. He adds, "The overall purpose in this study is to explain, albeit preliminarily, why Ghana, a materially poor country, has a National Health Insurance Scheme (NHIS) and the United States, a materially rich country, did not."[53] Assensoh compares the state of health of the United States of America with Ghana, which is one of the developing nations in Africa. Ghana, as described by Assensoh, is economically unstable and undeveloped compared to America, which is one of the world's major powers. A brief history of the political undertone and ambiance of the country is recounted as the memoirist, a historian, could not escape from infusing it into his work. Assensoh opines that:

> In 2003, the Parliament of Ghana passed the National Health Insurance Scheme (NHIS) bill, which was signed into law by President John A. Kufuor. The law provides health coverage for most illnesses of

all residents of Ghana. The fact that this relatively small and materially-poor country in West Africa has been able to enact such a law is, in itself a great feat because it is probably one of the few, if not the only, African country to have enacted such a law.[54]

This is a major accomplishment for the African country to have enacted this kind of law, which ensures that the health of the citizenry is well taken care of. Assensoh makes a comparison between the United States of America's healthcare system and the Ghanaian one, putting the African country on top of America. He outlines four reasons and perspectives to explain and account for the success of the Ghanaian healthcare system and the less-than-successful American healthcare policy.

As the first British colony to gain independence from colonial rule south of the Sahara, Ghana had passed into law a healthcare policy known as the National Health Insurance Scheme (NHIS), which enables quality health to be provided to the Ghanaian citizenry almost free, unlike the developed counterpart America, which has no such law and policy.

CONCLUSION

This chapter has explored the journeys of the author (A. B. Assensoh) in the memoir *Migrant Stories*. It begins with a preliminary note on journeys and the conceptual outlook of what the chapter explores. A journey, in itself, is the relative travel or trip of a migrant from one place to another in search of something. In this chapter, Assensoh's journeys to the West and Asia is a memoir layered with exciting hypertext of people, faces, celebration, and immortalization of friends, experiences, and family members. Furthermore, the study explores the author's flight from his home country during the regime of a dictator in Ghana. The author of this memoir started as a journalist with the zeal and zest to pull down structures of oppression and dictatorial leadership in his country. This was the beginning of his almost exilic journey to the West. The memoir does grow from his many travels to different parts of the world to acquire knowledge in several fields and as a researcher. In one of his journeys, Assensoh brings up some topical issues, such as racism and the modern relationship between a young African man and an older white woman.

This particular journey was to Sweden, where he encountered racism and racist comments. The debate over whether his encounter with a young girl was to be termed racism or ignorance was fueled by the people's reaction to a Black man whom they had never seen before. According to his opinion and experience with the Swedes, racism was due to their fear of the unknown and ignorance of his race, and not a blatant case of discrimination against black pigmentation. This experience is weighed against his "baptism" of racism in America, whereby he and a friend were asked to leave an eating place in the early 1970s because it was losing customers due to the presence of the two Black men. In any case, he did not make a total conclusion on racism in America based on that single experience. The foregoing incident led to an interesting encounter, whereby the memoirist had to experience a scene of a white female "cougar," who claimed to be in love with a much younger African man. Assensoh was shocked to know that in the West, there are different standards and opinions about adult relationships and age gaps. There is the element of culture shock in the West that Assensoh witnessed and expressed in his memoir.

This chapter also explored the seeming existence of modernity and tradition in the memoir by Assensoh. Though briefly discussed, Assensoh makes comparisons between the polygamous system of marriage and the fairly new modern, serially monogamous situation that also prevails. Assensoh also discusses traditional education in Africa while making a comparison with colonial or Western education. In his discussions on this issue, he supports the notion that the West and other European colonialists have contributed to the underdevelopment of the African continent. And so, Assensoh encourages African leaders to overhaul the educational systems that their colonial masters left behind and plan to educate the African youths with Afrocentric and pan-African educational values. This chapter goes on to discuss his journey to China as a law student in an exchange program, which he describes with so much fascination that he divides this section of his trip into different parts to fully capture his experience.

The trip to China gave Assensoh the opportunity to gather information about the origin of the country, its vast population, culture, law, people, and leadership. He went on to describe the history of China in the memoir as an accomplished historian who is genuinely fascinated by the political and legal history of China. He confesses, "My summer of 2015 SWUPL trip and stay were very worthwhile academically, intellectually, culturally and a social experience that I recommend to anyone, who wishes to follow our footsteps to travel from UO School of Law to SWUPL."[55]

The memoir also explores Assensoh's interest in the copyright law in Africa and other countries. It reveals the exploitation of Africa by the former colonial countries and colonizers, who plundered the wealth and artwork of these African nations. Assensoh delves into his knowledge of the legal world to discuss the issue of copyright legislation in different countries in Africa as well as the West. And before the epilogue, he discusses the healthcare policy in Ghana, his home country. From his discussion of the healthcare policy, it is obvious that the author is proud of the achievement of this African nation in implementing what America could not achieve.

In conclusion, this publication on the journeys of A. B. Assensoh, written as a memoir with the title *Migrant Stories: A Memoir of Living and Survival in the West and Asia*, successfully explores the journey of survival of an African who has experienced a lot to become a scholar in law and history. Assensoh lived a life that many would envy, even though it was initially filled with many ups and downs. This chapter concludes that Assensoh's memoir is a rich spice of memories, experiences, people, journeys, and celebrations. It is, indeed, not only about the author; instead, it is a shared collection of stories of friends, family members, colleagues, and associates. The memoir is spiced with pictures of many scholars, friends, achievements, deaths, births, and survivals in Africa, Asia, and Europe.

Chapter 6

MIGRANT (UN)HOMELINESS

Universalism and Global Identity in the Memoirs of A. B. Assensoh and Cherno Njie

INTRODUCTION

Memoirs consistently revolve around identity creation, and many movements developed by Blacks and Africans—including the Francophone Negritude movement, Afrocentrism, and Black Nationalism—were developed to propagate identities. Paul Zeleza, in his diachronic survey of the growth of African literature, stated that "the post-independence African intelligentsia had a trinity of dreams—for purity, parity and personhood . . . African intellectuals are adamantines of reinforcing African authenticity, history and humanity."[1] Zeleza's claim emphasizes the fact that a dogged insistence on promoting pan-African culture, identity, and humanity not only remains relevant but has also been widely discussed in contemporary African literature in general.

Many diasporic writers and thinkers have discussed and debated the African identity. The creation, definition, and substantiation of the African identity forms a large corpus of the migrant discourse in diasporic spaces. Migrant writers constantly negotiate the ambiguous meaning of home, the crisis of "being," and the politics of belongingness in creative works of fiction and nonfiction. Major thematic engagements center on what it means to "be African outside Africa and as a returnee to Africa." These writers primarily present their sense of loss, confusion, and struggle to adapt, along with race issues. As a result, they establish their affiliation with Africa and reveal the issues that triggered their mass departure, making commentaries on the shortcomings that cripple growth and development in their countries of origin. They also adopt different variations of universalism to survive in the cosmopolitan world. On their own, migrant writings have proven to be vibrant and fertile, reproducing mass literary works in and outside the continent.

A. B. Assensoh and Cherno Njie are contemporary, cosmopolitan migrant writers from West Africa. Although domiciled outside their places of birth, they are still very much involved with their homes. Their work addresses a universal readership, revealing the fact that migrant literature and its authors have made a substantial contribution to the periodization of African literature. Their decentralized writing is not subject to conventionally erected structures or ideologies, maintaining fluid plots and faster-paced narratives. Tejumola Olaniyan describes their literary productions as "an overall healthy development of cultural creativity, the type that continually breaches accepted boundaries and invents new forms and suggests new meanings."[2]

Assensoh and Njie can be called Afropolitans because they emerged on the literary scene through personal accounts, exposing their cultural underpinnings. Taiye Selasi, originator of the term "Afropolitanism," states that Afropolitans are a "generation of African emigrants, coming soon or collected already."[3] They renegotiate and challenge the stereotyped identity that social conventions confer on migrants, promoting the idea that marginalization, alienation, and racial segregation—along with homelessness and nostalgia—are subjective. These ideas are evident in the memoirs of Assensoh and Njie. According to Ngozi Cole, "In exploring my identity as an Afropolitan youth, I have broadened my mind to so many levels of understanding how geography, nostalgia and the drive for change are not just homogenous ideas, they are different for many young Africans who live in the Diaspora."[4]

Afropolitans are products of the cosmopolitanism and transnationalism that characterize postcolonial Africa and the present-day world. Incessant migrations, extreme modernization, and globalization have encouraged individuals to develop multiracial identities. Afropolitans conceptualize and propagate these new and emergent identities in a fast-changing world. The barriers created by "difference" or cultural diversity are not recognized by members of this radical and vibrant group.

Ugochukwu Nzewi affirms that Afropolitanism "articulates a social identity and identification for Africans who are at home in the world ... Africans devoid of Afropessimist mindset."[5] In Afropolitan works, the average migrant is redefined and represented in unfamiliar and positive ways to foreground the notion that trans-culturalism and hybridity is a phenomenon that is compatible with the contemporary world. For Nzewi, "Afropolitans insist on re-inventing the African narrative by shifting the conversation from that of victimhood to assertion."[6] The seemingly inherent negativity and pessimism that bedeviled the African continent—as depicted in earlier works of art—is neither refuted nor rebuffed in the memoirs studied in this chapter. Instead, the focus of Afropolitans is the reappraisal of Africa's conventional story against the backdrop of globalization and borderlessness. Selasi expresses a "willingness to complicate Africa . . . to engage, critique, and celebrate the parts of Africa that means most . . . understand what is ailing in Africa . . . rather than essentialising the geographical entity."[7]

Ghana-born Assensoh's *A Matter of Sharing* and *Migrant Stories: A Memoir of Living and Survival in the West and Asia* can be viewed alongside Njie's *Sweat Is Invisible in the Rain* as memoirs that reflect, represent, and subvert notions of home and identity in the "New Diaspora." Alienation, racism, pan-Africanism, Trumpism, global issues, multiculturalism, intermingling, immigration, hybridity, and other tropes appear in these works of art that also reflect the "Afro-returnee" relationship with the authors' natal home. The different redefinitions, reconstructions, and deconstructions of migrant identities—and new perspectives on the concept of "home"—as depicted in Assensoh and Njie's works are the focus of this chapter.

A critical reading of Assensoh's *A Matter of Sharing* and *Migrant Stories* and Njie's *Sweat Is Invisible in the Rain* uncovers a perfect mirroring of the concept of "home" described by Homi Bhabha as a place of stable identity where one has been and is understood. In nations and cultures experiencing oppression, home is linked to a positive version of the past that references life before oppression; the concept is inherently tied to open-mindedness, inclusion, and freedom. Njie and Assensoh problematize the concept of home as they experience the variant trends of multiculturalism, universalism, and cosmopolitanism. The stories in the memoirs express the reliability and interconnection of universalism's ideas—in contrast to particularism—seeking to produce and mold a globally and universally identified identity.

Sweat Is Invisible in the Rain,[8] by Gambian-born Njie, is a narrative of an African childhood, life in the American space, and Njie's essential quest to topple a dictator in his natal home. In the memoir, Njie discusses cultural aspects of his native country, The Gambia, which informed or contributed to his upbringing from childhood to his coming of age in a foreign country. This consciousness contributed to his involvement in his country's politics, and these tenets of cultural politics can be analyzed in different formats.

Assensoh's *A Matter of Sharing* is a personal narration that includes moments of pain and comic relief; its recounting is "a matter of sharing" for global readers. His second memoir, *Migrant Stories*, is about living and surviving in the West, Oriental countries, and Europe, straddling different worlds and cultures. Its postcolonial and postmodernist leaning projects an echo of believability for the readers, establishing the necessary relationship between history and memoir that was described by James Baldwin, quoted in the text "that we human beings carry within us, [and that we] are consciously controlled by it in many ways, and [that] history is literally present in all that we do."⁹

In the works of Assensoh and Njie, basic terms such as home and identity can be evaluated and negotiated as diasporic redefinitions and reconstructions performed by the writers of memoirs. The variant approach taken by these new writers can be interrogated, placing the lives and experiences of the authors and other personalities under scrutiny to evaluate perceptions of home, identity, racism, belongingness, world politics, and other recurrent themes from the literature of Africans in the diaspora. This chapter performs a close reading of Assensoh's *A Matter of Sharing* and *Migrant Stories*, coupled with Njie's *Sweat Is Invisible in the Rain*, placing emphasis on "a new dawn," or change in the topicality and familiar subject matter of migrant writings. It also explores the issues in intercontinental and intracontinental spaces, using texts as primary data to explore the new "living experiences" at home and abroad that are radically propagated by Africans in the diaspora.

The works of these successful Africans have demonstrated a radical and logical approach. The new social constructs in their climes cultivate new belief systems and dispositions to life and living in the diaspora. By foregrounding the thematic engagements in Assensoh and Njie's writing, their texts demonstrate the changes that migrants propagate, which reveals new approaches to life in the diaspora as depicted by cosmopolitan writers. Nationhood, borders, and boundaries have acquired alternative meanings and interpretations through their work.

Topical issues discussed in the literary sphere are dynamic and dependent on societal trends. Globalization, transculturalism, multiculturalism, modernization, immigration, effective world leaders, Trumpism, and many other factors have created a difference in the current experience of African migrants. Successful and forward-thinking Africans in the West, including Njie and Assensoh, have responded by posing radical new ways of thinking, understanding, and visualizing the world. This study critiques and interrogates their approach, which deserves scholarly appraisal.

MIGRITUDINAL TENDENCIES AND THE ROLES OF RETURNEES FOR THEIR HOMELANDS

Migration is defined as the movement or shift of a person or a group of people from one space to another, occurring over a significant distance.¹⁰

Migration can either be voluntary or involuntary, and the migrant's new space is usually a "Third Space" that can be temporary or permanent. Migrations are driven by factors that can either pull a person toward a new space or push them away from the space they occupy; these factors can be physical, psychological, or sociocultural. The texts under study are post-independence African memoirs that describe the movement of characters from one continent or country to another. These movements, which are often voluntary, are the results of both push and pull factors.

Njie's *Sweat Is Invisible in the Rain* opens with a sort of grand, migritudinal impulse where individuals who are sane, competent, and underappreciated in their natal home seek after the idea of moving to other lands to flourish. This feeling is what Njie adopts to explore the idea of home, and he embellished the idea with a Wolof proverb. The author explores the migration impulse, its push and pull factors, the complexities of home, and the role of diasporas and writers in correcting these ills. He explains:

> An attempted coup in The Gambia staged on the grounds of the State House in Banjul failed. A number of the plotters died at the State House, while I, waiting apart from the assault, and a few of the others involved separately escaped to Senegal after having been informed by one of the survivors of the failed attempt. From Dakar I flew to the United States, stopping in Baltimore, as I tried to make my way back to the quiet neighborhood in Austin, Texas, where I live. I was arrested, however, when I got to Maryland.[11]

A similar theme is present in Assensoh's memoirs, which describe several push factors that drove the narrator out of his natal country to other lands. These forces are evident in the narrative as civil unrest, political instability, and socioeconomic challenges in his host space. In *A Matter of Sharing*, Assensoh recounts how he was brutally dehumanized by the Ghanaian military regime during his time as a journalist. His newspaper, *The Pioneer*, was banned, and he was not allowed to express basic human rights, including free speech. Subjugation by military leaders is rampant in African countries, from the past to the present, and they exert control over the lives of citizens and deny them rights and freedoms.[12]

In a bid to escape subjugation and the denial of human rights, these authors migrate to other lands that offer relative peace and freedom. In both Njie's and Assensoh's memoirs, they moved to the West and started new lives with assistance from international circles. Assensoh writes: "Thanks to pressure from West Africa Magazine of London as well as the London-based

Amnesty International, International PEN writers' association and other overseas-based crusading human rights organizations and Journalist groups, we were released from the detention camp, where we had been held incommunicado for about two weeks."[13]

Flahaux and Haas wrote that "Millions of Africans are believed to be waiting to cross to Europe at the first opportunity,"[14] driven by the gap in the world economy. The widening inequality between the rich and poor nations is evident in the narrative through decisions made by Assensoh and Njie to study abroad using scholarships. The migrant's decision to cross borders is spurred by the ego, which advocates for liberation from the unfavorable stimulation of the current space. Migrations prompted by "pull" factors usually indicate the elevation of the self, in identity and social status, by moving into a preferred space that is presented as a European El Dorado or Utopia.[15] This is why "migration is seen as a form of achievement—a form of upward class mobility in itself. The very act of getting out is seen as getting ahead."[16] Assensoh writes:

> Sadly, I still felt unsafe because of the treatment Mr. Ofori and I suffered at the hands of the Kumasi-based military officers. Most certainly, I also saw clearly the dangers in continuing to be a full-time Journalist in Ghana. Therefore, I started to think about professional alternatives, especially as I had done very well in History and Government subjects when I studied and took the external examinations administered by the University of London as well as the West African Examinations Council (WAEC), respectively . . . To be trained as a historian in order to follow in the intellectual footsteps of the above-named erudite History Professors and others in the field, all of whom I regarded with much respect and affection, I sought admission to enter USA-based Dillard University, a well-regarded liberal arts institution that is situated in New Orleans in the southern State of Louisiana.[17]

Migration is a function of the laws of uneven development. Aderemi Ajibewa and Sola Akinrinade, quoting Harris, state that "increased migration is inevitable in an integrating world economy, that is increasingly characterized by widening inequalities between the rich and poor nations."[18] The high level of development attained by industrialized countries, leading to higher per capita income, attracts migrants. For the author, uneven education is a pulling factor accompanied by a pushing need to traverse a world other than his natal home. Njie stated the factors that led to his migration:

I LEFT MY JOB at Standard Chartered and traveled to Texas to pursue an undergraduate degree. I was twenty-five years old. They were bittersweet moments when the day came for me to leave. I wanted to go, to get to know another world apart from The Gambia, outside of Africa. But, naturally, I was very attached to 2 New Street. I had become, into my working years, even closer to my mother and father. My family shuttled me and my few possessions to the airport and saw me off. Everybody was there except Baboucarr, who was then in the Soviet Union studying.[19]

It is important to look at diasporic activities in home countries, host nations, and at the transnational level. Memoirs can help us gain a better knowledge of the roles that people in the diaspora play in their home nations, including how they contribute to the dynamics of war, peace, and social and economic growth.

The neoclassical approach to return migration holds that a returnee's migratory experience is an individual failure in relation to the diaspora's migratory goals abroad. In contrast, the return-aggression approach contends that the migratory experience of returnees is only successful when they have exhibited superior agency and advantages over those who stayed at home. The success or failure of returnees is measured by their ability to reclaim all that once belonged to them before leaving the homeland. The structuralist approach is similar, arguing that the success or failure of a returnee is gauged by measuring the "reality" of the homeland against the hopes of the returnee. For the structuralists, the returnee's intent to return to the homeland forms his or her hope, while the return-aggression approach argues that the survival of returnees depends on their level of agency and display of superior abilities regardless of whether they had intended to return. The return-aggression approach differs from the social-capital-network theory by arguing that the success of returnees goes beyond mere possession of or access to resources.

From a return-aggression perspective, the narrator in *Sweat Is Invisible in the Rain* has successfully developed agency: the sitting president, condemned for his government's totalitarian behavior, is removed from office. Although the narrator was jailed, it was worth the pain and effort! The return aggression would also be classified as a success by residents of The Gambia, which further substantiates the role of the diasporic community in contributing to its homeland and assisting with national matters, especially related to national peace, stability, and development. In the memoir, Njie writes:

> The opportunity was lost when he was not opposed from the beginning, probably sometime in his first term as president of the country.

In the year after my release from prison, I traveled to my native country. Jammeh was no longer there. I was speaking with another Gambian, a prominent businessman, who lived through the Jammeh years. He thanked me for the action we took in 2014 and said to me then, as almost a sort of apology, "The signs were there, we should have acted sooner."[20]

Assensoh's presentation of Africans in the diaspora playing roles in their home country is more subtle than that of Njie. Assensoh suggests that individuals who have moved to Europe or to the West from Africa have an obligation to take care of their immediate family back home, showing a sort of family privilege. While Assensoh was in the United Kingdom, his father sent a letter instructing him not to forget his role or family ties; the letter explained that he had an obligation to "take care" of his father. In the memoir, the narrator also recounted making remittances to his mother in Ghana—murmurs from other family members hinted that it would be appropriate to distribute the funds more widely, ensuring the successful transition of other individuals to the West rather than concentrating solely on his mother. It showed the expectations of those back home and how they show their privilege to relatives abroad.

In addition to subtle presentations of the roles that Africans in the diaspora must play in developing their natal home, Assensoh shows African nationals trying to assume different professional roles in their home countries. This is evident in the narration recounting his arrival in the United Kingdom and describing his political exile in Sweden. Assensoh describes fascination when meeting Africans from other regions of Europe who were important personalities ready to take up leadership positions in their home countries. His tone holds a sense of optimism for young Africans ready to return home and make their continent a better place; they would discontinue the acts of subjugation and denials of human rights that pushed them away from their natal lands.

GLOBAL CITIZENSHIP: AFROPOLITAN AND PAN-AFRICANIST MODELS

The concepts of global citizenship, Afropolitanism, and pan-Africanism are obvious from the presentation of different characters and global leaders in the memoirs of Njie and Assensoh. These concepts are presented as standard models of global citizenship, devoid of strands of particularism. Different philosophers have used these concepts to explain human behavior from one generation to another, based on rules, codes, and societal relations. In validating Aristotle's description of a universal citizen, Scalise and Sestico state, "A group is all the more particularistic, the more its networks, its norms of reciprocity and trust and its aims are confined to the members of the group, whereas a group is all the more universalistic, the more its networks, its norms of reciprocity and trust and its aims transgress the boundaries of the group and encompass other citizens and groups in society."[21]

In this cosmopolitan world, an individual must have a broader outlook, mutual respect, and empathy for others by envisioning their perspective. Humans must look beyond themselves and see what unites the self with others and people from other cultures. Njie and Assensoh can be regarded as Afropolitans presenting Pan-African ideals to birth model citizens. The significance of identity in African literature has sparked a kaleidoscope of ideas, debates, and conversations.

Since the beginning of African literature, the identity question has evolved, passing through many periods that include the Francophone Negritude movement, pan-Africanism, Afrocentrism, Black nationalism, and other ideas and movements. Sterling describes pan-Africanism as a political movement created to invoke the concept of African unity, which is tied to the decolonization of African states. Recent scholars have interpreted Afropolitanism as a new term for the pan-African movement. Sterling argues that "the aim of earlier intellectuals was to write themselves into a re-vision of black people in the global world; hence Pan-Africanism is as much about the unity of subjectivity as cosmopolitanism."[22] Sterling maintains that the purpose of pan-Africanism is consistent with Afropolitan goals.

Amatoritsero Ede captures Afropolitanism within "the complexity of identity in a hybrid, postmodern world where centre/periphery models have become inadequate for analyzing global cultural flows, and in which African identity can no longer fit into the next historical Pan-African uniformity."[23] Ede's assertion acknowledges the new dynamics and social constructs that transcend the scope of pan-Africanism. The modern world has witnessed radical changes, and it is expedient to develop new ideologies to accommodate them. For migrants, negotiation of identity and creation of the sense of self is an integral life formation process—the need to appreciate, appraise, and adapt to new spaces takes center stage in the life of the average migrant. Afropolitans emphasize personal identity and self-perception over social, cultural, or historical identity.

A Matter of Sharing, *Migrant Stories*, and *Sweat Is Invisible in the Rain* give insights into their characters' configuration of identity and sense of self.

The characters (and some personalities) in the memoirs are privileged and duly acknowledged in their spheres of influence, yet the historical identity conferred on them hinders the recognition of their essence. Characters in the novel are erudite, as typical of Afropolitans, and affiliated with prestigious Ivy League universities. In the foreword, written by Dorothy V. Smith, Assensoh is presented as a reputable scholar at Stanford University, which was not a common achievement in the United States when he assumed his teaching position.[24]

It is also relevant that the Afropolitan model, which presents characters and personalities that meet global standards and who are fit to be world icons, is showcased in Assensoh's *A Matter of Sharing*. The chapter "Encounters and Personalities Galore" is a rich exploration of African intellectuals, scholars, writers, and leaders who meet international and universal standards, as well as individuals who are cosmopolitan in their attitudes and beliefs. The personalities presented in Assensoh's memoir—Soyinka, Achebe, Mazrui, Awoonor, King, Mandela—are coupled with formidable women, such as Christie Achebe and Corretta King. They can all be regarded as Afropolitans. These individuals, who impact the world positively and are not racially biased, have fluid identities and believe that anywhere is home. The perfect illustration is that of Nelson Mandela, whose actions have inspired the world and united people as citizens of a global village. Assensoh writes that Mandela's

> humanity, humility and reconciliatory spirit unite all of us as citizens of the global village. On the historical plane, Mandela was our moral compass in the world that Franz Fanon (himself a fierce anti-colonialist) described as a wretched earth. Without qualms, Mandela nobly gave his all to the world: his overall noble life as well as his natural and creative intelligence, his devotion to nuclear and global family, and the freedom that all of us treasure, mostly serve as a shining example of a leader, who wanted to see his people free.[25]

Njie also incorporates Afropolitan ideals into his memoir. The lived experience of his narrator is extremely cosmopolitan, exhibiting intense erudition and existing primarily as a cultural hybrid. In her essay, Taiye Selasi (2005) describes cultural hybrids thus: "Some of us are ethnic mixes, e.g., Ghanaian Canadian, Nigerian Swiss . . . American accent, European affect, African ethos. Most of us are multilingual."[26] Their affiliation with two or more cultures is reflected in their lifestyle. The narrator is multilingual and has a talent for cultural interpenetration and intermingling within and outside of the continent. As primary adherents of interracial mixing and inclusiveness, Afropolitans desire to be understood beyond the limits of statehood; being part of a nation should never be the foundation for understanding humans. This is evident in the narrator's success in the United States, where he works at a housing ministry and understands basic cultural expressions, later practicing cultural entrepreneurship. The Afropolitan, as portrayed in memoirs, is not a helpless immigrant bedeviled by lack of privilege. Stereotyped notions of color and race are mythical social constructs, and they will be overcome by these Africans. In the long run, the constructs that are erected in society will lose their validity in the modern age of dispersal.

Assensoh gives primacy to interracial marriages and interethnic relationships. In the text, it is surprising that there are marriages during the Nigeria-Biafra war, joining the Yoruba and the Igbo ethnic groups. This is fascinating, even to Nigerians, because it occurred despite the massacre of countless Igbo indigenes in the country. This phenomenon not only typifies Nigeria but also cuts across the African continent. The complexity of this racial intermingling is accentuated when Kwame Nkrumah and Sedar Senghor marry women from the nations of Egypt and France. Assensoh writes:

> As pressmen, who had the opportunity to travel far and wide, we were also aware that Senegalese President Leopold Sedar Senghor's wife was from France and, as a result, Senegal's First Lady was a French woman. Then, with a lot of attractive women around in Ghana, the late President Kwame Nkrumah went to Egypt to pick a wife, who subsequently became Ghana's beautiful and worthy First Lady. Mrs. Fathia Nkrumah (popularly called Madam Fathia) lived with her Ghanaian husband at the Flagstaff House in Accra until the overthrow of the Convention People's Party (CPP) government of President Nkrumah on February 24, 1966.[27]

Across generations, these personalities promote cultural hybridity. This interracial fusion and partnership foreground the need for cultural interpenetration and its beauty in the postmodern world.

Assensoh's ideas of pan-Africanism presenting a global identity, shown through the personality of Kwame Nkrumah, is also noteworthy. Although Stephanie Santana believes that pan-Africanism "served as a powerful ideological weapon in the first-half of the twentieth century,"[28] she goes on to reference Toyin Falola and Kwame Essien's argument that "the 'one-dimensional' focus on race and racism could not sustain Pan-Africanism after the demise of colonialism, segregation, and apartheid, leading to its steady eclipsing by diaspora studies."[29] Thus, pan-Africanism may have lost relevance in the postmodern era that favors cultural hybridity and multiculturalism. Santana, recalling her interview with a successful Malawian writer called Chikoti, argues that the thinking known as pan-Africanism has changed: "To be a pan-Africanist is to be someone who wants to contribute to the discourse of the future of Africa . . . this is a different form of pan-Africanism than that of the 1960's, [Chikoti] notes that as 'a kind of protest movement against the West.'"[30] Rather, he argues, "The problems that Africa is facing are not necessarily from external forces."[31]

In a lecture delivered in 2012, Kenyan writer Binyavanga Wainaina openly rebuffed the term "Afropolitanism," which Santana described as an effort to exorcise the concept. Wainaina claimed that the term had been commoditized. In an interview with Gemma Soles, he stated, "I'm a pan-Africanist . . . of a pan-African movement to open borders, to trade, think, imagine freely across the continent is something that's very deeply important."[32] Wainaina's pan-Africanism, which entails migrating across borders, can be equated with Afropolitanism.

The presentation of Afropolitan characters like Wole Soyinka, Achebe, Nelson Mandela, Kofi Awoonor, Dr. Justin, A. B. Assensoh, and Cherno Njie, in memoirs written by other important personalities, shows that individuals should be gauged and viewed as global citizens. They should not be considered as indigenes to rule certain nations, and the indigene/nonindigene dichotomy should be abolished to benefit the greatest number of African countries. This will create global and universal citizens in all countries.

FAR AWAY FROM HOME: RENEGOTIATING HOME AND IDENTITY

Assensoh's and Njie's memoirs are multivocal texts that examine the migrant experience from a new perspective. The memoirs re-present issues that revolve around "belongingness," identity, self-perception, and the ideal home. The plot's apparent focus on relevant narration from the lives of the authors is a smokescreen—the works reveal the dynamics of contemporary diasporic experiences in relation to their homelands and newfound homes. The seemingly dysfunctional events in their natal homes are hidden portraitures of lived experience in the new diaspora and the quest for survival. Through their contributions to new homes and discussions of former homes, Njie and Assensoh reiterate that the panacea for the average migrant's challenges involves undermining barriers posed by race, eradicating self-inflicted feelings of difference and unworthiness, and understanding the limitations of the conventional "home," as well as what it means to exist "being at home in the world."

Njie delivers an engaging critique that celebrates the parts of Africa that ought to be celebrated. He reveals the fluidity of "home" and its relativity in his memoir *Sweat Is Invisible in the Rain*. For Ayo Kehinde, home "is not a private sphere, but a space where the private coexists with the public. It poses a complex relationship between subject and space due to the rapid growth of globalization."[33] Home is a location of many points in space, which makes it a multidimensional concept; people should be able to respond by adapting and facing multiple cultural forms. Ana Maria Sanchez-Arce posits that "human beings should define and re-define themselves every day and celebrate transgressed identity in areas where cultural identities collide."[34] This is evident in the text when the author explains that he fell in love with Texas and had given up hope of returning home:

> By that time, I had given up my intention to move back home after finishing with my degree at UT. Frankly, I fell in love with Austin, and I did not want to live anywhere else. I wanted, rather, to see what I could make of myself and of my career in Texas. The two and a half years at UT passed, it felt, incredibly fast, so fast that I was not yet ready to leave. The Gambia was at the back of my mind, and because communication with my friends and family at home was slow and difficult, it was natural for my attention to gravitate toward what was in front of me in Texas. Calling home was prohibitively expensive, and, of course, The Gambia was not on the radar of any American news outlets.[35]

Networking within diasporic communities is an important element of dealing with the fluidity of home—it offers a way to build African networks in new lands. Researchers describe diaspora as an untheorized or undertheorized concept, especially in a world where identity politics and ethnicity are regularly invoked. As James Clifford puts it, it is "loaded with a political meaning."[36] Various ethnicities, nationalities, races, and religions claim diasporic identities around the world. The origin, current meaning, and usage of the word diaspora add context to scenes from the memoir, such as the one where the narrator and other African students move with purpose to protest against inequality. The diversity of the diasporic community's network is also described:

> There was much more to do, the student body was more diverse, there were greater opportunities for involvement in student and social life,

and there were far more resources available to university students. I was, as far as I knew at the time, the only Gambian at the University of Texas, but there were plenty of other Africans in Austin. I met South Africans, many Nigerians and Ghanaians, and a few from Sierra Leone; they studied at UT, or at Austin Community College, St. Edward's University (a private Catholic school), Huston-Tillotson University (a private, historically black college), or simply worked and lived in the city. Many have remained good friends and live still in Austin or elsewhere in the United States—in particular, Louis Secka, Steven Frimpong, Sam Atere Roberts, and Robert Adams. Besides joining the African Students Association, I was also a member of the Black Students Union at UT, where I met more black Americans than I ever did in Lubbock.[37]

In A. B. Assensoh's memoirs, *A Matter of Sharing* and *Migrant Stories*, the fluidity of home as a concept relates more to national issues than personal ones. Despite this difference, Assensoh still promulgates the notion that home is where you are at the moment. This message is present during his experience as a child in Ghana when he moves back and forth between Father's house and Mother's house without being challenged. He navigates these spaces and makes himself comfortable in adulthood. In the chapter "Far Away from Home," Assensoh has positive experiences while meandering through three continents: Asia, Europe, and North America. These narrated experiences show him straddling different worlds, existing as an individual who understands cosmopolitan terrain despite the military problems in his country of origin.

Assensoh's concept of home can be critically examined in light of the internal strife present in African countries. He subverts the idea of home by tying his identity and sense of belongingness to his profession as a journalist and historian. In essence, his existence as an immigrant is approximated to his profession. His color, nationality, and race consciousness inflect his narration, and his expertise and relevance in his environs have enabled critical readers to perceive how his memoirs subvert the idea of home. This subversion is revealed by viewing countries in West Africa through the lenses of secession, coups, and counter-coups. In Assensoh's narration, the resounding address made by Kwame Nkrumah, the first elected indigenous president of Ghana, illustrates the concept of home to a global audience. Dr. Nkrumah told his huge audience, part of the new Ghanaian citizenry as well as foreign guests and dignitaries, including then Vice-President Richard Nixon of the United States, that "the independence of Ghana is meaningless unless linked to the total liberation of the African continent."[38]

An examination of the preceding quote shows the exaltation of Ghana, the home country, as a symbolic stand-in for the African continent. Nkrumah, as narrated by Assensoh, is concerned with the growth of Africa as a model for a home where any individual can be comfortable and stable. The mention of the Caribbean, Asia, and other parts of the world shows that Africa is a home that is open-minded, incorporating the spirit of inclusiveness.

To support the symbolic representation of Ghana as a home for people of the world, Assensoh presents the personality of Kwame Nkrumah as one that galvanizes the Black race and its leadership. Such overwhelming portraiture of Nkrumah encouraged American leaders, such as Malcolm X and W. E. B. Du Bois, to trace their ancestry to Ghana, making meaningful contributions to the country that helped in the advancement of Black history and culture. The galvanization of the Black race and leadership in Ghana is described by Assensoh:

Ghana's Kwame Nkrumah, whose 100th birthday is being celebrated worldwide this year, galvanized the black race and black leadership throughout the world. In fact, it was because of the respect that he commanded worldwide that Malcolm X, the radical black leader from the United States, arrived in Ghana on May 10, 1964 for what he termed, in his published autobiography, a pilgrimage-type of trip in 2006. Mayfield told Malcolm that there were about 300 African Americans in Ghana in 1964, who were working hard to help the Nkrumah government at various levels of involvement, to which Malcolm reportedly replied: "Beautiful. That's beautiful. . . . That's what I call making a real revolution."[39]

This fluid concept of home is replicated in Du Bois's request to be buried in Ghana, which birthed the Encyclopedia Africana. The idea would endure for ninety years: "This month, his [Dr. Du Bois's] dream became reality as Microsoft, in collaboration with two Harvard University editors, launched Encarta Africana, the first comprehensive encyclopedia on black history and culture."[40]

In projecting the idea of home as inclusive, peaceful, and a place where individuals feel stable, Assensoh promotes the idea of politics and secession. Most African countries, such as Nigeria, Rwanda, and Congo, have faced varying degrees of internal crisis and civil war among rival ethnic groups—Nigeria experienced the Biafran secession and insurrections in the Niger Delta region. Internal wars are not a universal standard, and they defy the concept of home as a unified place. Assensoh appeals for internal and external recognition of the concept of home as not only global but also localized.[41]

Assensoh condemned the bloodshed and appealed to Ghanaian society to espouse peace, castigating African leaders during historical secessions in which African countries held one ethnic group as superior to another. Such a limited worldview is neither universal nor cosmopolitan in nature, and the secession incidents show how they tend toward particularism that does not allow open-mindedness and prevents people from learning the values of other cultures. The current global age requires the equal promotion of all different cultures, recognizing the universal need for unconditional acceptance that transcends factional interests. Assensoh and Njie see clinging to one's natal home as subjective; everyone must learn to feel at home across all spaces in the world.

In modern times, spaces and the right of passage belong to no one in particular—having a home requires a huge sense of possession. The identity of individuals can be redefined after crossing to other lands. Psychological and sociocultural estrangement can result from a change in space; the distinct norms and ideologies in the new space—and the ego's conscious attempt to absorb these differences and adapt to the new culture—can lead to hybridity and syncretism. In extreme cases, it can cause personality disorder and disillusionment. In the words of David Ralph and L. Staeheli, "Individual migrants often fail to meet normative expectations of behavior, language, appearance, dress, eating habits, and countless other materialities and context-dependent etiquettes, and are in consequence perceived and discursively constructed as a group as being different to dominant others."[42] Estrangement and feelings of alienation cause the necessary identity formation and adaptation that precedes migration. This is evident in the text, as Njie was overwhelmed with the feeling of nostalgia and gripped with culture shock:

> To tell the truth, I was, after a day or more of traveling, too excited to be in Texas to spend very much time missing my home or feeling lonely. It was a new world; it was a new time and space. I met Basiru Njie (my friend who was already studying at Texas Tech) that week, and he quickly introduced me to the community of African students in Lubbock. There were maybe four or five other Gambians, as well as Senegalese, Nigerian, Malian, and Zimbabwean students; it was a tightly knit community. Lubbock, to be sure, was not the city that I had expected it to be; it was far from the metropolis I had imagined. I laugh at myself now, to have expected so much from the flat, scruffy West Texas town.[43]

In the formation of identity, Donald Cuccioletta asserts that transculturalism proposes "a new humanism of the recognition of the *other*, based on a culture of métissage, is in opposition to the singular traditional cultures that have evolved from the nation-state."[44] Transculturalism views the concept of culture as the redefinition or disappearance of the nation-state. He further states that transculturalism is not a total objective reality; it requires a conscious subjective component that is expressed in the public space and in a democratic fashion free from political interference.[45] Assensoh includes this in his memoirs when he states that there are many Black leaders in Africa, the Caribbean, the United States, and Asian countries. These leaders have played formidable roles in the advancement of their communities and the Black race, ensuring the formation of other identities through intermingling and marriages.

Assensoh recounts a time when he was in London and had to travel to Liberia to research ritual murders in the country. He noted the mixed-race identity of Liberians and Americans, who were proud of their identities and who helped to rebuild the country despite hatred. This type of identity formation breeds love and humanity, which is needed in this multicultural world. There is no more ethno-racial purity, and mixed ethnicity is increasing across the globe. Assensoh narrates:

> I was involved during my sojourn in Europe Asia and the United States, some parts of Southeast Asia and, later, in the United States of America, the Liberian story deserves a brief overview because of certain circumstances, including the fact that Liberia is often seen as a nation that emancipated American slaves—who called themselves Americo-Liberians—moved to and helped to rebuild in the midst of bitterness between them and the natives they met in the West African nation. The standing joke was that the coat-of-arms that the Americo-Liberians created had the inscription: "Love of liberty brought us here," but the native Liberian leaders had their own inscription: "Love of liberty met us here."[46]

ALL WALLS MUST FALL: RACISM, TRUMPISM, AND ANTICOSMOPOLITANISM

Cultural and racial hostility is an extension of the shock and alienation experienced by immigrants. In this case, it is spurred by intense contrast in physical differences and sociocultural ideologies that are manifestations of the psychological perception of others. These racial and cultural clashes manifest others" psychological perceptions and attempts to establish a difference between one's identity and that of others. It also serves as a criterion for the stratification of society on political and socioeconomic levels.

Racial tensions are well represented in Assensoh's *Migrant Stories*. The narrative's first indication of cultural and racial tension occurs in a moment of disillusionment during the narrator's time at NYU. It is internalized racism, where an individual thinks that members of a specific race look identical. In the text, the narrator suffers. The "Super," an individual who is a white woman, allows a thief to steal the narrator's bags from his hotel because the two people look the same to her. This sort of flawed racism is centered around biology and a dismissive view of other races. As recounted by the author, "However, when I returned to the rooming house, my two suit cases were gone and, of course, my entire savings were also gone. In tears, I did report the theft to the 'Super,' who told me that she saw my suitcases being taken out of my room and, also, out of the building. She did not bother to ask why I was leaving so soon because she thought I was leaving for Louisiana, as I told her that I would one day."[47]

The author counters this experience with an example from his childhood. Through a flashback, it is perceived that colors are just a social construct to divide individuals of different races—children cannot tell that Black is superior to white or vice versa. This is shown when the author sees a man from a different race, insisting that the man is red despite the adults naming him the "white man." He says:

> Why are you running so fast and panting as if you are being chased by a lion or a leopard?" Madam Abena Amoatemaa (Madam Hannah), my mother, asked me. That was after I rushed to our bedroom with anxiety etched all over my face. "I saw a man made of blood. He is totally red!" I exclaimed. "I am sure it is the Education Officer from the Queen's country. It must be the Whiteman," my maternal grandmother, who was listening attentively, said to me. "Awo, the man was not white. He is red, made of blood," I responded firmly, trying to impress upon both my grandmother and mother, at the same time, that the person I saw was totally mysterious.[48]

Racism is more than just a personal belief; it is also a means of cultural messages and institutional rules and systems. This system works in favor of whites and does not put the Black man on the map to be recognized. It can be used to discriminate when combined with social interactions because the underprivileged are disregarded. It can happen in any social space, including churches. The narrator describes how white people failed to recognize his humanity:

> Being their first encounter with a black man, they felt anxious to touch and rub my hands to see if the blackness would peel off to reveal another type of skin, possibly white skin. That did not happen. Then, curiously, one of the youngsters sought to know if I could talk at all. So, she asked in Swedish: "Hur mar du?" ("How are you doing?") My response was that I was doing well, and I added, "Tack, bra," which in Swedish simply meant: "Fine, thank you." She turned to her mother and, pointing her finger at me to say: "Mama, it talks." At that time, I was an "it." There were some more incidents, but Mr. Arild Berglof of the Swedish Institute would always explain that it was due to either ignorance or the fear of the unknown, not blatant racism.[49]

Racism surfaces in Assensoh's personal life in Sweden, demonstrating how racism can be taught from one person to another to establish feelings of superiority over others. The mother of Assensoh's girlfriend has convinced her daughter that kissing a Black person will bring terrible spots to her body. His girlfriend states that, "My mother said to me that if I kissed any black person, there would be spots in my face and on my neck for everyone to know what happened with a black man."[50] This incident shows that racism can become so entrenched in every facet of life that some individuals are unaware of it—the narrator's girlfriend only recognizes her racist indoctrination after spots fail to materialize on her body.

Another of the author's experiences shows the extent to which racism affects society: the narrator was part of a group that experienced racism at a restaurant where different people commonly gather to eat food. Assensoh hints that society is not safe when a place set aside for eating and drinking is vulnerable to racial division. Friends of the narrator explain that they:

> saw that several white customers came inside, but they hurriedly left, and they did not return. At the time, we had been served our meal, but a manager invited us outside and suggested that we could leave without paying for our half-eaten meal. "Sorry, we are losing customers because of your presence, and we can't have that" the female restaurant manager told me. "So, you want us to leave?" I asked in bewilderment. We obliged and left! A sad lesson in racism![51]

Color is another construct that can be used to create social identities. It is often seen as interchangeable with race or ethnicity, but color crosses divisions between and within various ethno-racial groups. White and privileged people do not generally view themselves in terms of race. Discussions about race usually refer to people who are marginalized, and individuals can become involved in an interracial conflict when one "black" skin color is seen as superior to another variation. Assensoh denounces this, noting it in his memoir and recognizing its irrelevance along ethnic lines:

> There were incidents that could have made me come to such conclusions, but I often considered the possibility that they were not mere racism, but probably competitiveness in the job place, which made a couple of colleagues nervous. Some foreign colleagues strongly felt that our African-American colleagues, our own black kith and kin merely tolerated us, as continental Africans, but that they did not really accept and like us as professional colleagues. In fact, a female colleague told me in a conversation that those of us from Africa had countries to return to if we came and muddied the professional working place for them in America.[52]

Assensoh expresses his displeasure at the thinking prevalent among white scholars that depicts Africans as a lost, clueless race that can only be saved by the white man. He ridicules the idea that ordinary white men can consider themselves able fit to fix the "broken continent" of Africa. He describes his professor:

> Consequently, he urged me to plan to write either a master's degree thesis or a doctoral dissertation later, which would discuss or extol good aspects of colonialism or imperialism. That was, to my ears, a bad music sang in a bad voice and I knew that it was time to move on. "Are you really serious, Professor, about me writing a thesis or dissertation in future to praise Africa's colonial exploiters?" I queried. His response was an interesting one, as he felt that that I spoke and wrote such decent English that, in his opinion, I might have gained a lot from the colonial masters or their education back in Ghana during colonial rule. "Was Ghana not under British colonial rule?"[53]

Assensoh's remark and his obvious disgust at the idea of Africa being perceived as constantly in need of salvation depict how he is daunted by the notion that Africa is a continent to be belittled and dismissed. However, other white individuals in his narrative understand the notion of equality, and they do not seek to subjugate other races—they treat them as equals. One such person is Dr. Spears, a Harvard University educator who employed the narrator and treated him with respect. He describes Dr. Spears: "He, therefore, informed me that he needed my shorthand-writing and editing expertise, but that he was not going to treat me like the way those big universities treated enslaved Blacks: to get their labor to erect the buildings on their campuses as free labor because they were enslaved persons. 'In my case, I will compensate you well,' he told me with a solemn face."[54]

Assensoh's critique of racism relies on the idea that it is anti-cosmopolitan to avoid embracing the new world order or disrespecting other cultures. He frames these views through the personality of US President Donald Trump. In his memoir, *Migrant Stories*, Assensoh criticizes Trump's negative comments about Africa and Haiti (describing them as "shithole" places). Assensoh writes:

> Imagine, for some of us from Africa, waking up and hearing the unbelievable as U.S. President Trump—in anger about congressional insistence that he should not undermine immigration laws of the country of immigrants—reportedly said, degradingly, that he did not want to see any more immigrants from "shithole" African countries as well as Haiti. Wow!! Reportedly, Mr. Trump was also quoted as saying that all postearthquake immigrants from Haiti had AIDS. Another Wow!![55]

As noted by Andrew Fiala, individuals:

> have already been "cosmopolized" (to adopt Beck's terminology). The fact is that in the sciences and humanities we hold international conferences, read translated works, and correspond with international colleagues. International, intercultural, and interfaith dialogues have a long and productive history. The same cosmopolization occurs in technology, commerce, financial markets, and so on—even including in friendship and family life.[56]

Andrew Fiala's perspective is validated by Assensoh, who notes that Trump had no respect for immigrants. The US president was an eco-terrorist who was neither cosmopolized nor a good leader for the free world; he did not espouse the tenets of an Afropolitan or a pan-Africanist. In his 2018 address, Trump stated that "we reject the ideology of globalism, and we embrace the doctrine of patriotism,"[57] a statement that was disregarded by world leaders at the United Nations. The administration's stance was not beneficial to the continent of Africa.

The US president's harsh immigration laws, disregard for third-world countries, and environmental negligence rejected the positive, open-minded approach relevant for a globalized world. This global age requires the ability to forge oneness from the transcultural and diversity from the multicultural. One must condemn monoculturalism and avoid racism and tyranny. Humans need cultural attachments and a sense of inclusiveness that welcomes immigrants from every part of the world—this contributes to the essence of global safety that Trump blatantly disregarded. There are merits in the power of unity and the enriching properties of transculturalism and multiculturalism: "New ideas, knowledge will erupt and be shared; freedom will be guaranteed, and there will be ability to cross boundaries. There will be no racial segregation, which will be confined by cultural particularity. It will only give a worldwide community under multiple cultures. However, it is not a state of Utopia. What is needed is a multicultural identity, not a pan-cultural one."[58]

Multiculturalism enables mutual acceptance of the widest range of human differences among the largest number of people. It helps people overcome manifestations of racism, ethnic favoritism, and other forms of discrimination. A shift from multiculturalism to transculturalism will broaden perspectives and foster a cosmopolitan identity that compels people to see the world through a cultural lens. Thus, culture would serve as the lens through which people will examine, project, and resolve challenges. Recognizing relationships across races without barriers enables culture to become all-encompassing as the foundation of global perspectives. At the grassroots level, the concepts of social multiculturalism and transculturalism have fostered a conscious ebb and flow of interculturality and hybridity.[59]

TOWARD A SYNCRETIC CULTURE AND AFRICAN DEVELOPMENT

Africans must create a channel for adapting to the new environment that confronts them with new values, cultural mores, schemas, relationships, and socioeconomic systems and challenges. Africa faces a cultural challenge today when it considers development for any aspect of life. Culture is a lens through which the continent must view development—words such as development and modernization are attached to culture and deeply rooted in values and norms.

The development of Africa hinges on creating a culture that allows the continent to evolve an industrial civilization that achieves prosperity. These norms and values are buttressed by Assensoh in his memoir; the chapter "Not All Is Political" reviews how education affects progress in Africa. In his analysis, Assensoh identifies the traditional educational values that were undermined and downplayed by colonial leaders. The exploitative rule over the continent did not consider traditional values from the precolonial period, which were more in line with the culture of the British and French. In validating this claim, Assensoh writes:

> For example, before the colonial period, legal education throughout Africa, as research has shown, was provided through apprenticeships, whereby sages and elders—referred to at times as Griots, with indigenous legal wit and aphorisms—were asked by parents and local leaders known as chiefs to impart their legal acumen or knowledge to the younger generation. There was, therefore, no formal legal education at that time, dating back to pre-colonial Africa. Instead, there other forms of law in addition to customary or traditional laws in countries like Nigeria and Ghana in West Africa; there were such forms of laws as "Muslim law, Islamic law or the Sharia [law] as part of the applicable law."[60]

The African community possesses the knowledge, skills, and modes of behavior that are necessary to attain standard education. The Europeans' flaw was that they did not consider the cultural values of the African community when developing educational opportunities. The colonizers' refusal to conduct education in indigenous languages encouraged imitation and overdependence on the Western way of learning.

In order for African development to occur, African intellectuals must imbibe the communitarian nature of Africans. A policy of self-reliance and reflection would allow Africa to be free from external economic domination, and policies can ensure mutual relationships and cooperation among ethno-religious societies. To make this point, Assensoh quotes Dr. Ki-Zerbo:

> The time has come for African decision-makers as well as leading educators to end the embrace of Eurocentric (or Western) education wholesale as well as its attendant human capital theories and the transparent flaws. It should, however, be pointed out that while African countries are not being urged to go into isolation, whereby educational and cultural exchanges are concerned. Instead, the former

colonies should overhaul the educational systems that their colonial masters left behind for the education or training of the citizenry.[61]

Some African scholars believe that training pan-African and Afrocentric youths will ensure the continent's development. This sustainable, multicultural outlook would enable national integration, aiding social reconstruction and exporting the most important aspects of African culture. Africa would need to reject some aspects of its culture and tradition that are no longer fit for globalized living, borrowing beneficial cultural aspects from numerous other cultures.

Cultural integration can produce a Third-Space attitude to kick-start development, which is another cultural orientation. Assensoh postulates and shares this lesson, which is applicable to most African countries—they are multiethnic by nature. He proposes a government that encourages a healthy relationship between individual ethnic identities and broader cultural attitudes, assisting national integration that promotes freedom and fluid identities. The lesson is that a culture avoiding critical self-renewal will ensure its own death. In this globalized world, the cosmopolitan identity is favored over monoculturalism; a kind of progressive cosmopolitanism is necessary, along with a dash of enlightened localism, to hasten the development of Africa culturally, educationally, and socially.

CONCLUSION

African postcolonial writers, such as Assensoh and Njie, have creatively interpreted and highlighted the concepts of home and identity by describing the forces that affect our individual, continental, and globalized existence and realities. These interpretations can be evaluated to determine their effectiveness in confronting and understanding African life and culture. African memoir writings, Afropolitanism, and "localization" have been appraised from the broad-spectrum perspective of universalism, pan-Africanism, and cosmopolitanism.

This chapter has surveyed biographical writings from the viewpoint of Africans in the diaspora, discussing how these works have presented African portraiture in line with cultural realism in the global sphere. (Other writers, who also explore the essence of multiculturalism, transculturalism, and hybridity, are not presented here.) Despite generational differences, these writers have advocated for peaceful coexistence. They believe that no single culture should dominate others, and people should imbibe solidarity and love with a view to satisfying their needs for cultural identity in a completely heterogeneous locale. An understanding of the way that migrant writers in Africa and other worlds present and educate the reader about cultural diversity, history, and democracy is essential for understanding where African literature is headed in this twenty-first-century postmodern world, as well as in the coming centuries.

Chapter 7

CONTRASTING EXPERIENCES OF OLD AND NEW HOMES IN THE NEW AFRICAN DIASPORA MEMOIRS

INTRODUCTION

African lives have been shaped by diverse experiences. Since colonialism, the African experience cannot be defined without acknowledging its interaction with foreign cultures. During the transatlantic slave trade, people were shipped to the Western Hemisphere in slavery. During colonialism, young Africans migrated to the West for education, military training, and to fight under the flags of their colonial masters in the world wars. In the postcolonial era, people migrate for reasons that include political exile and the search for greener pastures.

Despite the end of colonialism, many Africans maintain connections with the West, and Africans have left their homelands to search for a better society that can provide missing amenities. Many migrated for jobs, to acquire education, and to set their children on a path that had a better chance of overcoming poverty. In Africa, many leaders who claimed power after self-government have abused that power and become dictators. Their regimes of fear and terror compel citizens to flee their countries. Political opponents are oppressed and eliminated. The press is stifled, and journalists are threatened, forcing many to seek political asylum. After their migration, Africans have had to reexamine the realities of their homelands in comparison to the realities of the new cultures in which they find themselves.

The history of Africa has endured the transatlantic slave trade, colonialism, political and religious instability, civil wars, and other impairments to development. Before slavery and colonialism, Eurocentric scholars, including G. W. F. Hegel, Hugh Trevor Roper, and Lucien Levy-Bruhl, were convinced that Africans had no history and that they were not capable of logical reasoning before contact with Europe. They claimed that Africa existed under a mantle of darkness before its contact with Europe, and by eliminating a group's history and capacity for logic, they declared that it had no sense of consciousness. However, Africans had a long history before contact with Europe. These histories were unwritten because Africa had an oral tradition of sharing and retaining knowledge. But because these histories were not found in written texts, they were dismissed.

It is redundant to dismiss any history's authenticity because of its orality; the justification itself is in the orality. Despite the erroneous and Eurocentric view that Africa did not exist before European contact, the continent had its own heterogeneous identities before the slave trade and colonialism. Africans had unique systems, experiences, and identities that enabled "native intelligence," an African way of rationalizing issues. Although the perception of the African experience stems intrinsically from an aspect of being, there is a sociological aspect that dominates the essence of what it means to be an African. The sociological aspect of human life considers how social factors and norms affect individuals and groups—African experiences during the precolonial, colonial, and postcolonial eras shaped the experience of Africans and how they internalized it.

The African past determines how Africans experience the present. Rwandans, for example, understand humanity, war, and genocide in a subjective sense because they have already faced these dilemmas. Their experience of genocide interprets reality and humanity in ways that are different from those who have not shared that experience. Growing up in an urban, suburban, or rural setting influences how people perceive and evaluate issues. The availability of formal and informal education determines a group's epistemic basis. The sociopolitical structure and history of countries and communities influence the experiences of their residents. Sociopolitical circumstances cause different reactions to phenomena.

Colonialism has affected European and African minds in different ways—Africans, in particular, experienced it from the position of the oppressed. This has created a dichotomy between Africa's past, as traditional Africa and its encounter with colonialism, and the present, as the postcolonial encounter and what has been made of it. Unfortunately, the postcolonial experiences of self-governance have commonly involved corruption, bad leadership, tyranny, nepotism, and genocide. These events have led to new experiences that are different from the precolonial and colonial eras.

Experience can compel people to take up the pen and record their plights, struggles, and triumphs—many Africans have written their subjective reactions to historical events. Most importantly, African intellectuals write as a form of documentation, which has led to Ngugi Wa Thiong'o, Chinua

Achebe, Wole Soyinka, and others who write extensively about their experiences and the African experience in general. Political leaders have also written about their inspirations, failures, and successes. Common topics in many African memoirs are governance, politics, migration, and civil wars. In a real sense, everyone wants to recount these events to discuss how happenings in society have shaped their decisions, actions, and lives in general.

African authors have told stories that discuss what it is like to grow up in rural towns in Nigeria and The Gambia, the forces that led to their eventual migration, and their experiences with culture shock after moving to new countries and communities. The corruption and tyranny of many African leaders led citizens to flee their homelands and seek better lives elsewhere. It is worth considering how authors reminisce about the years spent in their homelands and the events that made them leave those homes behind. These events have their own political, philosophical, communitarian, and intellectual undertones. Paying attention to the undertones, looking beyond the stories and snapshots, allows readers to analyze and criticize the actions and inactions of authors. Stories and narrations can be examined as media to perform a deeper investigation of the rot that invests postcolonial African systems. The stories examined in this chapter have been carefully curated to consider power dynamics, infrastructural deficiency, poverty, and other sociopolitical factors.

The authors under consideration have tried to elevate the traditional African sense of reasoning, showing sagacity in African ways of life without taking an Afropessimist approach. Despite the shared African experience, the authors were shaped by the immediate history of their people and the culture in which they grew up—the sociocultural differences in their societies are evident, but their work rationalizes multitudes of experiences in Africa and the West.

THIS IS US: AFRICAN COMMUNITARIANISM AND FAMILY CARE SYSTEMS

Analysts agree that the social nature of precolonial Africa was essentially communitarian—the aim of their analysis is to distinguish what traditional African society was like before European contact. African societies are described as elevating the interest of the community above that of individuals, commonly categorized as "we-social." John Mbiti, the famous Kenyan religious scholar and philosopher, said, "I am, because we are; and since we are, therefore I am."[1] One cannot define a person in the African sense without their community; the person's existence is affirmed through the existence of others. Traditional African societies adhere strictly to principles of togetherness over principles of individualism and solipsism. An African person who lacks this communal spirit is considered abnormal and often treated as an outcast.

The communitarian aspect of traditional African identity has been elevated to such a degree that nationalists and African leaders at the end of colonialism clamored for a return to the precolonial sense of community and brotherliness. Kenneth Kaunda, Julius Nyerere, Kwame Nkrumah, and other leaders urged Africans to see themselves as brothers and sisters, as it was in precolonial African societies. There may be countless opinions on the nature of communitarianism in precolonial Africa, but even during the colonial era, there were some elements of communitarianism amongst African people. They still cared for each other and looked after one another.

However, it is a stretch to categorically say that precolonial Africans were essentially communitarian. Even with their sense of community, people owned slaves, sold their own people into slavery, and waged war against each other. The common notion is that if Africans were truly communalistic, they would not have perpetrated such callous and evil acts against one another. The relevant point is not that evil acts were absent from Africa's precolonial era—the communitarian spirit did not completely eradicate such acts—but that acts of solipsism and selfishness were reduced by a sense of community and a desire to support the greater good.

Communitarianism is a utilitarian principle of community that does not eliminate evil acts. It is a principle of "We" over "I" that promotes the greatest amount of good for the largest number of people. Every society includes evil deeds and bad actors, but communitarianism worked to minimize the damage they caused. African communitarianism promoted togetherness and a sense of belonging over individual exceptionalism.

Michael Afolayan's *Fate of Our Mothers: The Collected Memories of An African Village Boy* displays the belongingness and togetherness that are basic tenets of communitarianism. The author emphasizes that the stories collected in the memoir are not only his own but also shared experiences of the places where he grew up and those who nurtured him. One of the most significant stories emphasizing the sense of community is that of the man called Dalemo. Afolayan writes:

> Each family house was a large compound. They housed extended families. It was relatively easy to build houses in Oke-Awo. It was always a community venture. The owner of the house to be built simply announced his request for help to the people in the village on

a particular day. Often, the job was done in one day, except on rare occasions when they had to return the second day due to inclement weather conditions or some other emergencies. There was only one person in the history of Oke-Awo who was said to have built his house without inviting anyone to help him. He was nicknamed "*Dalemo,*" meaning "one who builds his house alone." Dalemo was considered a loner. I was not born when he did the unthinkable, but I knew him by that name as I was growing, and I knew the house that he built himself. He was always the gossip topic of the village.[2]

The central idea is that of Oke-Awo: the custom of people helping one another in times of need. Dalemo is independent, exhibiting the spirit of individualism. In modern times, an attitude like Dalemo's would be praised—for metropolitan sensibilities, the idea of individuality is celebrated as a way to encourage people to stand on their own without inconveniencing others. Their idea of inconvenience is that which Oke-Awo would interpret as togetherness. When young Afolayan questions Mama Debi, asking whether Dalemo should be celebrated for not imposing his problem on the other villagers, Mama Debi retorts by stating the importance and value of accomplishing feats in unison by employing the image and rhetoric of lifting a heavy load, which is aptly presented with the different functions of the leg in comparison with the hand, stating, "Do you ever lift up the load onto your head with one hand? You cannot. You lift the load up with two hands. If one leg can do it alone, do you think Olodumare, the creator God, would give us two?"[3] This is just to show the lapses and flaws in Dalemo"s character.

In Afolayan's memoir, Mama Debi and the other villagers believe in communitarianism. It is not like the socialism of Karl Marx or any sophisticated form of modern communism. Their idea of community is simply based on the idea that one cannot survive without depending on others—this dependency shapes the activities and destinies of communities. The same idea is present in some Ifá cantos. A verse in *Otuurupon Meji* states:

> For Odukeke, the heavenly priest,
> Elebutee's divination thrived, so was Odukeke's,
> We rubbed our hands together and they are clean
> We thus become wise men of divine gifts.[4]

This Ifá verse corroborates Mama Debi's claim that one needs assistance in achieving a goal. The canto emphasizes the need to cooperate with others to live a good and communal life. With this notion, one fulfills one's essence. It supports the Yoruba notion that walking together brings success to any endeavor.

Communitarianism starts from the family. Yoruba people believe that only four eyes give birth to a child, but two hundred eyes raise that child. Even within polygamous families, it is difficult to identify who has given birth to whom. At the family level, mothers are identified by their complexion, stature, and seniority, not by who their children are. According to Afolayan in his memoir, mothers like Mama Kekere and Mama Agba were identified by their age group, and they could be women from family and non-family members as they are still called "Mama" despite that "they could be wives of uncles, cousins, neighbours and so on. But in my father's house, we talked of Mama Agba (older or senior mother) and Mama Kekere (younger or junior mother)."[5]

This is generally the case in most Yoruba societies. A passage from Toyin Falola's *A Mouth Sweeter Than Salt* states, "The Mamas were so many that I was confused about my real one . . . before you ask me, let me tell you right away that I did not know their real names other than to call Mama plus an object associated with them. I am sure there were those who knew their names, but I never did until I saw them in the notices announcing their deaths and the printed programmes of their funerals."[6] This is not an examination of polygamy. Instead, it demonstrates the sense of unity in the family that transfers into the community.

Communitarianism is possible in Oke-Awo because unity transfers from the family level to the community level. Mama Debi was not the only one teaching young Afolayan the spirit of togetherness. The family house in which he grew up offered a lived experience of doing things together. The idea of living together in family houses is summarized by Mama Agba when she says, "The lone ranger dies alone."[7] The idea is that by living together, the "illness" of one becomes the "illness" of the others. Similarly, a lone wolf dies, but the pack survives during an attack. Dalemo is a lone wolf who spurns help from the pack.

Afolayan's father emphasized the importance of walking and working together in one of his folktale sessions with the young Afolayan. Baba Agba lectures on accommodation through the familiar animal folkloric genre that children are usually interested in, especially lions and leopards and how they settle disputes.[8] Baba Agba's lecture suggests that risks that have been taken on by Dalemo stand as an element of individualism while the rest of Oke-Awo embodies communal unity.

Amongst the Yoruba, different families commonly occupy a single compound of houses. The compound is separated into different rooms, housing different members of the family or others who have been taken in as family members. Accommodating large groups of people in a single space embodies the idea of hospitality as found in communitarianism. Dalemo might have built his house by himself to avoid housing extended family members or other members of the village in need of accommodations.

Villagers might have gossiped about Dalemo, not because he built his house alone, but because he planned to break the chain of shared hospitality amongst the Oke-Awo people. African discussions of hospitality talk about the need to treat strangers and people from other groups as bona fide members of a single family. When humanism is considered, it does not involve the concepts of race and ethnicity. For Africans, humanity is the family affiliation to which everyone belongs—not Xhosa, Zulu, Igbo, Yoruba, Fon, Ewe, or others. According to Julius Nyerere:

> Those of us who talk about the African way of life and, quite rightly, take a pride in maintaining the tradition of hospitality which is so great a part of it, might do well to remember the Swahili saying: "Mgeni siku mbili; siku ya tatu mpe jembe"—or in English, "Treat your guest as a guest for two days; on the third day give him a hoe!" In actual fact, the guest was likely to ask for the hoe even before his host had to give him one—for he knew what was expected of him, and would have been ashamed to remain idle any longer.[9]

This was the atmosphere in which Africans lived together; no one was considered to be a stranger after a few days. No one abused the African sense of hospitality and community for a "free lunch" or handouts. Dalemo failed to embrace these concepts. This African communitarianism, beginning with the family unit inside a compound, was a way of life for Afolayan in Nigeria and for Cherno M. Njie in The Gambia. In *Sweat Is Invisible in the Rain*, Njie writes that his family revolves around that community and "two of my uncles and their families lived with us —-our two mothers and all the kids. So, of course, we all lived very closely, but it was no problem."[10]

Njie shows that in a rural African setting, communal living forms the basis of existence. In *Fate of Our Mothers*, Afolayan describes his family setting in Oke-Awo as one that is filled with numerous family members and exhibits a high level of communal living. Njie and Afolayan show the essentiality of communal living amongst Africans. Family units extend beyond the Western idea of a nuclear family, encompassing various members of the community who share experiences. Afolayan's family compound included his immediate family, extended family, and other people who were not blood relations. In Njie's narrative, he writes:

During the Eid al-Adha celebrations, we kids from 2 New Street went together around the city visiting the compounds of friends and relatives; then the other kids visited us, and it was all a lot of fun. (Over the years I came to appreciate that Wolof proverb my father kept close to his heart, especially after reading the economist Julian Simon's brilliant *The Ultimate Resource*. It occurred to me then, reading the book, there was another apt translation for my father's lesson: humans are indeed the ultimate resource.)[11]

Njie's and Afolayan's childhoods engraved lessons on their hearts: there is a need for cooperation and complementarity in human relations. In the affairs of the world, no man is an island. In an African society that maintains traditional values, it takes a village to raise a child. The community's interdependence is not an attempt to abandon the sense of the self. Instead, the notion reminds community members that they are parts of a greater whole. Without belonging to a whole, the personhood of the self is meaningless; it is akin to priesthood without parishioners.

With Dalemo"s character in *Fate of Our Mothers*, only one tree cannot make up the forest. It is considered insanity among the Yoruba for an individual to say, "We have arrived." Afolayan believes that such settings of communal living were "enriched by the scores of individuals, families, languages and cultures often residing under our roof."[12] It was within this family system that many Africans gained their first ideas of schooling. In this context, it meant lessons that were pragmatic and often different from the ones learned in orthodox Western institutions. Njie learned about duty and humanity from his father, and he writes about how he learned the practical usefulness of everyday life and the level of cooperation that are primary features of living a decent life in the community.

Humanity, compassion, integrity, and discipline are taught and learned in practical terms, not merely as abstractions and theoretical concepts. Children learn from many sources within compound life, sharing lived experiences. They learn good principles and reasons to avoid bad behavior. In traditional African societies, most parents use their actions to model appropriate conduct and teach valuable lessons to guide the lives of their wards and children. Not only do parents teach life lessons, but relatives and other members of the community work to set individuals on the right path. Mama Ogunyoyin"s character helped young Afolayan begin school, and he would later be thankful for it. Afolayan narrates:

I have not told you about my aunt whom we called Mama Ogunyoyin. She is the one who forced me to start school. She never told me I would start school before, but one day, she came to my father's room and found me sleeping and started yelling, "What are you doing here?" she yelled. Before I could say anything, Mama Ogunyoyin grabbed me by the right ear, dragging me out of the room, pounding me with a barrage of questions.[13]

Mama Ogunyoyin did not ask for an opinion from Afolayan's parents before taking their child to school, which was possible because "a child is born by four eyes but raised by two hundred eyes." Her motivation was to set Oladejo (Afolayan) on a path to success, ensuring that he sought a better life outside Oke-Awo. Afolayan did not regret her decision. This African sense of community and family is not an overstatement of traditional African values. It is no longer as common as it was in the past, but these values remain part of the lives of Africans, especially in rural areas where familial cooperation is still shared.

According to Emmanuel Babatunde, in *An African Journey through Celibate Priesthood to Married Life*, "Yoruba tradition taught collective responsibility."[14] This is another criticism of the individualism practiced by Dalemo. However, Babatunde soon regrets this sense of collective responsibility and communitarianism after he takes on the responsibilities of his relatives. He narrates how Fr. Ayinla realized the notion of loyalty is fast becoming an obsolete one among family members and ties as his dependents stole, worked as individual units rather than help build together, which is the African communitarian nature he hoped for through bringing and helping members of the extended family to the fold to put them in a better place and hope they do the same to the next generations. This cyclical node of communitarianism is what Babatunde hopes for in his memoir and the typical African society.[15]

In his memoir, Babatunde highlights trends amongst the younger generation that have made it difficult to maintain the collective sense of African responsibility. That remains the case in Africa today, where the sense of community is neither apparent nor cherished. Many younger Africans are now a bunch of Dalemos.

YES, SHE CAN: UNDERSTANDING ROLES OF WOMEN AND ESSENCE OF COMPLEMENTARITY

The common view of African women is that they are subjugated beings without rights or influence in a family setting. Men are assumed to be the ones who wield power, controlling the home and the destinies of the women within it. One of the loudest rebuttals of such claims, Chinweizu Ibekwe's *Anatomy of Female Power*, asserts that women actually rule men: "In the last couple of decades, feminist propaganda has sought to persuade the world that women are powerless in society, and the men are natural oppressors of women. It claims that wives are subordinates of their husbands in the home; and that, outside the home, men have excluded women from political, economic and cultural powers."[16]

The suggestion is that women are more powerful than commonly acknowledged. Chinweizu describes a deliberate attempt by "African feminists" to portray traditional women as subordinates whose main work is only child rearing and housekeeping. Concerned parties have asked whether motherhood is the zenith of womanhood. It may not be a woman's greatest accomplishment, but Chinweizu declares that it is one of many ways in which they exert authority over men. It is an extreme position, but a more moderate position would note that men seek the counsel of their wives and mothers more frequently than they may be willing to admit. In *Fate of Our Mothers*, Afolayan's daughters tell him that the television claims African men do not respect their wives, and he quickly debunks the idea. In his words:

> Our father respected our mothers more than I have seen men respect their wives in our time. Let me tell you a little bit about the relationship between our mothers and our father. It was one of mutual respect and admiration. In my mind today, I am convinced that in our family we cannot celebrate fatherhood without first venerating motherhood. Concealed behind the veil of our father's courage and convictions were the faces of our mothers. When serious matters were brought to our father, it was not uncommon for him to say to the people, "Come back tomorrow." I knew dimly then, but quite clearly now, that between the time he dismissed the people and the time of their return, he leaned on our mothers for counsel.[17]

In African societies of the past, fathers depended on their wives more than has been written or discussed. The relationship is more than the mere subordination that Western-inspired feminism attributes to the relationship between women and men in Africa. The dynamics of the relationship are shaped by the identification and separation of roles between men and women—it is a relationship of complementarity, not subordination. Afolayan notes how different chores are carried out naturally by the parents in a convincing manner. This notion of complementarity excites Afolayan as he notes his parents "never complained. They were never exhausted. We owe them all that we are worth, if anything at all."[18]

This points out the multitude of tasks that women performed in African societies. Their roles frequently differed from those of men because there is an African understanding that men and women are gifted with different traits and abilities. The most prominent abilities of women are caring and nurturing, which most men lack. Women who are successful in their roles do not make men into inferior subordinates; men have their own abilities that can be difficult for women to imitate. Afolayan realizes this in his narration, understanding that complementarity of social and biological differences exists between fathers and mothers in Yoruba societies. In his own case, he writes, "Most of what Baba did was on the advice of the two mothers, but nobody knew or was supposed to know this. Only he and the mother were privy to that information. Our two mothers were always around to support and advise him. I had always felt that the tower of our father's success was built on the fates of our mothers. He lived on the breath of their fate."[19] His success, built on their fates, does not undermine their essence. They enabled his accomplishments; without their advice, counsel, and support, he would have achieved nothing. The unique strengths of African women hold families and communities together.

Njie also recognizes that African fathers and mothers perform different functions. As Afolayan has noted, it is not the relationship of subordinates—they are equal partners with complementary attributes. Family dynamics are not merely that of men commanding women or issuing decrees. Women in African society are as industrious as men, and they enjoy the same basic liberties that are available to every human. Babatunde, in *An African Journey through Celibate Priesthood to Married Life*, describes a similar relationship between men and women, noting the significance of women in society. He writes:

> Ketu culture was gender sensitive and female empowering Yoruba sub-culture. It saw the woman as the more important partner in marriage and more important than the man in parenting and raising offsprings. The father usually worked hard outside the home to provide victuals for his wife and children as best he could. It was the mother who worked the miracle of virtually making something worthwhile out of the little resources extracted from the daunting Ketu environment. The woman, as the mother, was the savior of Ketu society. Her tireless effort to carry the fetus to term during pregnancy transformed the identity of the man as husband to that of a father. The man is proudly identified as such in social gatherings.[20]

Women, by nature of their fertility and reproductive activity, cement the place of their husbands in Ketu society—this is true in most African societies. Babatunde captures the strength of his mother and the power wielded by African women when he writes about the subversion of power and the predominant figure men would have respect for at all times. He notes that "like most powerful African women who lived in male-oriented societies, she had perfected the act of totally controlling the menfolk, all the while giving them the impression they were in total control."[21] Beyond that, Babatunde's position alludes to the one held by Njie and Afolayan: women manage the family's affairs. They complement their partners in areas where the men's capabilities are lacking, and men do the same in areas where women are lacking. It is not a competition but a simple relationship of symbiosis.

Feminism is now a global issue, but some of its concerns may not be present in Africa. Babatunde classified his mother as a feminist because she was fierce and fought for her rights.[22] Social events are viewed subjectively, and the history of a people determines the struggles that they experience.

LET'S DEVELOP OUR HOME: POLITICS, WAR, AND CORRUPTION IN POSTCOLONIAL AFRICA

With the end of colonialism came self-governance. Africans who were privileged enough to receive Western education began clamoring for independence after the end of the Second World War. After India gained independence, many Africans wanted to regain their own freedom from colonial oppressors. By the 1950s, African countries began gaining independence. However, the geographic borders of most African countries were arbitrarily fashioned by colonial masters because colonizers merged diverse groups into larger entities that were easier to rule. Preexisting tribal and cultural differences meant that most African countries were already at war with one another. Political conflict, motivated by tribal sentiment, led to killings and civil wars.

Babatunde applied the prophecy and philosophy of Adunni Oluwole, a democracy activist, to evaluate the discord, corruption, military rule, and civil war in Nigeria. Oluwole was a women's rights activist who lucidly warned against self-rule, believing that Nigerians were not ready. She stated that within ten years, Nigeria would be at war with itself. Oluwole's prophecy became a reality by 1966. As Babatunde writes:

> Within six years of independence, the first Military Coups occurred, confirming the stark reality of Adunni Oluwole. The decline and

decay in Nigeria predicted so clearly by Adunni Oluwole began in earnest under politicians who were products of Christian and Muslim missionary schools. They were all invariably educated, but they were largely devoid of conscience. They employed every means necessary, particularly those means perfected by their erstwhile colonial masters, to acquire and hold on to office. Nothing was too mean or too despicable for this purpose. The sacred goal of collective liberation for meaningful independence through the improvement of the lot of the many was discarded as nonsensical. This was touted by the mainly all male Pan-Africanists before independence.[23]

When Africans finally gained independence, it was handed to people who were hungry for power. These new leaders used the differences among Nigerian citizens to divide them further. It soon became evident that they fought for independence just to increase their own power, which Babatunde laments about on the new group of leaders and their obsession with control. Babatunde's lamentation is a shared frustration at the results of self-government. In the years after independence, most Nigerians could see that democracy and self-government were on a destructive trajectory. Afolayan expressed the general feeling shared by many in the early years of Nigeria's independence: initial excitement was followed by disappointment. He succinctly states how the political leader "won election easily and became premier of the region. His administration was peaceful for the first term. But it would not be long before we experienced another election. This was a different type. It was—very violent."[24] Violence broke out ahead of Nigeria's second election, beginning the history of political conflict in the country. The head is sick for as long as the rest of the body is sick, and Nigeria's leadership was an example of the rot afflicting the minds and moral compasses of its people.

This was how things stood at the end of colonial rule—they were so bad that some people openly wished for a return to colonialism. People who were aware of Adunni Oluwole's prophecy became convinced that she was right and that Nigeria was not ready for self-rule. Afolayan's Mama Debi claimed that "with this ominira (independence), our chicken was standing on the tight rope; neither the rope nor the chicken was at ease."[25] Independence, which is ominira, then became omi inira (water of discomfort). In most African countries, the years after independence were characterized by moral decay and a reign of terror, corruption, and tyranny. This was also the case in The Gambia. The country's independence is often attributed to the resistance of elites in The Gambia who opposed a foreign government. According to Sulayman S. Nyang, "The first reason why the British colonial office decided in 1964 to grant independence to the Gambia was the general feeling that the Gambian elites were not too keen about a federation with Senegal and, for this reason, nothing short of independence was acceptable to them."[26]

The first president of The Gambia was Dawda Kairaba Jawara. His post-independence rule enjoyed a reasonable amount of peace, and the country's diplomatic efforts were focused on maintaining political stability. As a result, The Gambia supported Nigeria in the Nigerian civil war (also known as the Nigerian-Biafran war):

> The Gambia did not wish to undermine her own domestic stability by encouraging secession, a political act which could be carried out by one of her own ethnic children (the Wolof). Again, the Gambia did not like the idea of being associated with a radical and minority position such as supporting the Biafrans. These two points are closely related to the third consideration of the Gambian leaders, which suggests that they did not want to antagonise the British, the major donor of aid to their country and one of the chief suppliers of arms to Nigeria during the civil war.[27]

President Jawara remained in office for twenty-two years until Yahya Jammeh and other officers of the Gambia National Army overthrew him in a bloodless coup on July 22, 1994. The event was a profound shift in The Gambia's political history. According to Arnold Hughes, the coup "brought to an end one of the most open political systems in Sub-Saharan Africa."[28]

Jawara was guilty of embezzlement and mismanagement of public funds, but Njie believes that "mismanagement of a transfer of power from the founding generation of nationalist politicians to a younger leadership who could develop a post-independence politics remains the defining failure of Jawara government."[29] After Yahya Jammeh assumed leadership of The Gambia, Njie summarized the administration as one of unchecked evil. Njie suffered directly and indirectly during the years of callousness and brutality that characterized Jammeh's time in power. Njie's brother, Baboucarr, was arrested and later fired from his job. Njie was also arrested, spending more than a year in prison for trying to restore governance to the people.

Afolayan, Babatunde, and Njie describe the disturbing situation in post-colonial Africa and the disappointment that people felt during the years that followed colonialism. Despite corruption and uncertainty, the three authors hope for the best for their countries as they write from the diaspora. Their work shows a sense of optimism, believing that their countries will eventually get it right. Afolayan recounts that "Nigeria was changing fast. We had been independent for a few years, but nothing exciting had ever happened in the country except for an upsurge of corruption, the magnitude of which we had never experienced in the colonial days. Yet, Nigerians remained optimistic and resilient."[30] This kind of optimism filled the hearts of Nigerians during Afolayan's childhood. Yahya Jammeh's removal from office in The Gambia brought a new dawn. However, Njie expressed concern that the country's mindset had been harmed by Jammeh's time in office, as he notes that "twenty-two years of Jammeh's rule seems to have had a stultifying effect on the possibility of creating a new political culture and reform in the country which won't deter the reconstruction and transformation of the Gambian society."[31] Njie's position is similar to that of most Africans—they fear that the much-needed change may never happen, but they remain hopeful that their countries will improve.

In Babatunde's memoir, he conducts a diacritical analysis of Botswana and Nigeria. There has been a major divergence between the paths taken by the two countries. Botswana has become an economic and political force to be reckoned with; it has found ways to eliminate greed, individualism, and corruption, and its people adhere to the principles of Ubuntu. The principal notion of Ubuntu is embodied in the famous John Mbiti aphorism, "I am, because we are; and since we are, therefore I am."[32] This means that one cannot define a person in the African sense without defining their community—a person's existence is affirmed through the existence of others. Ubuntu discourages leaders from pursuing selfish and corrupt practices, making every decision about "us" and not "me." They do not seek to benefit themselves but to advance Botswana's people, the Batswana. Strict adherence to the principles of Ubuntu, which are strongly linked to religion, holds Botswana's leaders accountable to its people. Unlike Nigeria, in Botswana:

> Generations of groups of their elite did not band together to steal what belonged to their country, leaving the rest of the citizens poor and dejected. Neither are they envious of others who are lavish, flamboyant or overzealous. With an assured sense of traditional justice rooted in sharing to care for the needs of all in their nation, they spend the money from their mineral resources wisely and under strict accountability and oversight. They invested in health and infrastructures. They took care of the sick and employed their youth, thereby giving them hope for the future. Their politicians do not beg representatives of foreign governments who visit them to give them money.[33]

Any Botswana leader who neglects the principles of Ubuntu would forfeit his right to rule. If Nigeria could subscribe to similar principles, such as that of Omolúwàbí and the ideas of communitarianism, then the country's fortunes might change. This also applies to other African countries harmed by corruption and bad leadership.

These authors are genuinely concerned about their homelands, and their efforts have inspired people to look inward for solutions. They have recognized that they cannot sit back and watch while their countries sink into sociopolitical and moral decline. Despite being far from home, Africans in the diaspora keep their home countries in their hearts and maintain their efforts at social commentary. Their time abroad has shown them what functional, effective institutions look like. Some suggest that it may be easier to share commentary from a distance than to experience the plight of a people firsthand. However, these authors maintain relationships with friends and relatives who reside in their homelands. They receive regular updates about the hardships caused by bad leadership, tyranny, and corruption. These authors are not strangers who have left their homelands; they carry their homelands with them in their hearts, attitudes, and behaviors. A careful reading of their memoirs shows the pain the authors feel whenever they talk about their countries.

Postcolonial Africa has been marred by corruption. In many African countries, the early years of independence set the tone for the bad leadership, corruption, dictatorship, and tyranny that is currently practiced. However, by maintaining the right attitude and being willing to hold politicians accountable, Africa still has a hope of getting it right.

HERE AND THERE: CULTURAL SHIFTS AND SIMILARITIES AT HOME AND ABROAD

Adjusting to a new culture or way of life can be challenging; the differences in a new location are immediately apparent. Apart from the climate, most Nigerians who travel out of Nigeria first notice how widely available electricity is in their new environment. In Nigeria, blackouts are common, and the electric company is a frequent target of criticism and curses. When electricity is restored, it is met by cries of "UP NEPA" in an attempt to praise the company for restoring service. Most African migrants are shocked by the ordered aspect of life in Western countries. People obey traffic lights without a traffic warden in sight. The roads are free from potholes. It is also surprising to move from a country that bases its perspective on spirituality to one that values pragmatism and scientific objectivity. Njie compares life in The Gambia and America based on differences in superstitions, taboos, and human agencies. He notes that "confidence in human agency is, to me, a sine qua non, and, being one of the governing myths of the American ideal, among the most attractive features of American life. By contrast, in The Gambia, it often seems that agency belongs only to the spirit to which it has been prescribed."[34]

These differences are immediate sources of culture shock; people from Africa can be overwhelmed by this way of life. Cultural differences become more noticeable as more time is spent relating to people of different races, and it becomes important to navigate these differences successfully and acclimate to new ways of life. At the same time, migrants must maintain connections with their homeland while participating in their new society. Njie describes the dialectic problem of a man torn between his native land and his new home. While seeking greener pastures elsewhere, the home left behind also requires attention. Babatunde experienced a similar culture shock after landing at Heathrow. He writes:

> Compared with his home country, everything looked organized, austere, and individualistic. No one greeted anyone or laughed at anything. People looked stern, taciturn, and happy to be on their own and not bothered. He felt suddenly alone in the huge crowd at the station. How could one be part of so many other people and yet be so alone? Could he ever have imagined this severe loneliness with so many people around him if he were still stuck in Nigeria?[35]

Different approaches to life are often obvious, but efforts must still be applied to cope with those differences and adapt. Babatunde explains how he was able to cope despite the loneliness and the desire to be back home. However, these instances show both a nostalgic feeling for the past and a need to forge ahead; it is important to maintain balance. Njie and Babatunde understood that despite the need to cherish the past and the homeland, it is also important to keep sight of that which is in front of them. The interrelation of cultures means that some convergences exist between the cultures of homelands and the new cultures that migrants experience. In some cases, the nature of racial differences between Africa and the West is implicit instead of overt.

Immigration, for any purpose, is a psychological test that challenges the mind. Njie was not troubled by racial differences in his new country. He talked about his experience with racial differences in relation to housing and economic advantages in Texas, explaining that his background helped him to see beyond those differences:

The assumption that, in a multicultural society, participation in the housing program and development should somehow comport with an ethnic or racial group's share of the population itself reflected rather wishful thinking. And, having grown up in a multiethnic society, with many disparities along ethnic lines, I am, perhaps, conditioned not to look at racial discrimination as the sole cause of disparity in cases such as these. The Serahules, a small ethnic group, for example, were the leading businessmen in my youth and still own a disproportionate number of businesses in the Gambia.[36]

Njie's cultural background clearly shaped his perspective when assessing differences in the distribution of wealth or other issues. Africa is a heterogeneous entity that contains several ethnicities, creating an incentive to interact with others despite cultural or tribal differences. This encourages most Africans to develop tolerance and open-mindedness. When Njie was sent to prison for conspiring to overthrow the Jammeh government, he adapted quickly—he met other Africans and they supported each other because of the African sense of brotherliness.

Different social conditions create different individuals. Authors who grew up underprivileged raised children who received the resources that their parents lacked. The children were also raised in environments that were different from those of their parents. New environments bring new social conditions, which can involve individualism, racism, multiracial existence, and other factors. Despite these changes, the children were raised in what could be called a functional society. Despite his generosity, compassion, and desire to maintain a strong family unit, Njie's father could not afford to sponsor his son's tertiary education. But Njie walked so his children could fly; Cherno Njie's son, Dukuray, attended a private university in the United States.[37] Resources that were inaccessible to Njie were provided to his children, which creates generational conflict. Njie had differences with his father because they were from different generations, and he also had differences with his children, who are from their own generation. These differences create conflicts between the beliefs, attitudes, and privileges of each generation.

A similar cultural shift occurs when raising children in homelands and abroad. The way that people were raised in the past is different from the way that they are raised now. The Afolayan girls, who learned from television how African men treat their women, are one example.[38] If they were growing up in the time when Afolayan was raised, Mama Debi, Baba Agba, Mama Agba, Mama Kekere, or any other person from the community would have lectured them about how men should treat women. This was not because they lacked television but because they believed in giving first-hand lessons to their children and wards.

Additional cultural differences arise from the fact that these children, though born in America, have African ancestry while holding American citizenship. Their parents also needed to navigate ancestral identities alongside the identities into which they were born. It is their task, as much as it was the task of their parents, to ensure that they do not become the river that has forgotten its source. In their memoirs, Njie and Babatunde highlight how their children visit family in The Gambia, Nigeria, and Botswana. These are intentional efforts to ensure that they stay connected to their roots.

CONCLUSION

The three major African memoirs examined so far are Babatunde's *An African Journey through Celibate Priesthood to Married Life*, Afolayan's *Fate of Our Mothers*, and Njie's *Sweat Is Invisible in the Rain*. They tell the stories of three men from different African countries, and this chapter examined the challenges they faced and how they responded. Some of the central themes in these memoirs are culture, African communitarianism, corruption, motherhood, bad leadership in Africa, and the navigation of new cultural terrain. The memoirs also address various misconceptions about African women, who are mistakenly seen as inferior, subjugated, and subordinate beings. In different ways, the authors capture how such women take on much more responsibility than people normally acknowledge.

The authors were raised in an era when there was still an appreciation for communal cooperation, and their communitarian attitude has helped them handle the complicated nature of human relations. A careful reading of the memoirs also shows the authors' concerns for their countries—they all predict that there is a long way to go before postcolonial Africa can repair the damage done by years of tyranny, mismanagement, corruption, and civil war. However, they are all optimistic that the situation will improve when there is a reorientation that encourages open-mindedness from the people and a desire to hold leaders accountable. The authors also explain how they combined the cultures and concerns of their homelands with their new realities—one cannot easily displace one's origin despite new affiliations. It is important to recall the past and how it affected us so that we may predict what is to come. The memoirs are not only filled with personal stories; they are also didactic. Intriguing personal stories can pass different messages and lessons to guide a myriad of endeavors.

Conclusion

FROM SLAVE NARRATIVES TO FREEDOM NARRATIVES

A Genealogy of Immigrant Stories

The value of memoirs lies in their ability to provide phenomenological accounts of history. African memoirs tell their stories through Afrocentric worldviews with African epistemologies, creating grounded narratives that paint history's lived realities. Literature from the African Diaspora—from slave narratives to freedom narratives—provides an understanding of the historical context in which these authors were writing, allowing us to examine their representation of Africa.

More importantly, the theory of spatiality denotes and ascertains who belongs to a community, and it is a motif of membership. The idea of space helps to examine how the world is viewed and structured and the way people relate with each other in a community, which ultimately is the backbone of the community. As noted by theorists, space has a relationship with the idea of place, especially in an urban context, and the place is shaped by culture, social imaginings, and culture. Space cannot be eradicated in the freedom narratives and the selected memoir in the book. A space can be the physical part of a society; a signifier of general attitude; an index of a specific portion of history; a landscape, conditioner, character, or system of related living persons; or related matrices of difference. These multiple conceptual realizations of space lead literature to approach it or conceptualize it as lived, real, or imagined space.

A space, as an entity, is shaped by perceptions of it, which is exhibited through placement within it and ideological proximity to it. Where space is definable in relation to the perception of people, what is real and imagined (as types of places) becomes subjective—they are shaped by subjective positioning. This complication has been addressed by arguing that space is not generally fixed in its definitions or representations; it represents unity between reality (real) and perception (ideal). Space refers, in the general sense, to the environment where everything occurs.[1] This environment has been theorized as having an immense number of symbolic meanings for exactly this reason: it ferments a multitude of essentialities and nonessentialities. Often, space is portrayed as an embodiment of the sum of those who inhabit it and the sum of their differences.

Two of the important concepts in this work are narrative and space, and one complements the other. Narrative theory or narratology in relation to space helps the reader to understand the role space plays in narration, especially the ability to reveal the relationship between the space and each character of narration.

Freedom Narratives

Freedom narratives relate to the larger field of memory studies, which tends to comprise two disciplines: psychology and sociology. In cognitive psychology, memory is studied as an individual phenomenon taking place due to the activity in the brain. Through sociology and some extensions of social psychology, memory is studied as a cultural and societal phenomenon. Society constructs memories through a variety of social processes in which memory is constantly constructed, reconstructed, and renegotiated. Geoffrey Cubitt describes memory as "the reconstruction of past experiences, both individual and shared," which can be linked to "culture, religion or social institutions."[2] Through memory studies, history is not a fixed narrative; it is a critical framework where memories are contested or confirmed.[3]

The current "memory crisis" in Africa exists because postcolonial African memories are full of contradictions between individual accounts and official state narratives.[4] Efforts that involved actors such as UNESCO's attempt to standardize the atrocities of slavery, colonialism, and transitions to statehood have often produced generalizing histories. Although these clean histories preserve heritage, they may also silence individual memories that contradict the dominant narrative. As a result, individual memories are often expressed through nonformal forms of collective memory or storytelling.

The "official" historic memories provided by UNESCO or the state are often secular. They may not include important phenomenological aspects of history: not just what happened, when, and to what effect, but how those events were experienced by the individuals involved. A further gap is left in how those individuals and their communities made meanings of these memories. Memoirs fill this gap by offering firsthand accounts of events that include the relevant emotional, religious, and cultural aspects. In this way, memoirs are better positioned to express history from the African epistemological perspective.

In a memoir, one has the control to tell a story from lived experience. This is what Zussman has called "narrative freedom," meaning "the ability to tell stories about ourselves in the ways we want," including the ability "to draw meanings and morals about our own lives."[5] The African Diaspora's ability to exercise narrative freedom has, in many ways, been restricted by the system of colonial powers. In Western countries, published works often dictated what the African Diaspora could write through explicit or implicit restrictions. The Western publishing system incentivized the diaspora to represent Africa through a Eurocentric lens.

This chapter analyzes the narratives of the African Diaspora, including accounts of slavery, freedom, migration, and discrimination. These powerful stories are analyzed within their historical contexts and compared to ideas about what it means to be Black and the imaginations of Africa. All the stories were intended to be narratives of freedom, advocating for African liberation, but the extent to which authors had narrative freedom is not always apparent.

Slave Narratives

The Interesting Narrative of the Life of Olaudah Equiano (1789) was written by Olaudah Equiano, also known as Gustavus Vassa.[6] The memoir followed Equiano's life from the kingdom of Benin—modern-day Nigeria—where he was captured as a slave. It recounted his abduction and that of his sister, who was separated from him. It also described the inhumane conditions of his passage to America. Equiano's journey through slavery took him from the plantations of America to the United Kingdom, where he eventually purchased his own freedom. His narrative focused on his struggles with the Christian faith, in which he eventually found salvation. Equiano helped establish a plantation in Jamaica before returning to England and advocating for the abolition of slavery.

Equiano's narrative can be analyzed on the basis of the themes of duality in his identity. This is revealed by the use of his African name from birth and the English name imposed on him in Virginia. Equiano expressed amazement at the West's technology, describing his homeland as "uncivilized and even barbarous."[7] However, Boulukos notes that Equiano contradicted white slave owners—he "insists that the degradation entailed by slavery is far greater than that resulting from living in an 'uncivilized' culture."[8] Equiano took great pride in describing his "Englishness," often expressing a desire to return to the United Kingdom and a strong love of the country.[9] Equiano's experience working on a plantation complicated his positions on slavery and the nature of Africans—these views must be contextualized by the fact that his native kingdom of Benin practiced voluntary slavery, where individuals served the king in a way that was neither exclusionary nor dehumanizing.[10]

Equiano's relationship with Africa was complex. His writing combined his historical moment with his personal experience, education, and cultural and religious beliefs. The narrative took the form of a religious salvation story, and its emphasis on Christianity supported underlying European values. While Equiano did not see Africans as lesser than Europeans, he identified himself through European values, religions, and nations. His construction of personal identity suggested that he viewed African identities as able to "apply only in Africa, while the terms of European identities should be applied consistently to all people."[11] He portrayed Africans as human but possessing less knowledge, especially due to their lack of Christianity. Equiano often emphasized the "innocence of Africans," making Europeans solely responsible for the atrocities of slavery.[12] This portrayal of Africans as innocent victims, ignorant of the ways of European technology and religion, reflects the colonial ideology underlying Equiano's writings.

Although Equiano's memoir was one of many narratives describing the captivity and slavery of Africans, it was particularly influential in Europe's abolition movement. Slavery was abolished in the United Kingdom in 1833, but the Thirteenth Amendment outlawing slavery was not added to the US constitution until 1865. More than fifty years after Equiano's memoir was published, African American writer Frederick Douglass published *Narrative of the Life of Frederick Douglass*.[13] Douglass's work was one of the most influential slave narratives that shaped the abolitionist movement within the United States.

Douglass's memoir detailed his enslaved childhood, separated from his mother and witnessing the abuse of family and friends. He moved to Baltimore, where his owner began teaching him how to read; he continued his studies independently. Douglass ended up under the control of a particularly cruel master, and after trying to escape his new plantation, Douglass was put in jail and then sent to Baltimore to work at a shipyard. He finally fled from slavery and traveled to New Bedford, where he became involved in the abolitionist movement and recounted his experience. Douglass's memoir and other narratives of slavery shared common themes of cruel and hypocritical slave owners followed by eventual escape. Douglass emphasized literacy as a means to overcome captivity, portraying himself as a self-made man—this image appealed to white Americans. His ability to fully analyze the issue of slavery was limited, and he did not fully discuss what it meant to be African. Abolitionists helped Douglass publish his story and likely discouraged him from theorizing, which limited him to descriptive narratives that could appeal to a larger audience.[14] Ironically, Douglass had a limited amount of narrative freedom even though his memoir was described as a freedom narrative.

Douglass refrained from larger assertions about African Americans in his memoir. However, in other lectures and newspaper articles Douglass was "singularly dismissive" of the relation of Black Americans to Africa.[15] At times, he implied that the slave trade had severed the link between Black Americans and Africa, citing the role of Africans in the slave trade. Although Douglass did see Africa as part of a common struggle with Black Americans, he saw any discussion of African affairs as a distraction from abolitionism.[16] During his time at the *North Star*, he maintained the narrative that innocent African victims were sold into slavery, employing images of "dark, savage Africa" to illustrate the difference between Black Americans and Africans.[17]

A strong collection of slave narratives was collected through the WPA project in the 1960s, as well as by independent researchers. An example of an independent collection of narratives compiled by John W. Blassingame entitled *The Slave Community: Plantation Life in the Antebellum South*.[18] In his work, Blassingame went beyond known slave narratives, seeking untold stories from the South. He constructed slavery as an institution where a subculture amongst slaves was able to transcend oppression and retain cultural heritage such as music, folklore, and religion. Blassingame analyzes the problematic nature of slave narratives, which have often been published by white publishers, thus compromising their integrity. He states that as a result, many narratives reflect Western stereotypes of slavery rather than accurate portrayals of the times. Blassingame emphasizes Harry Stack Sullivan's interpersonal theory of personality development in slaves. This theory suggests that personality develops from the expectation of others and their environment.

However, whereas previous scholars on slave narratives suggested that slaves' personalities and culture developed from the expectation of slave owners, Blassingame argues that the Black slave family was the stronger determinant of personality development. He argued that while families were often torn apart through the exploitation and rape of Black women or selling of family members, the slave nuclear family was often able to preserve itself. While Blassingame's work sometimes overgeneralizes the experience of slaves, as little differentiation is made between plantation work and other forms of slavery, it is integral to a critical reading of slave narratives.

Tales of Progress, Reconstruction

Before the American Civil War, African American literature focused on the abolitionist project. Africa was either portrayed as the origin of the trauma of slavery or as an "uncivilized" place when compared to the Western world. The end of slavery in the United States allowed African Americans to gain literacy. Although they continued to face significant oppression, they began writing about what Africa and the identity of "blackness" meant to them.

In 1901, Booker T. Washington published his autobiography *Up from Slavery*,[19] which details his childhood as a slave during the civil war and continues through his education at the Hampton Institute. It also details his work establishing vocational schools for minorities. Washington saw himself as a self-made man, arguing that even the most disadvantaged African Americans in society could do the same by being productive and obeying the law. Washington expected political rights for African Americans to be granted after they proved their worth through productivity. The work has been criticized as "an overly sunny view of black life and prospects in America," an aspect that also was integral to its popularity at the time.[20]

Washington's portrayal of Africa was not substantially different from that of slave narratives. He believed that "the uncivilized Negro of Africa could improve himself and his society through individual initiative and the acceptance of Western religion and cosmology."[21] Indeed, Washington appealed to white audiences by attributing his success to the "puritan work ethic that white men had taught him."[22] Despite this portrayal of Africa, Washington coordinated with African leaders and many were influenced by his philosophy of self-help and self-determination.[23] As a historical figure, Washington is complex—he has been criticized for compromising Black rights to appeal to white audiences.[24] His autobiography, which was allegedly written "as a way to present himself in an unthreatening manner to his potential white donors,"[25] reflected this complexity. For example, Washington focused on the successes of Reconstruction and claimed lynching was a thing of the past.

While the complexities of Washington's views and the motivation behind his rhetoric cannot be understood by viewing his autobiography in isolation, *Up from Slavery* largely portrayed Africa as a "dark" continent. Although Washington did not self-identify with Africa, he viewed the continent, like Black Americans, as capable of rising from its position through economic productivity. This approach, giving up the fight for political rights and focusing on economic productivity, has been called the "Atlanta compromise."

Washington's greatest critic, W. E. B. Du Bois argued that economic rights were not a precondition for political rights. He argued in a review of

Washington's autobiography that it was a "partial history of the steps which made [Washington] a great leader" and that while it was an example of Black success, Washington's racial philosophy was "far short of a complete program."[26] Du Bois wrote three autobiographies, but his seminal work, *The Souls of Black Folk* (1903), drew on his personal experiences to build his theory of double consciousness.[27] This memoir gave Du Bois's experiences with racial prejudice, starting from his childhood. He described the history of slavery and emphasized the haphazard transition into freedom, mentioning Washington's "Atlanta compromise" as partially responsible for the lack of political rights received by Blacks after Emancipation. The book recounted Du Bois's personal experiences teaching and traveling from Tennessee to Georgia, relating his experiences in rural Georgia to the continued oppression of Black Americans. Du Bois emphasized the Black church from an outsider's perspective and from his own experience. He noted that spirituals were an important form of religious and artistic expression for the African American community, although they were not accepted by the country's white majority.

Du Bois explained the theory of double consciousness through his personal experiences and observations in *The Souls of Black Folk*. Black Americans must constantly consider how they view themselves in comparison to how the outside world sees them, which is double consciousness. Du Bois argued that this experience leads to a nonidentity that continues to marginalize the individual; the duality of identity leads to a renegotiation of the Black identity within the context of the United States.[28] To Du Bois, Black Americans were torn between white and Black identities. This Black identity was not synonymous with Africa—it was a new culture created by African American experiences with slavery and emancipation.[29] Du Bois imagined Africa as a place of origin for Black Americans, but he saw the African American identity as distinct from the continent.

In the Americas, a new imagination of Africa emerged while the debate between Washington and Du Bois continued. The Ethiopianism movement contended that Black Americans could and should go back to Africa. It was inspired by Psalm 68:31: "Princes shall come out of Egypt, Ethiopia shall soon stretch forth her hands unto God."[30] In a historical analysis, John Gruesser argued that "black American literary depictions of Africa cannot be fully understood without being read in the context of Ethiopianism,"[31] which spread along with Christianity and pan-African movements. Gruesser also noted that Black literature before the 1900s had a little description of Africa. The turn of the century saw neither the embrace that would be illustrated in the writing of Langston Hughes nor the rejection of Richard Wright's works or the back to Africa movement. Both Washington and Du Bois neglected Africa as a central point of their narratives, focusing instead on the experience of Black Americans.

Harlem Renaissance

Although Reconstruction reimagined what it meant to be Black in America, portrayals of Africa were limited to Eurocentric stereotypes. The Harlem Renaissance, starting in the 1920s, embraced African roots and African culture in America. Leaders such as A. Phillip Randolph described the "New Negro" of the 1920s as one who "demands political equality," "better working conditions," and "a society composed of social equals."[32] An embrace of African culture through art, music, and literature was central to the period.

A key poet of the Harlem Renaissance was Claude McKay, whose work included poems such as "If We Must Die" and "Outcast" and the novel *Home to Harlem*. His 1929 novel, *Banjo: A Story without a Plot*,[33] inspired pan-Africanism through his use of the term "roots" in discussing Black culture.[34] The narrative described McKay's time living in Marseilles, France. The book's main character escaped American society to live a pleasure-seeking lifestyle in Europe, and its episodic chapters did not follow an overarching plot. The port town discussed in the book changed to become predominantly white, and its characters expressed disillusionment with society before departing the town to pursue individual goals.

It can be argued that McKay's work "anticipates migritude" through its exploration of themes such as migrancy, diaspora, racism, and postcoloniality.[35] His novel explored how Black Americans returned from Europe after the First World War, experiencing contradictions between the decreased racialism of Europe and the nationalistic propaganda of America.[36] McKay's novel, along with other works exploring transnationalism in the Black community, began to deconstruct borders. Characteristic of the Harlem Renaissance, it was done through an artistic format that emphasized the embodied experiences of being a Black American abroad.

Alain Locke was another key author of the Harlem Renaissance. He published a collection of fiction, poetry, and essays called *The New Negro*, which was a landmark in Black literature and often considered to be the key text of the movement. One of his additions, "Harlem, Mecca of the New Negro" was originally featured in the 1925 issue of *Survey Geographic*. Locke describes the "Old Negro" as a work of "historical fiction" created by white America and Black Americans forced into a "protective social mimicry."[37] The New

Negro was defined as active and thinking, engaging with social problems and creating artwork of advocacy.

Langston Hughes may be the most well-known voice of the Harlem Renaissance. Unlike Randolph and other authors, Hughes advocated for the lowest income group of Black Americans. He mixed high and low literature through references to folk art and oral tradition, influencing Black American culture. Hughes's narrative structure was often emotional and descriptive, rebelling from white forms of art and advocacy. Unlike some authors of the Harlem Renaissance, Hughes saw a deep connection to the land of Africa, often writing about Africa in a romantic fashion. One example is this passage from his poem "The Negro Speaks of Rivers":

> I bathed in the Euphrates when dawns were young.
> I built my hut near the Congo and it lulled me to sleep.
> I heard the singing of the Mississippi when Abe Lincoln
>   Went down to New Orleans, and I've seen its muddy
>   Bosom turn all golden in the sunset.[38]

Hughes's poem compared the blood that runs through him with rivers in America and Africa, borrowing from ideas of African "roots" and discussing a personal experience in a land he had not visited. This is contrary to the Reconstruction thinkers who viewed the Black American experience as limited to America; they embraced the trauma and cultural history of African Americans. Hughes's poetry mainstreamed the perspectives of African Americans and did not conform to the art of the time. It created foundations for pan-Africanism and reoriented the ontology of what it meant to be Black in America.

The Harlem Renaissance marked a turning point for Black Americans. It represented a shift in identity—sometimes borrowed, as in "The Negro Speaks of Rivers"—to Ethiopianism and a connection "back to Africa." Black Americans were represented as active agents capable of creating a new culture, which set the foundations for Negritude. At the same time, narratives that emphasized a connection to Africa began to deconstruct borders and inspire a reconnection with African forms of art and culture.

Negritude

A new framework for the African Diaspora, known as Negritude, arose in the 1930s and 1940s. The movement originated in France and francophone Africa, and was inspired by intellectuals such as Cesaire, Senghor, and

Damas. It moved from Europe and Africa to America, bringing a Marxist political philosophy and a strong sense of common cause amongst the diaspora. Although the movement advocated for Afrocentric ideas, it was inherently rooted in European critical discourse; it referenced Hegel's *Phenomenology of the Spirit* and European ideas of Marxism.[39] Negritude focused on roots, condemning colonial practices and drawing from Ethiopianism.

In 1953, *Libretto for the Republic of Liberia* was published by Melvin B. Tolson.[40] The book was an extension of a series of poems commissioned by William V. S. Tubman, former president of Liberia, that had been published in the 1940s. The book was an epic poem, organized in the European style of oralities through a past, present and future, and it synthesized Black culture through ideas of Africa, Europe, and America. The work narrated the history of Liberia, constructing a new memory of the nation meant to counter the standard Eurocentric version. The conclusion portrayed a Marxist-democratic version of the world centered in Africa and overcoming the barriers of race.

Negritude is reflected in Tolson's work through Afrofuturism, which combined Afrocentricity with optimism about the diaspora's future. It represented a negotiation of cultural categories entering into the politics of optimism.[41] This cyclical nature of history, where humanity begins in Africa and ultimately returns to its cultural roots, reflected the values of Ethiopianism. However, while Tolson's work initially embraced Ethiopianism, he began to move away from it as the conflict of the Second World War escalated.[42] In *Libretto*, Tolson's Afrofuturism also differed from Ethiopianism by framing optimism not from a biblical perspective but on the historical precedent of Liberia's success.[43] Tolson used African proverbs and ruminated on great moments in African history, marking a turning point in African American literature that moved away from Afro-pessimism.

In contrast to Tolson's Afrofuturism, the Black American author Richard Wright joined the realist literary tradition during the period of Negritude. Wright's literature was influenced by the Great Depression and the unfulfilled promises of the Harlem Renaissance. He produced several narrative works that were also autobiographical, including *Black Boy*[44] and *Black Power*.[45] The former described Wright's upbringing in the American south and his eventual involvement in the Communist party. The latter was a narrative that described Wright's trip to Africa, detailing his struggles with his own identity and his attempts to place the African American in relation to the continent.

Black Boy explored themes related to Du Bois's double-consciousness, following Wright's struggles to place his identity within the white gaze of Mississippi. Wright's struggle to place his identity in relation to Africa was most fully explored in *Black Power*. He insisted that "there was some sort of connection between the native African and the American Negro,"[46] but never managed to articulate that link. His expectations of connection were met with disillusionment—he reacted with disgust after witnessing beggars, nudity, and local tribal rituals. He again felt a double-consciousness or a duality of identity. However, his book articulated what Appiah has called a "rhetoric of distance" from what Negritude would consider his African roots.[47] *Black Power* described a new kind of pan-Africanism, contrasting with the rivers of Africa that Langston Hughes described flowing through his blood. In Wright's perspective, there is no biological similarity among members of the pan-African community; the similarity is political and oppressive.

Lorraine Hansberry's *Raisin in the Sun* was another narrative work influenced by the Negritude movement.[48] First released in 1959, it took the form of a Broadway play that followed Black families' experiences in south Chicago. The story explored themes revolving around the embrace and rejection of African heritage in an African American family, drawing on themes of Ethiopianism through its main character, who traveled back to Nigeria to become a doctor. Hansberry's work reinterpreted Negritude, displacing the movement's binary logic and reconstituting the African American identity within the realities of the time.[49]

Frantz Fanon's *Black Skin, White Masks*[50] was the broadest critique of the Negritude movement. It combined genres, giving Fanon's personal experiences along with historical critique and psychological analysis. He expressed his concern over Antilleans, who frequently traveled to France, acquiring prestige by learning the ways of Europe. He discussed colonization's psychological effects on people of color by using the ideas of Octave Mannon and Hegel's master-slave dialectic. Fanon's work echoed Du Bois's double-consciousness, describing racism as engendering a feeling of alienation from oneself, and his psychological analysis transcended Freud's ideas of childhood trauma to employ the idea of a traumatized society.

Fanon criticized the romanticized version of precolonial Black culture as able to confirm stereotypes.[51] Fanon analyzed three autobiographies as critiques of Negritude, justifying his traumatized society hypothesis. In *I Am a Martinican Woman*, by Mayotte Capecia,[52] Fanon found that the author was desperate for white approval. Fanon supported his argument by identifying "whiteness" entrenched in Capecia's standards for beauty and her desire to marry a white man. A similar critique was performed on Abdoulaye Sadji's *Nini*,[53] in which a biracial Senegalese woman also expressed a desire to marry a white man. Fanon also analyzed Rene Maran's *A Man Like Any Other*,[54] finding that the author struggled as a Black Antillean living in

Bordeaux—Maran's protagonist is ultimately accepted by the white community after being forced to renounce his Blackness. Fanon uses these three autobiographies to apply psychological analysis and identify how they have internalized inferiority complexes and acceptance of Eurocentric philosophy.

Writings on Negritude, such as Tolson's, encouraged a new level of optimism for Africa and Afrocentrism; the movement brought pan-Africanism to the forefront through a variety of perspectives. For some, Negritude represented a romanticized return to African culture that was similar to Hughes. For others, such as Locke and Randolph, Negritude was a political movement that united Blacks around the world in solidarity against oppression. While Wright's work was much more political, both his and Hansberry's narratives show the contradictions in African American identities. Fanon's analysis of Black autobiographies and historical critiques marked a shift to postcolonialism and complexity in representations of Africa amongst the African Diaspora.

Civil Rights Period

Negritude began to achieve its political potential through the civil rights movement. While this was a period of turbulent protests and historic advances in America, nations began gaining independence in Africa. The entire pan-African community joined together in a global fight for liberation from colonialism, bringing the relationship between Black Americans and Africa back to the forefront of the movement.

The narrative works of James Baldwin, published from the 1940s through the 1980s, showed the evolving imaginations of Black Americans and Africa. Baldwin was a prominent Negritude writer who put the Black American identity "in old roots, the singular ancient root: the geographic and spiritual wellspring of Africa."[55] John Drabinski organized Baldwin's works into three portrayals of Africans that express the complexity of identity. The first is the "virtual African," which Drabinski argued is "constituted in the imaginary," giving the example of Haile Selassie as a powerful leader of Ethiopia. This provided an optimistic representation of power, disrupting the narrative of marginalization present in the civil rights movement. The second portrayal was the "para-African." This was a projection of African roots set upon African Americans; the Black American is at "most a screen on which . . . the para-African can be projected."[56] Baldwin's final representation was the "Actual African," a recognition of the differences between the Black American and the African. This is exhibited by the following excerpt from *The Price of a Ticket*:

> An American Negro, however deep his sympathies,
> or however bright his rage, ceases to be simply a black man
> when he faces a black man from Africa. [57]

Throughout his writing, Baldwin describes many versions of Africa. His earlier works exhibited the optimism of Negritude, and later texts expressed a realism that rejects an inherent affinity amongst the Black community. Baldwin did not advocate for Ethiopianism or any return to Africa. Unlike Fanon's work, Baldwin's writing focused on inspiration instead of critique. For example, *Closets of American Power* explored African American Pentecostalism and viewed the church as simultaneously hypocritical and a source of inspiration and community.

Maya Angelou also wrote in the 1960s, and her work was often mixed with activism for civil rights. She wrote seven autobiographies, the most famous of which was *I Know Why the Caged Bird Sings* (1969).[58] The book explores Angelou's life experiences to show how a young Black American overcame racism and trauma to achieve success. Angelou wrote on issues of identity, inferiority, women's rights, and the key role of education. Her work was exceptional for being one of the first honest works of identity produced by an African American woman, leading her to achieve unprecedented fame for her race and gender. Hence, it is pertinent to note that the term "slave narrative" can be regarded as a "freedom narrative," which is under the umbrella term autobiographies too. For instance, individuals who had regained their freedom wrote stories and dedicated such accounts to slavery.

Furthermore, it is argued in this volume that there is a difference between narratives constructed by people who had been free in Africa and those born into slavery in the Americas and those who were eventually born free in Africa and searched for a new life in America, which will be viewed through a literary lens by selecting appropriate memoirs. Angelou's poem "Africa," published in *Oh Pray My Wings Are Gonna Fit Me Well*,[59] presented Africa through the metaphor of an African woman. It began with a description of Africa's landscape using feminine features. A scene of destruction followed, recounting colonialism, leading to a reemergence of the woman from her lowest point. The personification of Africa as a woman emphasized the African roots of the diaspora, reminiscent of Negritude. However, the poem's focus on trauma and struggle iterated the challenges for liberation that Angelou witnessed. Terminology such as "remember her pain" invoked ideas of trauma similar to those of Fanon, and the final phrase, "she is rising," expressed optimism for Africa's future. Angelou's poem romanticized

Africa and focused on struggle, taking a political focus while presenting a psychological victory over historical trauma.

Toni Morrison emerged as another female African American author at the turn of the decade. Her works *The Bluest Eye*[60] and *Sula*[61] involved themes similar to Angelou's work. However, Morrison encouraged thinking beyond binary constructs, reconceptualizing the racist ideologies of America and deconstructing standards of beauty and internalized inferiority caused by colonial ideology.

Another influential African American author whose works were woven throughout the 1970s and 1980s was Alice Walker. Walker's works reflect the struggles of Black Americans, women in a patriarchal society, and diaspora imaginations of Africa. Her most famous work, *The Color Purple*, follows the journey of a group of African American missionaries to Africa.[62] The book includes a series of letters that ultimately follow the journey of two sisters, Celie and Nettie. At home in Georgia, these two women face double exploitation as Black Americans and women. Nettie begins to read about Africa and is influenced by Ethiopianism and the missionary project to civilize Africa. Beginning with initial optimism, Nettie and her fellow missionaries descend into disillusionment as they struggle with the history of colonialism and fundamental epistemic differences between them and the subjects of their work. In the end, Nettie states, "My father, Samuel, was a missionary also, but by the time we returned to America he had since lost his faith; not in the spiritual teachings of Jesus, the prophet and human being, but in Christianity as the religion of conquest and domination."[63]

Similar to Nettie's conclusion Walker's books often struggle with decolonization and frame Christianity as a colonial project. In doing so, the idea of internalized coloniality is explored. An emphasis is put on the inherent differences between the African missionaries and Africans, where Blackness in itself was not a grounding commonality. This difference is complicated by the internalized coloniality the African Americans come to realize through their missionary efforts. The book challenges Ethiopianism's romantic portrayals of Africa or calls for African Americans to return. Through Nettie's story Walker "investigates political, racial, sexual, and spiritual colonization that occurred in both America and Africa in the first half of the twentieth century."[64] The story can also be interpreted as perpetuating African American exceptionalism, as an almost hierarchical difference is portrayed between the missionaries and the people of Africa.[65]

Gloria Naylor brought African American women's voices to the center stage again with her 1982 debut novel, *The Women of Brewster Place*.[66] The novel was eventually adopted into two miniseries in America as well as a musical based in Atlanta. It is organized through seven smaller stories, each centered on an individual character. All the stories involve the women living at Brewster Place, a housing development in an unknown city with many African American migrants from the American south. A key theme in the novel is the hope of migration for African Americans migrating to Northern cities after the civil rights movement for the hope of a better future. The stories reflect a sense of disappointment with these aspirations as the women face challenges from failed relationships and abandonment to discrimination. Many of the women's challenges emphasize their gender and sexuality, suggesting that while they have tried to escape the racism of the South, they cannot escape their identity as Black women.

Naylor portrays Brewster Place as a community held together by the relationships between women, reflecting a feminist philosophy.[67] The intersectionality of gender with class is explored as Brewster place was originally a low-cost housing development meant to serve the Irish community—eventually serving the Black poor. Naylor examines the geography of the urban poor through Brewster Place's proximity to richer neighborhoods as well as the physical and metaphorical location at a "dead end." This dead end is further supplemented by a "wall imposed on them by white city officials who want them separated from more 'respectable' folk."[68] Eventually Brewster Place residents are forcibly displaced, making them "as powerless as they were when they first came."[69] The book effectively demonstrates how the African American community is gendered and rejects "solutions" to equality as both theoretically and practically ineffective.[70]

The civil rights period saw a shift from Africa as the roots of African Americans to a distinct "otherness" but retained solidarity with the continent. The independence of new African nations created a new wave of Black power. The prominence of women's movements also allowed for the greater contribution of Black African American authors. The combination of these events produced the Afrocentric narrative literature of the twenty-first century.

The Twenty-First Century

The twenty-first century has brought on a wave of Afropolitanism embraced by the diaspora. Migratory patterns have added to the complexities of identity and politics—the greater opportunities for travel available to Africans and the diaspora have created an unprecedented clash of identity and space. Eddy Harris's *Native Stranger*[71] revisited the Black American in Africa. It created a situation similar to Wright's *Black Power*, where the author felt a contradictory disconnect from the continent as well as an uncanny sameness.

Harris's work experienced a duality in epistemology, describing personal connotations of Africa as an almost magical place that contradicts the poverty he witnessed. Harris and Wright both documented deep differences between themselves and Africans in terms of worldview and values. On his relation to Africa, Harris states:

> Because my skin is black you will say I traveled Africa [sic]
> to find the roots of my race. I did not—
> unless that race is the human race, for except in the color of my skin,
> I am not African.
> If I didn't know it then, I know it now.
> I am a product of the culture that raised me.[72]

Harris's book presented a distancing between his own identity and Africa, similar to critiques of Negritude. At the same time, he embraced the similarities of the pan-African movement. This perspective reflected what British theorist Gilroy articulated as the "black Atlantic," imagining the African Diaspora as having common roots in the transatlantic slave trade separate from nationalism.[73] Although the roots of slavery were common in past pan-African imaginations, the de-emphasis on national borders introduces complexity in migratory patterns and identity.

Perhaps the most influential African American narrative from the turn of the century is that of former president Barack Obama. In 1995, Obama published the book, *Dreams from My Father*,[74] which followed Obama's life from his birth in Honolulu, Hawaii. The book emphasized the role of Obama's father, who was born in Kenya and lived the majority of his life in the United States. Obama described the struggles of growing up as one of the only Black students in Jakarta and his involvement in the African American community. Before eventually going to Harvard, he decided to visit his relatives in Kenya—the experience caused him to reflect on pan-Africanism: "Whatever my father might say, I knew it was too late to ever truly claim Africa as my home. And if I had come to understand myself as a black American, and was understood as such, that understanding remained unanchored to place. What I needed was a community . . . A place where I could put down stakes and test my commitments."[75]

Obama's autobiography was significant because of its relation to identity. Obama struggled with his identity as either an American or African, congruent with the idea of double consciousness. As with other historical African American authors, Obama was unable to fully own his Kenyan identity because of his cultural upbringing. His perspective of race was often described as "post-racialism," an American concept seeking to move past ideas of race through reparations and focusing on similarities between groups.[76]

Obama's book showed how his relation to his Blackness and African heritage made him wary of ascribing to any single identity.[77] Obama is often described with an "Afropolitan personality" that embraces diversity and inclusion.[78] His African roots led to high expectations for US–Africa relations. At times, Obama did take significant action in Africa during his presidency, such as when he declared Darfur a humanitarian crisis. However, in a speech in Ghana, Obama stated that "Africa's future is up to Africans," an ontological orientation that may have led to "Africans' disappointment with Obama's Africa policy" in the long run.[79] Obama's representations of Africa were significant for mainstreaming postracialism. Intersectional movements of Black feminism have also influenced African narratives in the new century. African American feminist literature rejected the stereotypes created for Black women, such as the "mammy," "jezebel," and "matriarch."[80] In popular culture, African American feminist works have provided counter-narratives to these expectations, such as Beyoncé's album "Lemonade."[81]

Chimamanda Ngozi Adichie is an example of a modern narrative African feminist writer. Adichie is a Nigerian who has lived much of her life in America, breaking the boundaries between African and African American literature. Although her works are not autobigraphical, the narratives explore issues around identity and nationality. Her 2006 book, *Half of a Yellow Sun*, is a historical fiction set before the Nigerian Civil War; it involves themes of politics, identity, and Western influence in postcolonial Africa.[82] Adichie has also delivered a variety of infamous speeches, including "The Danger of a Single Story."[83] This modern narrative emphasizes the importance of storytelling, especially through literature, which provides a variety of perspectives about Africa. Adichie has also challenged the hegemonic colonial images of Africa, often portrayed through Eurocentric history and literature as a "dark continent." Unlike Negritude authors, Adichie does not advocate for romanticizing Africa. Instead, she works for an elevation of African voices able to speak their truth. Adichie asserts that while poverty is one side of Africa's story, it is not the only side. Her speech is an example of modern postcoloniality, which comes closer to realism than Afrofuturism, advocating for marginalized voices and Afrocentric storytelling above all else.

However, it is pertinent to state that the most recent theme developed within the selected African autobiographies or memoirs has been that of migritude. The term "migritude" was first used by Jacques Chevrier in 2003 but became solidified in 2010 through Shailja Patel's book,[84] which combined an innovative form of poetic personal narrative with political history.[85] The blending of genres mirrored Patel's blending of identities. Her book unveiled stories of migrant women crossing through Kenya, the United Kingdom, and the United States, focusing on the neocolonial context of migration in modern times and referencing politics in post-independence Kenya. Patel defined "migritude" as a movement of younger African authors, born after the independence movements of the 1960s, who have lived both inside and outside of Africa.

Negritude was typically used to describe a one-way transfer of Africans out of Africa. It provided romantic reimaginations, often by the diaspora, of what it meant to be African. Migritude differs through the complexities of the modern African Diaspora identity. This identity is complicated by the modern ease of travel that allows Africans to study or work abroad, while members of the African Diaspora can visit their African roots more easily.

Conflict in Africa and the Middle East has drastically increased the rate of migration in the past decade. While Negritude focuses on finding and maintaining roots, migritude looks at how these roots are disrupted by Africans entering new countries. A common theme in the literature of migritude is the phenomenology of borders. These borders are becoming cheaper and quicker to cross, but they are also secured and restricted by international politics to greater degrees. They are explored as both material and imagined through the literature of migritude.[86]

CULTURAL IDENTITY AND THE HOMELAND

It is evident that the purposively selected memoirs—Afolayan's *Fate of Our Mothers*, Cherno Njie's *Sweat Is Invisible in the Rain*, and *A Matter of Sharing* by Assensoh—critically examined in this volume reveal new perspectives on cultural identity in the postmodern world and globalized age. All the authors are seen to have a sort of preinstalled tendency to naturally categorize themselves into their environment and make them imbibe a sense of belonging to a culture. This belonging is justified with the shared set of companionship, principles, or beliefs of living that enable them to navigate their daily lives and resulting in making them have an unconscious judgment about different characters in their physical settings in the memoirs. Basically, it can be deduced or inferred from the memoirs that all the memoirists interact and make assumptions about different people and characters they come in contact with based on various boundaries of ethnicity, nationality, language, religion, gender, and other social identities.

Interestingly, these authors know that owning the culture means they embrace and understand the workings of all the traditions that have been passed down throughout the history of their natal locale, which they are first exposed to at an early age. As a result, the cultural identities of Njie, Babatunde, Afolayan, and Assensoh reveal that their history, heritage, and cultural education, as well as assisting them in recognizing and interacting favorably with individuals who share similar cultures or religious frameworks, coupled with those with different traditions and belief structures as well. In other words, it can be concluded that the concept of cultural identity has been redefined as the authors of the examined memoirs interact with both home and abroad, aided by African traditions and belief systems. This has helped to successfully project a sort of critical self-reflection and a well-developed identity, which is still an ongoing activity, as they participate in journeys that will help in the pursuit of humanity, which is not usually carried out in isolation or individualism but in communitarianism and fellowship. This subverted and redefined the idea of cultural identity invariably led to the several importance of the memoirists and the environment(s) they reside.

It is pertinent to note that the importance of cultural identities is reflected in the author's nationality, religion, education and even ethnicity, as these were critically analyzed in the chapters of the volume under different tenets and thematic preoccupations. One of the inferred benefits is that we learn to accept people, but we learn to dislike others too. Coupled with this, we consciously or unconsciously accept what we are taught without challenging the information, as it is more of a foundation or foreground on which every other boundary is established. As explored in the memoirs, the characters accept their parents' and grandparents' customs and traditions and cling to them as they grow into adulthood until they learn to redefine them and apply them in lands other than their own as they move on later in life.

However, it is obvious that the narrators of the analyzed memoirs explored their biases and approached each situation they encountered with nondeficit thinking. They understood that "people have their own customs, traditions, and values that are neither more valuable, nor less valuable, than our own."[87] Memoirists continue to do this because it gives them a sense of identity and helps them better understand others who share similar cultural traits with them, even in foreign lands. This does not only expand their relationships but also contributes to the further development of cultural activities that could have been overlooked if not for the sense of ownership they demonstrated and the understanding they have that humans "have multiple social identities that are complex, multidimensional, and in flux."[88]

Furthermore, Njie, Babatunde, Assensoh, and Afolayan understand that social identities are multifaceted, dynamic, and complex, as each person is unique and must act based on where they are. This was evidently showcased in their sojourns in the United States as they became aware of privilege and oppression in various patterns. Understanding that they are the marginalized helped them to quickly see the need to respond to their situations in a transcending and cosmopolitan way. They quickly learn to have a sense of cultural ownership and its direct effect on their cultural identity, which includes implementing the values of that particular culture. It defines how these characters can be identified as belonging to that culture or nationality. As a result, through tolerance, solidarity, and transculturalism, they persevered in the foreign land, which led to their character development as they chose several identities to integrate into their own personality.

Hence, the memoirists acknowledge the fact that mobility and flexible borders and boundaries have promoted cultural pluralism, contamination, hybridity, multiculturalism, and the like. The new global order makes it impracticable to lay claims to a single home or to tag one's home country "the only true home." As exemplified in this volume, the writers demonstrate this notion in their works by giving primacy to migration and cultural hybridity. They undermine restrictive factors like racism and tribalism in different spaces. They propagate a psychical sense of belongingness and dominance in diasporic spaces.

Njie, Afolayan, Babatunde, and Assensoh, as emblems of the new diaspora, demonstrate that home, in contemporary times, is contextual and emotional, not geographic. Incessant migration and cultural hybridity have created overlapping experiences that infringe on monolithic identity and mentality. In their works, they demonstrate that the order of things in recent times has changed. They maintain with certitude the fact that social issues and movements like racism, Afrocentrism, pan-Africanism, and other signifiers of difference and monoculturalism may have lost their credibility and relevance. The memoirs consciously and deliberately undermine markers of polarity.

CONCLUSION

In this brief history of African American autobiographies, which emphasizes African American literature, several key themes have been developed. Autobiographies allow for personal narratives to enter the discussion. Issues of the African Diaspora can be explored, not from the perspective of history, which has been standardized, but from the embodied experiences of autobiographers. These have often explored issues of identity, similar to Du Bois's double consciousness.

The literature examined in this chapter expresses a duality in identity. This duality evolved from a romanticization of Africa and a desire to return to roots, ultimately accommodating the complexities of Obama's postracialism and the new movement of migritude. Representations of Africa in antebellum America often exhibited Afro-pessimism, just as writing during the civil rights movement developed into hopeful representations of Afrofuturism. Modern writing has begun to explore Afropolitanism, where culture and borders are seen as symbolic, layered, and complex. Literature of the African Diaspora has maintained a sort of Eurocentric form, often drawing from Western literary traditions. However, it is also uniquely developed from the African Diaspora, starting from the traditions of Europe to produce something completely new.[89] Above all, these works have disrupted historical narratives and allowed the diaspora to reimagine Africa and its relation to the continent.

BRIDGING THE GAP: NEXUS BETWEEN SLAVE/FREEDOM NARRATIVES AND MODERN MEMOIRS

Freedom narratives relate to the larger field of memory studies, which tends to be divided into psychology and sociology. In cognitive psychology, memory is studied as an individual phenomenon taking place due to the activity in the brain. Through sociology, and some extensions of social psychology, memory is studied as a cultural and societal phenomenon—society constructs memories through a variety of social processes in which memory is constantly constructed, reconstructed, and renegotiated. One may distinguish between slave and freedom narratives as the period in which a character narrates his ordeals; in other words, the narrator's position determines what kind of narrative it is.

More importantly, the condition of the protagonist of a narrative is the determining factor of whether a narrative is a slave or freedom narrative. Slave narratives literature is founded by the oral testimonies of freed slaves. They are accounts of thousands of slaves who were freed from the clutches of their masters. They became fugitives and wrote personal memoirs of their encounter with slavery. Some of the popular memoirs of slave narratives are explicitly Olaudah Equiano's *The Interesting Narrative of the Life of*

Olaudah Equiano,[90] Frederick Douglass's *Narrative of the Life of Frederick Douglass*,[91] Harriet Jacobs's *Incidents in the Life of a Slave Girl*[92] and many others. The slave narratives of these former slaves reconstructed Africa in a way different from how it was known. The nature of these slave narratives was to pass on the terrible nature of slavery and how Africa was raided for the economic purpose of the Western world. The difference between the two is not enough to alienate one from the other. It is significant to lay from the beginning that without slavery, there would not be slavery narratives.

From inception, modern memoirs have generated a lot of reactions and criticism by scholars in different fields to accept it as a compelling genre in literature, politics, history and sociology. As noted, most of these critics regard the modern memoir as a subjective work of art with its own political machinations, which might not be considered to have wider significance because of the personal subject matter that arises in such work. The personal experiences of memoirists that are intended to address serious issues in society are not paid attention to, are considered sentimental, and have no major stronghold in wider settings.

However, the selected West African memoirs in this book are self- and community-reflexive coupled with the subversion of personalization of politics in memoirs, which are devoid of the common pitfalls of early memoirs. Even though the memoirists are influential personalities in their community and the continent, they still manage to make and link their subject matter and thematic preoccupations to contemporary issues, not only in Africa but in the other landscapes where they migrated. Babatunde, Afolayan, Njie, and Assensoh used their memoirs to serve as a meeting point for literary, political, and social criticisms, and this has propelled revisitation and regarding the memoir genre as a compelling one, especially in Africa and the United States of America. Despite these differences in complexities and dynamics, there are adequate and important connections between slave/freedom narratives and modern memoirs that will be discussed in this chapter.

Migration has metamorphosed from being a social phenomenon to being a culture in the contemporary world. It has played definitive roles in shaping people's cultural orientation, disposition to social issues, literature, and vocation, among other things. Contemporary African literature and slave narratives give primacy to the migration question because it is of great significance in the present-day world. Hence, journeying, migration, and their effects usually form the crux of the subject matter in many works of art by third-generation writers. Caren Kaplan points out that "changing locations and leaving home become central experiences for more and more people in modernity, the difference between the ways we travel, the reason for the movement, and the terms for our movement in this dynamic must be historically and politically accounted for."[93]

The transatlantic slave trade led to the movement of many Blacks from Africa and the Caribbean Islands to the Americas, or the New World. This trade began in the late fifteenth century and lasted until the beginning of the early 1860s. These Blacks were taken through a tortuous and horrific route known as the "Middle Passage," and many slaves died as a result of the abysmal conditions that they were forced to endure during the journey. The migratory pattern of these selected West African memoirists is a voluntary one they moved due to the conditions of their natal home. As a result, man has been known to display an engrained propensity toward living a nomadic lifestyle because of his desire for green pastures. However, migratory trends, patterns, and their effects differ through ages and traditions. Multiculturalism, transnationality, and other effects of human "dispersal" in the twenty-first century are germane to recent discussions in diverse kinds of diasporic literature today. J. K. S. Makokha makes this very clear when he avers, "The prominent writers at the turn of the century are evidently those who have given original and refreshing (re)presentations of the good, old and familiar narratives of relocation and recollection in contexts of the new forces and times of cultural mobility."[94]

The authors of the memoirs selected for this book grew up in Africa; they had to migrate for various reasons. In a new world, they reminisce about their homelands, which alludes to one of this book's central points: migration is one of the most prominent reasons that influence or even calls for the creation of a memoir. Babatunde reminisces on his experience as an immigrant, noting that:

> A major problem about migration, whether voluntary or involuntary, ancient or recent, is the tendency for the migrant to remain so fiercely loyal to memories of how things were when he or she left the native shores. Things as they were become frozen in the heart of the immigrant at the time of his exit. It is as if the native land must remain pristine and unchanged for it to deserve the unflinching loyalty of the traveler. Yet a cursory look at the society at the time of the migrants exiting would reveal that even then things were changing before their very eyes ... The immigrant who comes home at the end of the year misreads the conviviality and joyful expectancy and reciprocity in the community at Christmas and New Year celebrations as a sign that

all is well in the home front and that the ancestral lore, respect, and sanctions are still holding.[95]

This implies that migrants still carry nostalgia for home in their hearts, even after migrating to the new African Diaspora. Cherno Njie makes a similar observation in *Sweat Is Invisible in the Rain*:

> I moved to Texas from The Gambia, my native country, in the first years of the 1980s—in the beginning to Lubbock, to study at Texas Tech University, but I later transferred to the University of Texas in Austin not long after. I have since made Austin my home. I spend little time in Gambia from year to year—I have for the most part looked after my life and career here in the United States. Or, to what I have, so to speak, made of the American Dream.[96]

Although this is different from Babatunde's perspective on the dilemma of being an immigrant, Njie speaks of his new home and his native home.

Also, the United States has seen increasing amounts of violence committed against Black people, despite the fact that an African American held the office of president for eight years. This inhumane disposition to Blacks is greatly discussed in slave narratives consistently. However, the modern memoir showcases a different mode of violence in their texts. Assensoh and Njie aptly capture this subject matter as they narrate the political, social, and community violence perpetrated by rulers in their home country, which evidently led them to migrate to other lands and, at the same time, write against it as socially committed writers in their respective memoirs. Increasing demonstrations in support of white supremacy and ongoing brutality against Blacks have created growing unrest amidst a global pandemic. The suffering of Harriet Tubman, Olaudah Equiano, and Frederick Douglass is comparable to the violence committed against Cherno Njie and A. B. Assensoh. These Black Americans and West Africans suffered violence and death that were inflicted due to their skin color. Today's events show that the events described in slave narratives and modern memoirs were not exaggerations or filled with subjective discourses.

Slave narratives and modern memoirs have many uses and have served as historical references. They remind African Americans and Africans of how they have struggled while serving as a message of hope. Slave narratives have contributed to how the selected memoirists in this book give new ideas of what it was like to be unfree, exploited, and discriminated against. The best way to learn history is to study the memories of its participants. Slave narratives have gained a large amount of academic attention, and these works serve a different purpose in academia.

Researchers in this field should work to identify connections between the past and the present. They must advance the discourse by linking contemporary issues with the philosophical importance of these narratives. Current events in America and Africa are not new developments—if anything, they are repackaged conflicts from the past. Literary writers, important figures, and historians, which the memoirists in this book fit into, are custodians of knowledge, and they have analyzed slave narratives for comparisons with today's social order, making suggestions for reasonable legislation to curb the continued repression of African American and African rights and voices.

Just like slave narratives and freedom narratives, memoirs have been employed to highlight historical events at a personal level. A memoir is an important historical tool providing an opportunity to reconstruct the lives of people—they can reveal the implication of historical events and their sociological backgrounds. For Paula Fass, "Like all forms of writing, memoirs are deeply implicated in complex issues of representation; most writers reflect on, deal with, and overcome issues related to the authenticity of today's self."[97] Memoirs focus on a particular moment in time that stands out as an event worth sharing or a learning experience. Sometimes, they focus on a series of events with a specific purpose in mind. Memoirs are written with the intent to relate the life of the subject to selected events in history. They are historical sources, and writing memoirs may be considered as journaling the past.

It is pertinent to note that the connection between slave narratives and modern memoirs is not based on subject matter alone but also on techniques used by writers across genres. One of these is the use of songs and stories to embellish narrations and issues. The freedom narratives have a link with the vernacular tradition, which can also be found in some of the memoirs selected for analysis. The important context to note is the vernacular tradition, which is the foundation for this technique. It basically refers to the oral forms of African American literature. According to Gates and McKay, "The vernacular refers to the church songs, blues, ballads, sermons, stories, and, in our own era, hip-hop songs that are a part of the oral, not primarily the literate (or written down) tradition of black expression."[98] Therefore, the vernacular tradition includes the literary works of the Blacks, which were composed spontaneously and were transmitted primarily by word of mouth. The origins of the vernacular tradition can be traced to the Black slaves on the many plantations in the New World. Between the early eighteenth and nineteenth centuries, anonymous Black bards composed oral poetic forms as a channel through which they expressed their sorrow and asserted their humanity in a world where they were dehumanized.[99]

These poetic forms have been described as "slave songs"[100] and "sorrow songs."[101] However, the most popular name given to these songs is "negro spiritual." Regardless of their nomenclature, the fact remains that the slaves used these songs as a means of understanding and adapting to a strange, cruel new world. Du Bois describes the slave songs as "the most beautiful expression of human experience born this side of the seas."[102] This is also evident in the memoirs from the characters who are also elders in the stories. What is striking about the use of stories, songs, proverbs, and tongue twisters in these texts is that they are used for didactic purposes. They serve as lessons and templates for social and moral values for the authors, which they hold dearly and are transmitted to their children as well in the United States. They are considered sociocultural identifiers of the African moral value systems, which they intend to write about and other people, not just Africans, can adopt too.

Slave narratives and modern memoirs are connected to the African Diaspora and Black consciousness. Most African records from the period of slavery were not in a written form acknowledged by the Western world. Africans used orature for the communication and preservation of thoughts and history, which is evident in some of the African memoirs examined in this work, and it is important to state that the West African memoirs selected are written traditions. By understanding the concept of double consciousness and how it addresses issues in the memoirs selected. Du Bois's double consciousness gains greater nuance, even though it is sociological. Double consciousness means more than one consciousness, and Du Bois's concern is how to retain one's true self while maintaining the two consciousnesses of being Black and American. It is evident in the term "African American," acknowledging the African and the American; to be one and both at the same time.

Double consciousness affects everything African and American. Africans in the diaspora, while retaining their customs and traditions, must learn to present those customs and traditions in ways that will merge their old traditions and new ones. Africans are oral by custom, preferring orality as the mode and medium in which they store their knowledge. Frederick Douglass and others were from cultures that had been preserving their knowledge, history, and experiences in orality when they started recording their experiences in writing.

Some slave stories were narrated, and others were recorded in writing. Either consciously or subconsciously, the phenomenological world of the whites prevailed over African orality. The debate of writing versus orality is at the center of the Eurocentric–Afrocentric debate. Sticking to orality would have denied ex-slaves the ability to objectively store their encounters. Henry Louis Gates, an African American, believes that without writing, "there could be no ordered repetition or memory, there could be no history."[103] Euro-American scholars have argued about the superiority of the white race, and scholarly studies have disproved this notion. The movement of Hegel's absolute spirit has reached its full consciousness in America; the notion of superiority shows why those who suffer double consciousness are African Americans and not white Americans. Henry Louis Gates and Cornel West argue that:

> The specificity of black culture . . . lies in both the African and American character of black people's attempts to sustain their mental sanity and spiritual health, social life and political struggle in the midst of a slaveholding white supremacist civilization that viewed itself as the most enlightened, free, tolerant and democratic experiment in human history. . . . This unrelenting assault on black humanity produced the fundamental condition of black culture—that of black invisibility and namelessness. . . . Whites need not understand or live in the black world in order to thrive. But blacks must grapple with the painful "double consciousness" that may result [in Du Bois's words], "An almost morbid sense of personality and a moral hesitancy which is fatal to self-confidence."[104]

Both suggest that African Americans should not expect white Americans to understand or experience their history.

When Frederick Douglass said white people would have to go through what he had gone through to understand him, it would be contradictory to say that they do not need to understand. If participating in American values is what it means to be American or African American, then one expects white Americans to learn the history of African Americans—they are also Americans, and their history and contributions are a substantial part of the development of the United States. The proper American spirit calls for all cultures to be charitable to one another and not just for Black Americans to be charitable to the culture, customs, and values of others, which Babatunde, Njie, Assensoh, and Afolayan all did in their memoirs by allowing for the interrogation and acceptability of other cultures they encountered.

Gates and West observe that there is a racial gap between African Americans and white Americans, and they can be understood to mean that whites do not need to grapple with the difficulties of being Black in America before they show compassion. African Americans should not build their self-esteem or value on a need to be understood by whites. However, Gates and West are clear on the subject of orality: "The rich African traditions—including the kinetic orality, passionate physicality, improvisational intellectuality, and combative spirituality—would undergo creative transformation when brought into contact with European languages and rituals in the context of the New World."[105] From their perspective, the African orality that maintains African traditions, customs, and values must bow to the superior methods of the new world. When two worlds interact, one usually subsumes the other.

If one is to go by the analysis of Hegel and Du Bois to understand consciousness and double consciousness, then it is expected that the consciousness retaining one's African essence will be subsumed by the realities of the new world. In that case, African orality, which is part of African American ancestry, may suffer. However, writing does not guarantee objectivity. Instead, the constructive approach would fuse orality and writing together—orality is neither an improvised intellectuality nor is it inferior. Such a transformation, as revealed by analyzing the memoirs in this book, is how things were for Africans in Africa and the diaspora, as well as how things are in the new world. In the end, the double consciousness of Du Bois is not amiss. It is a delicate configuration of loyalties to ancestry, the African self, and the new American self. It is dialectic, but in this case, there must be a harmony of opposites. In many ways, the idea of double consciousness has helped African Americans to be the frontrunners of Afrocentricity and pan-Africanism that Babatunde, Njie, Afolayan, and Assensoh embrace.

These situations can be evaluated through the double consciousness of Du Bois. The authors are immigrants in new homes, but they cannot rid themselves of the affiliation with their native homes. Similar affiliations lead Africans in the diaspora to address causes in their native homes in varying forms and intensities. In the case of Njie, it was to end tyranny and dictatorship in The Gambia. He explains thus:

> In the last decade, however, I felt increasingly a tugging from somewhere over the Atlantic, in the direction of The Gambia. In 2011, Yayha Jammeh, a president who was becoming more and more a dictator, won a fourth term. I was at this point quite invested in his defeat; the outcome of the elections threw me into a cycle of detached apathy and despairing hopelessness. An acute sense of the uselessness of expanding my time and resources on legal actions to resist Jammeh

plagued me; from the United States, even with help of Gambians in diaspora and international advocacy groups, we accomplished very little. I was caught in a bind: I felt required to act concretely upon what I felt was a responsibility to the Gambia, upon a sense of civic duty as a successful Gambian of the diaspora.[106]

NOTES

CHAPTER 1: (SHIFTING) SPACES AND (FIXED) CROSSROADS:
THE AFRICAN DIASPORA AND THE IMAGINATIONS OF AFRICA

1. Black herein refers to all those with ancestral relations to Africa and is not limited to a particular sociocultural demographic in the United States of America.

2. While there have been specialized uses of terms like space as opposed to place. See, for instance, Michel de Certeau, *The Practice of Everyday Life*, trans. Steven Rendall (Berkeley: University of California Press, 1984)—this book uses both synonymously and as representations of the environment, especially given the confusion such distinctions are prone to create. Where usage calls for explanations, one will be given.

3. The notion of Africa as home here, in light of the arguments against this—Robert Elliot Fox, "Diasporacentricism and Black Aural Texts," in *The African Diaspora: African Origins and New World Identities*, eds. Isidore Okpewho, Boyles Davies, and Ali Mazrui (Bloomington: Indiana University Press, 1984), 367–89—proceeds from the act that for the first generation of enslaved Africans, home was present-day continental Africa.

4. Maureen Warner-Lewis, "The Oral Tradition in the African Diaspora," in *The Cambridge History of African and Caribbean Literature*, eds. Abiola Irele and Simon Gikandi (Cambridge: Cambridge University Press, 2004), 118–36.

5. Fox, "Diasporacentricism and Black Aural Texts."

6. William Shaw, *Migration in Africa: A Review of the Economic Literature on International Migration in 10 Countries* (Washington, DC: World Bank, 2007), http://documents1.worldbank.org/curated/en/248611468212384547/pdf/430960WP0Migra10Box327347B01PUBLIC1.pdf.

7. Thomas Faist, "Diaspora and Transnationalism: What Kind of Dance Partners?" in *Diaspora and Transnationalism: Concepts, Theories and Methods*, eds. Thomas Faist & Rainer Bauböck (Amsterdam: Amsterdam University Press, 2010), 9.

8. Maria Koinova, "Diasporas and International Politics: Utilising the Universalistic Creed of Liberalism for Particularistic and Nationalist Purposes," in *Diaspora and Transnationalism: Concepts, Theories and Methods*, eds. Thomas Faist & Rainer Bauböck (Amsterdam: Amsterdam University Press, 2010), 154, 159.

9. Emmanuel Babatunde, *Kelebogile—I Am Grateful: An African Journey Through Celibate Priesthood to Married Life* (Maitland: Xulon Press, 2018), 161.

10. Babatunde, *Kelebogile*, 163.

11. Pat Dudgeon and John Fielder, "Third Spaces Within Tertiary Places: Indigenous Australian Studies," *Journal of Community and Applied Social Psychology* 16 (2009): 396–409.

12. de Certeau, *The Practice of Everyday Life*.

13. Ibid., 37.

14. Dudgeon and Fielder, "Third Spaces," 400.

15. David Marshall et al., eds., *Contemporary Publics: Shifting Boundaries in New Media, Technology and Culture* (London: Palgrave Macmillan, 2016).

16. Fetson Kalua, "Homi Bhabha's Third Space and African Identity," *Journal of African Cultural Studies* 21, no. 1 (2009): 23–32.

17. Homi Bhabha, *The Location of Culture*, 2nd ed. (London: Routledge, 2004), 1.

18. Bhabha, *The Location of Culture*, 2.

19. Kalua, "Homi Bhabha's Third Space."

20. Dudgeon and Fielder, "Third Spaces," 400.

21. Pierre Bourdieu, "Social Space and Symbolic Power," *Sociological Theory* 7, no. 1 (1989): 14–25.

22. Ecocritics in general, and environment-conscious scholars like Kate Rigby in particular, have continued to see space and environment from a more active place in relation to humans. For more on this relation, see Kate Rigby, "Ecocriticism," in *Introducing Criticism at the Twenty-First Century*, ed. Julian Wolfreys (Edinburgh: Edinburgh University Press, 2002), 151–78. Other important works are Laurence Buell, "On Ecocriticism: A Letter," *PMLA* 114 (1999): 1090–92; Serpil Oppermann, "Theorizing Ecocriticism: Toward a Postmodern Ecocritical Practice," *Interdisciplinary Studies in Literature and Environment* 13, no. 2 (2006): 103–28; Laurence Buell, *Writing for an Endangered World: Literature, Culture and Environment in the US and Beyond* (Cambridge: Harvard University Press, 2002); Cheryll Glotfelty, *The Ecocriticism Reader: Landmarks in Literary Ecology* (Georgia: University of Georgia Press, 1996).

23. Irene P. Fernandez, "Representing Third Spaces, Fluid Identities and Contested Spaces in Contemporary British Literature," *ATLANTIS: Journal of the Spanish Association of Anglo-American Studies* 31, no. 2 (2009): 143–60; Joshua Parker, "Conceptions of Place, Space and Narrative: Past, Present and Future," *Amsterdam International Electronic Journal for Cultural Narratology* (2016): 74–101; Isabel Hoving, "Imagined Space/Lived Space, Alienation/Destruction, Singularity/Specificity," in *The Ideologies of Lived Space in Literary Texts, Ancient and Modern*, eds. Jacqueline Klooster and Jo Heirman (Cambridge: Academic Press, 2013), 111–24.

24. Edward Relph, "Place and Placelessness," in *Key Texts in Human Geography*, eds. Phil Hubbard, Rob Kitchin, and Gill Valentine (London: Sage Publications, 2008), 43–52.

25. Relph, "Place and Placelessness," 38.

26. Henri Lefebvre, *The Production of Space*, trans. Nicholson-Smith (Oxford: Basil Blackwell, 1991), 14.

27. Paul L. Knox and Sallie A. Marston, *Human Geography: Places and Regions in Global Context*, 7th ed. (London: Pearson, 2015).

28. Tim Cresswell, *Place: A Short Introduction* (Oxford: Oxford University Press, 2004).

29. Hoving, "Imagined Space/Lived Space," 112.

30. Cresswell, *Place*; Lefebvre, *Production of Space*.

31. Homi Bhabha, "The Third Space," in *Identity: Community, Culture, Difference*, ed. Jonathan Rutherford (London: Lawrence and Wishart, 1990), 207–21.

32. Claudia V. Camp, "Storied Space, or Ben Sira Tells a Temple," in *Imagine Biblical Worlds: Studies in Spatial, Social and Historical Constructs in Honor of James W. Flanagan*, eds. David Gunn and Paula McNutt (New York: Sheffield Academic Press, 2002), 65.

33. Marie-Laurence Flahaux and Hein De Haas, "African Migration: Trends, Patterns, Drivers," *Comparative Migration Studies* 4, no. 1 (2016): 1–25.

34. Omolola A. Ladele and Adesumbo E. Omotayo, "Migration and Identities in Chika Unigwe's Novel," *Studies in Literature and Language* 14, no. 3 (2017): 52–57.

35. Flahaux and De Haas, "African Migration."

36. Olivia Giovetti, "The World's 10 Poorest Countries," *Concern Worldwide USA*, July 17, 2019, https://www.corncernusa.org/story/worlds-poorest-countries/.

37. Yomi Kazeem, "Africa's Largest Economies Are Still Struggling to Kick Out Corruption," *Yahoo! Finance*, January 27, 2020, https://finance.yahoo.com/news/africa-largest-economies-still-struggling-180030352.html.

38. Flahaux and De Haas, "African Migration."

39. Ibid.

40. *Africa.com*, "The African Diaspora: Beyond Remittance," *Africa.com*, January 2020, https://Africa.com/the-African-diaspora-beyond-remittance/.

41. Meghan McCormick, "The African Diaspora Network Gives Africans Living Abroad a Pathway to Invest at Home," *Forbes*, March 16, 2020, https://www.forbes.com/sites/meghanmccormick/2020/03/16/the-african-diaspora-network-gives-africans-living-abroad-a-pathway-to-invest-at-home/#2f384610b6f8.

42. David Ralph and Lynn A. Staeheli, "Home and Migration: Mobilities, Belongings, and Identities," *Geography* Compass 5, no. 7 (2011): 518.

43. Ralph and Staeheli, "Home and Migration," 517–18.

44. August Meier, *Negro Thought in America, 1890–1915: Racial Ideologies in the Age of Booker T. Washington* (Ann Arbor: University of Michigan, 1963).

45. Adolph Reed Jr., "DuBois's 'Double Consciousness': Race and Gender in Progressive Era American Thought," *Studies in American Political Development* 6 (1992): 93–139.

46. Reed Jr., "DuBois's 'Double Consciousness,'" 95.

47. Robert Blauner, *Racial Oppression in America* (New York: Harper and Row, 1972).

48. David W. Blight, "Up From 'Twoness': Frederick Douglass and the Meaning of W. E. B. Du Bois's Concept of Double Consciousness," *Canadian Review of American Studies* 21, no. 3 (1990): 301–20.

49. Ralph and Staeheli, "Home and Migration."

50. Ladele and Omotayo, "Migration and Identities."

51. Ralph and Staeheli, "Home and Migration," 219.

52. Ibid.

53. David Morley, *Home Territories: Media, Mobility and Identity* (London: Routledge, 2000).

54. Magdalena Nowicka, "Mobile Locations: Construction of Home in a Group of Mobile Transnational Professionals," *Global Networks* 7, no. 1 (2007): 69–86.

55. Ralph and Staeheli, "Home and Migration."

56. Ibid., 250.

57. See Kalua, "Homi Bhabha's Third Space," on how the African identity is often erroneously essentialized as static to advance an afro-centric argument.

58. Ralph and Staeheli, "Home and Migration."

59. Ibid.

60. Ibid, 520.

61. Kalua, "Homi Bhabha's Third Space," 23.

62. Ralph and Staeheli, "Home and Migration," 520.

CHAPTER 2: CULTURE AND CULTURAL POLITICS IN CHERNO NJIE'S *SWEAT IS INVISIBLE IN THE RAIN*

1. Francoise Lionett, "Geographies of Pain, Captive Bodies and Violent Acts in the Fictions of Gayl Jones, Bessie Head and Myriam Warmer Vieyra," in *The Politics of (M)Othering: Womanhood, Identity and Resistance in African Literature*, ed. Obioma Nnaemeka (New York: Routledge, 1997), 205.

2. Hammed Oluwadare Adejare, "Final Master's Portfolio" (master's thesis, Bowling Green State University, 2019), 16.

3. Edward Said, *Reflections on Exile and Other Essays* (Cambridge, MA: Harvard University Press, 2002), 173.

4. Salman Rushdie, *Imaginary Homelands: Essays and Criticism 1981–1991* (New York: Penguin, 1991), 10.

5. Paul Zeleza, *Africa and the Disruptions of the Twenty-first Century* (Dakar: CODESRIA, 2021).

6. James Olney, "Autobiography and the Cultural Moment: A Thematic, Historical, and Bibliographical Introduction," in *Autobiography: Essays Theoretical and Critical*, ed. James Olney (Princeton: Princeton University Press, 1980), 1–27.

7. Paul John Eakin, *Living Autobiography: How We Create Identity in Narrative* (Ithaca: Cornell University Press, 2008).

8. Caroline Bretell, *Blurred Genres and Blended Voices: History, Autobiography and Ethnography of Women's Lives* (Oxford: Berg, 1997), 228.

9. Remy Oriaku, "Speaking to the Dead about the Living: The Nigerian Newspaper Obituary Publication as Covert Auto/biography," *Ibadan Journal of English Studies* 5&6 (2009–2010): 146.

10. Stephanie Newell, *Histories of Dirt: Media and Urban Life in Colonial and Postcolonial Lagos* (Durham and London: Duke University Press, 2020).

11. Cherno Njie, *Sweat Is Invisible in the Rain* (Austin: Pan-African University Press, 2020).

12. Njie, *Sweat Is Invisible*, xi.
13. Ibid., xvi.
14. Will Kymlicka, "Multicultural Citizenship: A Liberal Theory of Minority Rights," *Oxford Political Series* (Oxford: Clarendon Press, 1995), 76.
15. Kymlicka, "Multicultural Citizenship," 76.
16. Ibid., 76.
17. Ibid., 76.
18. Ibid., 16.
19. Ibid., 4.
20. Ibid.
21. Ibid., 6.
22. Ibid.
23. Kymlicka, "Multicultural Citizenship," 173.
24. Ibid.
25. Njie, *Sweat Is Invisible*.
26. Ibid., 47.
27. David Ralph and Lynn Staeheli, "Home and Migration: Mobilities, Belongings and Identities," *Geography Compass* 5, no. 7 (2011): 524.
28. Njie, *Sweat Is Invisible*, 48.
29. Ibid., 52–53.
30. Khachig Tölölyan, "The Nation-State and Its Others: In Lieu of a Preface," *Diaspora: A Journal of Transnational Studies* 1 (1997): 2.
31. Njie, *Sweat Is Invisible*, 51.
32. Ibid., 52.
33. Taiye Selasi, "Bye Bye Babar." *Callaloo* 36, no. 3 (2005): 529.
34. Selasi, "Bye Bye Babar," 528.
35. Ibid., 54.
36. Sulayman S. Nyang, "Ten Years of Gambia's Independence: A Political Analysis," *Presence Africaine* 104, no. 4 (1977): 30.
37. Nyang, "Ten Years of Gambia's Independence," 30.
38. Ibid., 31.
39. Njie, *Sweat Is Invisible*, 67.
40. Arnold Hughes, "Democratisation' Under the Military in the Gambia: 1994–2000," *Journal of Commonwealth & Comparative Politics* 38, no. 3 (2000): 35.
41. Niklas Hultin, Baba Jallow, Benjamin N. Lawrance, Assan Sarr, "Autocracy, Migration, and the Gambia's 'Unprecedented' 2016 Election," *African Affairs* 116, no. 463 (2017): 321–40.
42. Sait Matty Jaw, "Restoring Democracy in the Gambia?: An Analysis of Diaspora Engagement in Gambian Politics" (master's thesis, University of Bergen, 2017).
43. Hultin et al., "Autocracy, Migration," 2.
44. Aboulaye Saine, "The Paradox of Third-Wave Democratization in Africa: The Gambia under AFPRC-APRC Rule, 1994–2008," *Africa Today* 56, no. 2 (2009): 107.
45. Ibid., 76.
46. Saine, "The Paradox."

47. Emma Farge, "Gambia President Declares Country an Islamic Republic," *Reuters*, December 12, 2015, http://www.reuters.com/article/us-gambia-politics-dUSKBN0TU2TA20151211.

48. Alieu Sanneh, "Culture, Religion, and Democracy in The Gambia: Perspectives from before and after the 2016 Gambian Presidential Election," *Juniata Voices* 17 (2017): 125.

49. Ibid., 125.

50. Njie, *Sweat Is Invisible*, 89.

51. Awodiran Okanlawon Agboola, *Ifa Ohun Ijinle Aye* (Ifa: A Philosophy of Life) (Lagos: Fagbenga Ventures Nigeria, 2012), 67.

52. Ibid., 90.

53. Ibid.

54. Heather Saul, "Gambian President Says Gay People Are 'Vermin' and Should be Tackled Like Malaria-Causing Mosquitoes," *Independent*, February 19, 2014, https://www.independent.co.uk/news/world/africa/gambian-president-says-gay-people-are-vermin-and-should-be-tackled-like-malaria-causing-mosquitoes-9139119.html.

55. SDGLN, "Gambia's President Says No Gays Allowed; If Caught, 'Will Regret Being Born,'" *SDGLN*, April 1, 2013, http://ilga.org/ilga/en/article/o1VLiAB1wR.

56. Amnesty International, *Dangerous to Dissent: Human Rights Under Threat in Gambia* (London: Peter Benson, 2016).

57. Aboubacar Senghore, "Press Freedom and Democratic Governance in the Gambia: A Rights-Based Approach," *African Human Rights Law Journal* 12, no. 2 (2012): 508.

58. Senghore, "Press Freedom," 524.

59. Njie, *Sweat Is Invisible*, xii.

60. Liisa Laakso and Petri Hautaniemi, "Introduction: Diasporas for Peace and Development," in *Diasporas, Development and Peacemaking in the Horn of Africa*, eds., Liisa Laakso and Petri Hautaniemi (London: Zed Books, 2014), 1–2.

61. Ibid., 81.

62. Ibid.

63. Ibid., 99.

CHAPTER 3: THE REPRESENTATION OF TRADITION AND MODERNITY IN EMMANUEL BABATUNDE'S *KELEBOGILE*

1. Mani Joshi, "Tradition and Modernization (Conflicts and Challenges)," *International Research Journal of Management Science & Technology* 6, no. 6 (2015): 81.

2. Nelson Graburn, "What Is Tradition?" *Museum Anthropology* 24, no. 2–3 (2000): 9.

3. Ole Madsen, "Modernity," in *Encyclopedia of Critical Psychology*, ed., Thomas Teo (New York: Springer, 2014), 1200.

4. Madsen, "Modernity," 1199.

5. S. N. Eisenstadt, "Modernity and Modernization," *Sociopedia.iso* 25, no. 1 (2010): 1–15.

6. Emmanuel A. Babatunde, *Kelebogile—I Am Grateful: An African Journey Through Celibate Priesthood to Married Life* (Maitland: Xulon Press, 2018), 291.

7. Babatunde, *Kelebogile—I Am Grateful*, 227.
8. Ibid., 255.
9. Ibid., 234.
10. Ibid., 230.
11. Ibid., 281.
12. Ibid., 190.
13. Ibid., 193.
14. Ibid., 203.
15. Ibid., 12.
16. Ibid., 14.
17. Ibid., 6.
18. Ibid., 15.
19. Ibid., 316.
20. Ibid., 298.
21. Ibid., 189.
22. Ibid., 282.
23. Ibid., 40.
24. Ibid., 143.
25. Ibid., 251.
26. Ibid., 257.
27. Ibid., 88.
28. Ibid., 146.
29. Ibid., 68.
30. Ibid., 76.

CHAPTER 4: DERIVING MEANING: NUANCES OF LANGUAGE, NODES OF ORALITY, AND SENSE OF COMMUNITARIANISM IN MICHAEL AFOLAYAN'S *FATE OF OUR MOTHERS*

1. A. Bamgbose, "English and Inequalities: An African Perspective," in *The Domestication of English in Nigeria*, edited by V. Awonusi, E. Basim, and K. Lajiman). Lagos: University of Lagos Press, 2004), 3.

2. Amuseghan Adejimola, "Language Policy Provisions and Curriculum Issues: The Challenges for Secondary Schools in Nigeria," *US-China Education Review* 7, no. 11 (2010): 54.

3. Ayo Bamgbose, "English and Inequality: An African Perspective," in *The Domestication of English in Nigeria: A Festschrift in Honour of Abiodun Adetugbo*, eds. S. Awonusi and E. A. Babalola (Lagos: University of Lagos Press, 2004), 3.

4. Alamin Mazrui, *English in Africa After the Cold War* (Sydney: Footprint Books, 2004), 40.

5. Michael Afolayan, *Fate of Our Mothers* (Austin: Pan African University Press, 2015), xi.

6. Afolayan, *Fate of Our Mothers*.

7. Ibid., 4.
8. Ibid., 189.
9. Ibid., 87.
10. Ibid., 246.
11. Ibid., 234.
12. Ibid., 16.
13. Ibid., 21.
14. Ibid., 206.
15. Ibid., 191.
16. Ibid., 348.
17. Ibid., 119.
18. Walter Ong, *Orality and Literacy, The Technologizing of the Word*, 2nd ed. (Abingdon: Routledge, 2002), 12.
19. Eileen Julien, "Reading 'Orality' in French-language Novels from Sub-Saharan Africa," in *Francophone Postcolonial Studies: A Critical Introduction*, eds., Charles Forsdick and David Murphy (London: Edward Arnold, 2003), 122.
20. Afolayan, *Fate of Our Mothers*, 10.
21. Afolayan, *Fate of Our Mothers*, 48.
22. Afolayan, *Fate of Our Mothers*, 44.
23. Afolayan, *Fate of Our Mothers*, 81.
24. Solomon Babalola, *The Content and Form of Yoruba Ijala* (Oxford: Clarendon Press, 1996), v.
25. William Bascom, "Folklore and Anthropology," *Journal of American Folklore* 66, no. 262 (1953): 283.
26. John Mbiti, *African Religion and Philosophy* (Nairobi: East African Educational Publishers, 1959), 108.
27. Ifeanyi Menkiti, "Community, Communism, Communitarianism: An African Intervention," in *The Palgrave Handbook of African Philosophy*, eds. Adesina Afolayan and Toyin Falola (New York: Macmillan, 2017), 461.
28. Dismas Masolo, "Western and African Communitarianism: A Comparison," in *A Companion to African Philosophy*, ed. K. Wiredu (Oxford: Blackwell), 483.
29. Afolayan, *Fate of Our Mothers*, 33–34.
30. Afolayan, *Fate of Our Mothers*, 33–34.
31. Afolayan, *Fate of Our Mothers*, 54.

CHAPTER 5: THE DENSITY OF CULTURES: A. B. ASSENSOH'S *JOURNEYS*

1. Ayo Kehinde, "Writing the Motherland from the Diaspora: Engaging Africa in Selected Prose Texts of Dambudzo Marechera and Buchi Emecheta," *AfroEuropa* 3, no. 1 (2009): 2.
2. Akwasi Assensoh, *Migrant Stories: A Memoir of Living and Survival in the West and Asia* (Austin: Pan-African University Press, 2018), 1.
3. Assensoh, *Migrant Stories*, 3.

4. Ibid., 1.
5. Ibid., 2.
6. Ibid.
7. Ibid.
8. Ibid., 8.
9. Ibid., 10.
10. Ibid.
11. Ibid., 11.
12. Ibid., 19.
13. Ibid., 25.
14. Ibid., 32.
15. Ibid.
16. Ibid., 40.
17. Ibid., 21–22.
18. Ibid.
19. Ibid., 62.
20. Ibid., 65.
21. Ibid., 66.
22. Ibid.
23. Ibid., 66.
24. Ibid., 120–21.
25. Ibid., 68.
26. Ibid., 70.
27. Ibid., 72.
28. Ibid., 76.
29. Ibid., 77.
30. Ibid.
31. Ibid., 80.
32. Ibid., 83.
33. David French, "Racism and the Indelible Impact of Personal Experience," *National Review*, June 29, 2016, https://web.archive.org/web/20210520014728/https://www.nationalreview.com/2016/06/race-america-personal-experience-changing-perceptions/.
34. French, "Racism and the Indelible Impact."
35. Ibid., 56.
36. Ibid.
37. Ibid.
38. Ibid.
39. Ibid., 59.
40. Ibid., 57.
41. Ibid., 60.
42. Ibid., 51.
43. Ibid.
44. Ibid.
45. Ibid., 52.

46. Ibid., 88.
47. Ibid.
48. Ibid., 89.
49. Ibid., 92.
50. Ibid., 94.
51. Ibid., 89.
52. Ibid., 91.
53. Ibid., 97.
54. Ibid., 96–97.
55. Ibid., 81.

CHAPTER 6: MIGRANT (UN)HOMELINESS: UNIVERSALISM AND GLOBAL IDENTITY IN THE MEMOIRS OF A. B. ASSENSOH AND CHERNO NJIE

1. Paul Tiyambe Zeleza, "The Troubled Encounter between Postcolonialism and African History," *Journal of the Canadian Historical Association* 17, no. 2 (2006): 111.

2. Tejumola Olaniyan and James H. Sweet, *The African Diaspora and the Disciplines* (Bloomington and Indianapolis: Indiana University Press, 2010), 52.

3. Taiye Selasi, "Bye Bye Babar," *Callaloo* 36, no. 3 (2005): 585.

4. Ngozi Cole, "The Afropolitan Youth? The Albatross around Africa's neck," *Open Space* 1, no. 1 (2014): 52.

5. Ugochukwu Nzewi, "On That Fateful Journey Somewhere: Afropessimism, Afropolitanism and Agency," *Open Space* 1, no. 1 (2014): 65.

6. Nzewi, "On That Fateful Journey Somewhere," 66.

7. Selasi, "Bye Bye Babar," 526.

8. Cherno M. Njie, *Sweat Is Invisible in the Rain* (Austin: Pan-African University Press, 2020).

9. Akwasi Assensoh, *Migrant Stories: A Memoir of Living and Survival in the West and Asia* (Austin: Pan African University Press, 2018), xvi.

10. Paul Shaw, *Migration Theory and Fact (Bibliography Series, No. 5)* (Philadelphia: Regional Science Research Institute, 1975); Pieter Kok, "The Definition of Migration and Its Application: Making Sense of Recent South African Census and Survey Data," *SA Journal of Demography* 7, no. 1 (1999).

11. Njie, *Sweat Is Invisible in the Rain*, xi.

12. Akwasi Assensoh, *A Matter of Sharing* (Austin: Pan African University Press, 2016), 17.

13. Assensoh, *A Matter of Sharing*, 18.

14. Marie-Laurence Flahaux and Hein De Haas, "African Migration: Trends, Patterns, Drives," *Comparative Migration Studies* 4, no. 1 (2016): 1.

15. Philip Kelly, "Migration, Transnationalism, and the Spaces of Class Identity," *Philippine Studies: Historical and Ethnographic Viewpoints* 60, no. 2 (2012): 153.

16. Kelly, "Migration, Transnationalism," 175.

17. Assensoh, *A Matter of Sharing*, xxi.

18. Sola Akinrinade and Aderemi Ajibewa, "Globalization, Migration and the New African Diasporas: Toward a Framework of Understanding," in *Nigeria's Struggle for Democracy and Good Governance*, edited by Adigun Agbaje, Larry Diamond, and Ebere Onwudiwe (Ibadan: Ibadan University Press, 2003), 431–40.

19. Njie, *Sweat Is Invisible in the Rain*, 47.

20. Ibid., 99.

21. Guido de Blasio and P. Sestico, "Universalism vs. Particularism: A Round Trip from Sociology to Economics," *Questioni di Economia e Finanza (Occasional Papers)* 212 (2014): 11.

22. Cheryl Sterling, "Race Matters: Cosmopolitanism, Afropolitanism and Pan-Africanism via Edward Wilmot Blyden," *Journal of Pan-African Studies* 8, no. 1 (2015): 129.

23. Amatoritsero Ede, "The Politics of Afropolitanism," *Journal of African Cultural Studies* 28, no. 1 (2016): 89.

24. Assensoh, *A Matter of Sharing*, xv.

25. Ibid., 138.

26. Selasi, "Bye Bye Babar," 528.

27. Ibid., 49.

28. Stephanie Santana, "Exorcizing the Future: Afropolitanism's Spectral Origins," *Journal of African Cultural Studies* 28, no. 1 (2016): 124.

29. Toyin Falola and Kwame Essien, *Pan-Africanism and the Politics of African Citizenship and Identity* (New York: Routledge, 2013), 1.

30. Santana, "Exorcizing the Future," 124.

31. Santana, "Exorcizing the Future," 124.

32. Gemma Solés, "Wainaina on Afropolitanism," UrbanAfrica.net, accessed April 4, 2014, https://www.urbanafrica.net/urban-voices/wainaina-afropolitanism/.

33. Ayo Kehinde, "Engaging the Necessity of Multiculturalism and Transculturalism for Africa and African Development," *Journal of Black Studies* 37 (2011): 293.

34. Ana Maria Sanchez-Arce, "Changing States: Exile and Syncretism in Bucchi Emecheta's *Kehinde*," *Exile and African Literature* 22 (2000): 80.

35. Njie, *Sweat Is Invisible in the Rain*, 52–53.

36. James Clifford, *Routes: Travel and Translations in the Late Twentieth Century* (Cambridge: Cambridge University Press, 1997).

37. Njie, *Sweat Is Invisible in the Rain*, 51.

38. Assensoh, *A Matter of Sharing*, 74.

39. Ibid., 77–78.

40. Ibid., 78.

41. Ibid., 93.

42. David Ralph and L. Staeheli, "Home and Migration: Mobilities, Belongings and Identities," *Geography Compass* 5, no. 7 (2011): 524.

43. Njie, *Sweat Is Invisible in the Rain*, 48.

44. Donald Cuccioletta, "Multiculturalism or Transculturalism: Towards a Cosmopolitan Citizenship," *London Journal of Canadian Studies* 17 (2001/2002): 8.

45. Cuccioletta, "Multiculturalism or Transculturalism," 2–4.

46. Assensoh, *A Matter of Sharing*, 3.

47. Assensoh, *Migrant Stories*, 13.

48. Ibid., 55.
49. Ibid., 56.
50. Ibid.
51. Ibid., 59.
52. Ibid., 60.
53. Ibid., 17.
54. Ibid., 16.
55. Assensoh, *Migrant Stories*, xvii.
56. Andrew Fiala, "On Thinking Globally and Acting Locally: Resurgent Nationalism and the Dialectic of Cosmopolitan Localism," *Dialogue and Universalism—The Journal of the International Society for Universal Dialogue* 29, no. 1 (2019): 41.
57. Nahal Toosi, "Laughter, Frowns and Shrugs: Trump Speaks to the U.N.," *Politico*, September 25, 2018, https://www.politico.com/story/2018/09/25/trump-united-nations-globalism-840045.
58. Kehinde, "Engaging the Necessity of Multiculturalism," 312.
59. Cuccioletta, "Multiculturalism or Transculturalism," 9.
60. Assensoh, *Migrant Stories*, 63.
61. Ibid., 69.

CHAPTER 7: CONTRASTING EXPERIENCES OF OLD AND NEW HOMES IN THE NEW AFRICAN DIASPORA MEMOIRS

1. John Mbiti, *African Religion and Philosophy* (Nairobi: East African Educational Publishers, 1969), 108.
2. Michael Afolayan, *Fate of Our Mothers: The Collected Memories of an African Village Boy* (Austin: Pan-African University Press, 2015), 31.
3. Afolayan, *Fate of Our Mothers*.
4. Omotade Adegbindin, "Ifa and the Consequences of Literacy: A Philosophical Analysis," *LUMINA* 21, no. 2 (2010): 13.
5. Afolayan, *Fate of Our Mothers*, 18.
6. Toyin Falola, *A Mouth Sweeter Than Salt: An African Memoir* (Ann Arbor: University of Michigan Press, 2004), 66.
7. Afolayan, *Fate of Our Mothers*, 33.
8. Ibid., 12.
9. Julius Nyerere, "Ujamma—The Basis of African Socialism," *Journal of Pan-African Studies* 1, no. 1 (1987): 4–11.
10. Cherno Njie, *Sweat Is Invisible in the Rain* (Austin: Pan-African University Press, 2020), 4.
11. Njie, *Sweat Is Invisible in the Rain*, 5.
12. Afolayan, *Fate of Our Mothers*, 33.
13. Afolayan, *Fate of Our Mothers*, 22–23.
14. Emmanuel Babatunde, *Kelebogile—I Am Grateful: An African Journey Through Celibate Priesthood to Married Life* (Maitland: Xulon Press, 2018), 78.

15. Babatunde, *Kelebogile*, 139.
16. Chinweizu Ibekwe, *Anatomy of Female Power: A Masculinist Dissection of Matriarchy* (Lagos: Pero Press, 1990), 9.
17. Ibid., 18–19.
18. Ibid., 19.
19. Ibid., 53.
20. Babatunde, *Kelebogile*, 13.
21. Ibid., 78.
22. Ibid.
23. Ibid., 42.
24. Afolayan, *Fate of Our Mothers*.
25. Ibid., 161.
26. Samuel Nyang, "Ten Years of Gambia's Independence: A Political Analysis," *Presence Africaine*, no. 104 (1977): 30.
27. Nyang, "Ten Years of Gambia's Independence," 36.
28. Arnod Hughes, "'Democratisation' Under the Military in The Gambia: 1994–2000," *Journal of Commonwealth & Comparative Politics* 38 (2000): 35.
29. Njie, *Sweat Is Invisible in the Rain*, 66.
30. Afolayan, *Fate of Our Mothers*, 315.
31. Njie, *Sweat Is Invisible in the Rain*, 236.
32. Mbiti, *African Religion and Philosophy*, 108.
33. Babatunde, *Kelebogile—I Am Grateful*, 137.
34. Njie, *Sweat Is Invisible in the Rain*.
35. Babatunde, *Kelebogile—I Am Grateful*, 84.
36. Njie, *Sweat Is Invisible in the Rain*.
37. Ibid.
38. Afolayan, *Fate of Our Mothers*.

CONCLUSION: FROM SLAVE NARRATIVES TO FREEDOM NARRATIVES: A GENEALOGY OF IMMIGRANT STORIES

1. Teresa Bridgeman, "Time and Space," in *The Cambridge Companion to Narrative (Cambridge Collections Online)*, ed., David Herma (Cambridge: Cambridge University Press, 2007), 52.
2. Geoffrey Cubitt, *History and Memory* (Manchester: Manchester University Press, 2007), quoted in Elena Anca Georgescu, "Sites of Personal and Cultural Memories in Doris Lessing's Writings of Africa," *Kultura (Skopje)* 3, no. 4 (2014): 164.
3. Paul Ricoeur, *Memory, History, Forgetting* (Chicago: University of Chicago Press, 2004), 164.
4. Richard Werbner, *Memory and the Postcolony: African Anthropology and the Critique of Power* (London: Zed Books, 1998).
5. Robert Zussman, "Narrative Freedom," *Sociological Forum* 27, no. 4 (2012): 808.

6. Olaudah Equiano, *The Interesting Narrative of the Life of Olaudah Equiano, or Gustavus Vassa, the African* (London: G. Vassa, 1789).

7. Olaudah Equiano, quoted in George E. Boulukos, "Olaudah Equiano and the Eighteenth-Century Debate on Africa," *Eighteenth-Century Studies* 40, no. 2 (2007): 243.

8. Boulukos, "Olaudah Equiano," 243.

9. Ibid., 247.

10. Ibid.

11. Ibid., 249.

12. Ibid.

13. Frederick Douglass and Harriet A. Jacobs, *Narrative of the Life of Frederick Douglass, an American Slave* (New York: Random House Digital, Inc., 2000).

14. Maurice Lee, "The Old and the New: Double Consciousness and the Literature of Slavery," *ESQ—Journal of the American Renaissance* 49, no. 1–3 (2003): 95–105.

15. Daniel Kilbride, "What Did Africa Mean to Frederick Douglass?" *Slavery & Abolition* 36, no. 1 (2015): 41.

16. Kilbride, "What Did Africa Mean to Frederick Douglass?"

17. Ibid., 45.

18. John Blassingame, *The Slave Community: Plantation Life in the Antebellum South* (New York: Oxford University Press, 1972).

19. Booker T. Washington, *Up from Slavery* (New York: Simon and Schuster, 2013).

20. Louis R. Harlan and John W. Blassingame, eds., *Booker T. Washington Papers, vol. 1: The Autobiographical Writings* (Chicago: University of Illinois Press, 1972), xv.

21. W. Manning Marable, "Booker T. Washington and African Nationalism," *Phylon (1960–)* 35, no. 4 (1974): 398.

22. Harlan and Blassingame, *Booker T. Washington*, xv.

23. Ibid.

24. Kevern J. Verney, *The Art of the Possible: Booker T. Washington and Black Leadership in the United States, 1881–1925* (New York and London: Routledge, 2013), quoted in Pero Gaglo Dagbovie, "Exploring a Century of Historical Scholarship on Booker T. Washington," *Journal of African American History* 92, no. 2 (2007): 239–64.

25. Dagbovie, "Exploring Historical Scholarship," 256.

26. W. E. B. Du Bois, "The Evolution of Negro Leadership," *Dial* 31 (1901): 53–55, quoted in Harlan and Blassingame, *Booker T. Washington*, xxxiii.

27. W. E. B. Du Bois, *The Souls of Black Folk: Essays and Sketches* (Chicago: A. C. McClurg, 1903).

28. David C. Jones, "Apart and a Part: Dissonance, Double Consciousness, and the Politics of Black Identity in African American Literature, 1946–1964" (PhD dissertation, University of Manchester, 2015).

29. Anne Rawls, "'Race' as an Interaction Order Phenomenon: W. E. B. Du Bois's 'Double Consciousness' Thesis Revisited," *Sociological Theory* 18, no. 2 (2000): 241–74.

30. Psalm 68:31, KJV.

31. John Gruesser, *Black on Black: Twentieth-Century African American Writing About Africa* (Lexington: University Press of Kentucky, 2015).

32. Phillip Randolph and Chandler Owen, "The New Negro—What Is He?" *The Messenger* 2 (1920): 73.

33. Claude McKay, *Banjo: A Story Without a Plot* (New York: Harcourt Brace Jovanovich, 1957).

34. Christopher Foster, "Black Migrant Literature, New African Diasporas, and the Phenomenology of Movement" (PhD dissertation, City University of New York, 2015), https://academicworks.cuny.edu/cgi/viewcontent.cgi?article=1942&context=gc_etds.

35. Foster, "Black Migrant Literature," 38.

36. Jacqueline Kaye, "Claude McKay's 'Banjo,'" *Présence Africaine*, no. 73 (1970): 165–69, www.jstor.org/stable/24348789.

37. Alain Locke, ed., "Harlem," *The Survey Graphic* 6 (1925): 629.

38. Langston Hughes and Amos Paul Kennedy, *The Negro Speaks of Rivers* (New York: Disney Jump at the Sun Books, 2009).

39. Sandra Adell, *Double-Consciousness/Double Bind: Theoretical Issues in Twentieth-Century Black Literature* (Chicago: University of Illinois Press, 1994).

40. Melvin Beaunorus Tolson, *Libretto for the Republic of Liberia* (New York: Twayne, 1953).

41. Timothy Dejong, "Affect and Diaspora: Unfashionable Hope in Melvin B. Tolson's Libretto for the Republic of Liberia," *Research in African Literatures* 45, no. 3 (2014): 110–29.

42. Gruesser, *Black on Black*.

43. Ibid.

44. Richard Wright, *Black Boy: A Record of Childhood and Youth* (New York: Random House, 2000).

45. Richard Wright, *Black Power: A Record of Reactions in a Land of Pathos* (New York: Perennial, 1954).

46. Richard Wright, *Black Power*, quoted in David C. Jones, "Apart and a Part," 111.

47. Henry Louis Gates and Anthony Appiah, *Richard Wright: Critical Perspectives Past and Present* (New York: Penguin, 1993), quoted in Jones, "Apart and a Part," 109.

48. Lorraine Hansberry, *Lorraine Hansberry's A Raisin in the Sun* (New York: Samuel French, 1984).

49. Jones, "Apart and a Part."

50. Frantz Fanon, *Black Skin, White Masks* (London: Paladin, 1970).

51. Fanon, *Black Skin*.

52. Mayotte Capecia, *I Am a Martinican Woman* (Paris: Correa, 1948).

53. Abdoulaye Sadji, *Nini* (Montreal: Editions Hurtubise HMH Ltee, 2003).

54. Rene Maran, *Un Homme Pareil Aux Autres (A Man Like Any Other)* (Paris: Albin Michel, 1947).

55. John E. E. Drabinski, "Baldwin's Three Africans," *New Centennial Review* 16, no. 2 (2016): 82.

56. Drabinski, "Baldwin's Three Africans," 91.

57. James Baldwin, *The Price of the Ticket: Collected Nonfiction* (New York: St. Martin's Press, 1985), 286.

58. Maya Angelou, *I Know Why the Caged Bird Sings* (New York: Bantam, 1997).

59. Maya Angelou, *Oh Pray My Wings Are Gonna Fit Me Well: Poems* (New York: Random House, 2013).

60. Toni Morrison, *The Bluest Eye/Toni Morrison, with a New Afterword by the Author*, 1st Plume ed. (New York: Plume Book, 1994).

61. Toni Morrison, *Sula* (Milan: Sperling & Kupfer, 2012).

62. Alice Walker, *The Color Purple*, 1st ed. (New York: Harcourt Brace Jovanovich, 1982).

63. Walker, *The Color Purple*, 146.

64. Gruesser, *Black on Black*, 151.

65. Ibid.

66. Gloria Naylor, *The Women of Brewster Place* (New York: Penguin, 2005).

67. Barbara Christian, "Gloria Naylor's Geography: Community, Class, and Patriarchy in *The Women of Brewster Place* and *Linden Hills*," in *New Black Feminist Criticism, 1985–2000*, eds., Gloria Bowles, Giulia Fabi, and Arlene Keizer (Chicago: University of Illinois Press, 2010), 99–119.

68. Christian, "Gloria Naylor's Geography," 102.

69. Ibid., 108.

70. Ibid.

71. Eddy L. Harris, *Native Stranger: A Black American's Journey into the Heart of Africa* (New York: Vintage, 1993).

72. Harris, *Native Stranger*, 13.

73. Paul Gilroy, *The Black Atlantic: Modernity and Double Consciousness* (London: Verso, 1993).

74. Barack Obama, *Dreams from my Father: A Story of Race and Inheritance* (Edinburgh: Canongate Books, 2007).

75. Obama, *Dreams from my Father*, 115.

76. Michael Janis, "Obama, Africa, and the Post-Racial," *CLCWeb—Comparative Literature and Culture* 11, no. 2 (2009), https://doi.org/10.7771/1481-374.1466.

77. Robert E. E. Washington, "Obama and Africa," *Research in Race and Ethnic Relations* 16, no. 16 (2010): 3–26.

78. Washington, "Obama and Africa."

79. S. Relative, "Obama Ghana Speech, Cape Coast Castle and Self Determination in Africa," *Associated Content*, July 1, 2009, http://www.associatedcontent.com/article/1933208/obama_ghana_speech_capecoast_castle.html, quoted in Washington, "Obama and Africa," 9.

80. Patricia Hill Collins, *Black Feminist Thought: Knowledge, Consciousness, and the Politics of Empowerment*, 2nd ed. (New York: Routledge, 2002).

81. Welang Nahum, "Triple Consciousness: The Reimagination of Black Female Identities in Contemporary American Culture," *Open Cultural Studies* 2, no. 1 (2018): 296–306.

82. Chimamanda Adichie, *Half of a Yellow Sun* (New York: Alfred Knopf Incorporated, 2006).

83. Chimamanda Adichie, "The Danger of a Single Story," TED video, 19:16, October 7, 2009, https://www.ted.com/talks/chimamanda_ngozi_adichie_the_danger_of_a_single_story?language=en.

84. Foster, "Black Migrant Literature."

85. Shailja Patel, *Migritude* (New York: Kaya Press, 2010).

86. Foster, "Black Migrant Literature."

87. Lacey Sloan, Mildred Joyner, Catherine Stakeman, and Cathryne Schmitz, *Critical Multiculturalism and Intersectionality in a Complex World* (2nd ed.) (New York: Oxford University Press, 2018), 26.

88. Sloan, et al., *Critical Multiculturalism*.

89. Adell, *Double-Consciousness/Double Bind*.

90. Olaudah Equiano, *The Interesting Narrative of the Life of Olaudah Equiano, or Gustavus Vassa, the African* (London: G. Vassa, 1789).

91. Frederick Douglass and Harriet A. Jacobs, *Narrative of the Life of Frederick Douglass, an American Slave* (New York: Random House Digital, Inc., 2000).

92. Harriet Jacobs, *Incidents in the Life of a Slave Girl* (Brooklyn: Sheba Blake Publishing, 1961).

93. Caren Kaplan, *Questions of Travel: Postmodern Discourses of Displacement* (Durham: Duke University Press, 1996), 102.

94. J. K. S. Makokha, "In the Spirit of Afropolitanism," in *Negotiating Afropolitanism Essays on Borders and Spaces in Contemporary African Literature and Folklore*, eds., Jennifer Wawrzinek and J. K. S. Makokha (Amsterdam: Rodopi, 2011), 20.

95. Emmanuel Babatunde, *Kelebogile—I am Grateful: An African Journey Through Celibate Priesthood to Married Life* (Maitland: Xulon Press, 2018), 111–12.

96. Cherno Njie, *Sweat Is Invisible in the Rain* (Austin: Pan-African University Press, 2020), xi.

97. Paula Fass, "The Memoir Problem," *Reviews in American History* 34, no. 1 (2006): 107.

98. Henry Gates Jr. et al., "The Vernacular Tradition—Part 1," *The Norton Anthology of African American Literature, Vo1. 1* (New York: W. W. Norton & Company, 2014), 3.

99. Wilfred Samuels, Tracie Guzzio, and Loretta Woodard, eds., *Encyclopedia of African-American Literature* (New York: Facts on File, 2007).

100. Lauri Ramey, *Slave Songs and the Birth of African American Poetry* (New York: Palgrave Macmillan, 2007).

101. Samuels, et al., *Encyclopedia of African-American Literature*.

102. W. E. B. Du Bois, *The Souls of Black Folk: Essays and Sketches* (Chicago: A. C. McClurg, 1903).

103. Henry Louis Gates, ed., *Bearing Witness: Selections from African-American Autobiography in the Twentieth Century* (New York: Pantheon Books, 1991), 7.

104. Henry Louis Gates and Cornel West, *The Future of the Race* (New York: Vintage Books, 1996), 79–86.

105. Gates and West, *The Future of the Race*, 81.

106. Ibid., xii.

BIBLIOGRAPHY

Adegbindin, Omotade. "Ifa and the Consequences of Literacy: A Philosophical Analysis." *LUMINA* 21, no. 2 (2010): 1–23.
Adejare, Hammed Oluwadare. "Final Master's Portfolio." Master's thesis, Bowling Green State University, 2019.
Adejimola, Amuseghan. "Language Policy Provisions and Curriculum Issues: The Challenges for Secondary Schools in Nigeria." *US-China Education Review* 7, no. 11 (2010): 53–61.
Adell, Sandra. *Double-Consciousness/Double Bindowo: Theoretical Issues in Twentieth-Century Black Literature*. Chicago: University of Illinois Press, 1994.
Adichie, Chimamanda Ngozi. "The Danger of a Single Story." TED video, 19:16, October 7, 2009. https://www.ted.com/talks/chimamanda_ngozi_adichie_the_danger_of_a_single_story?language=en.
Adichie, Chimamanda Ngozi. *Half of a Yellow Sun*. New York: Alfred A. Knopf, 2006.
Afolayan, Michael O. *Fate of Our Mothers*. Austin: Pan-African University Press, 2015.
Africa.com. "The African Diaspora: Beyond Remittance." *Africa.com*, December 10, 2019. https://www.africa.com/the-African-diaspora-beyond-remittance/.
Amnesty International. *Dangerous to Dissent: Human Rights under Threat in Gambia*. London: Peter Benson, 2016.
Angelou, Maya. *I Know Why the Caged Bird Sings*. New York: Bantam, 1997.
Angelou, Maya. *Oh Pray My Wings Are Gonna Fit Me Well: Poems*. New York: Random House, 2013.
Assensoh, A. B. *A Matter of Sharing: My Memoir*. Austin: Pan-African University Press, 2016.
Assensoh, A. B. *Migrant Stories: A Memoir of Living and Survival in the West and Asia*. Austin: Pan-African University Press, 2018.
Babalola, S. A. *The Content and Form of Yoruba Ijala*. Oxford: Clarendon Press, 1966.
Babatunde, Emmanuel. *Kelebogile—I Am Grateful: An African Journey through Celibate Priesthood to Married Life*. Maitland: Xulon Press, 2018.
Baldwin, James. *The Price of the Ticket: Collected Nonfiction*. New York: St. Martin's Press, 1985.
Bamgbose, Ayo. "English and Inequality: An African Perspective." In *The Domestication of English in Nigeria: A Festschrift in Honour of Abiodun Adetugbo*, edited by S. Awonusi and E. A. Babalola, 1–14. Lagos: University of Lagos Press, 2004.

Bascom, William. "Folklore and Anthropology." *Journal of American Folklore* 66, no. 262 (1953): 283-90.

Bhabha, Homi. *The Location of Culture*. 2nd ed. London: Routledge, 2004.

Bhabha, Homi. "The Third Space." In *Identity: Community, Culture, Difference*, edited by Jonathan Rutherford, 207-21. London: Lawrence and Wishart, 1990.

Blassingame, John W. *The Slave Community: Plantation Life in the Antebellum South*. New York: Oxford University Press, 1972.

Blauner, Robert. *Racial Oppression in America*. New York: Harper and Row, 1972.

Blight, David W. "Up From 'Twoness': Frederick Douglass and the Meaning of W. E. B. Du Bois's Concept of Double Consciousness." *Canadian Review of American Studies* 21, no. 3 (1990): 301-20.

Boulukos, George E. "Olaudah Equiano and the Eighteenth-Century Debate on Africa." *Eighteenth-Century Studies* 40, no. 2 (2007): 241-55.

Bourdieu, Pierre. "Social Space and Symbolic Power." *Sociological Theory* 7, no. 1 (1989): 14-25.

Bretell, Caroline. *Blurred Genres and Blended Voices: Life History, Biography, Autobiography and the Auto/Ethnography of Women's Lives*. Oxford: Berg, 1997.

Bridgeman, Teresa. "Time and Space." In *The Cambridge Companion to Narrative (Cambridge Collections Online)*, edited by David Herma, 52-65. Cambridge: Cambridge University Press, 2007.

Buell, Laurence. "On Ecocriticism: A Letter." *PMLA* 114 (1999): 1090-92.

Buell, Laurence. *Writing for an Endangered World: Literature, Culture and Environment in the US and Beyond*. Cambridge, MA: Harvard University Press, 2002.

Camp, Claudia V. "Storied Space, or Ben Sira Tells a Temple." In *Imagine Biblical Worlds: Studies in Spatial, Social and Historical Constructs in Honor of James W. Flanagan*, edited by David Gunn and Paula McNutt, 64-80. New York: Sheffield Academic Press, 2002.

Capecia, Mayotte. *I Am a Martinican Woman*. Paris: Correa, 1948.

Christian, Barbara. "Gloria Naylor's Geography: Community, Class, and Patriarchy in *The Women of Brewster Place* and *Linden Hills*." In *Reading Black, Reading Feminist: A Critical Anthology*, 99-119. Chicago: University of Illinois Press, 2010.

Christian, Barbara. *New Black Feminist Criticism, 1985-2000*. Chicago: University of Illinois Press, 2007.

Clifford, James. *Routes: Travel and Translations in the Late Twentieth Century*. Cambridge: Cambridge University Press, 1997.

Cole, Ngozi. "The Afropolitan Youth? The Albatross Around Africa's Neck." *Open Space* 1, no. 1 (2014): 51-52.

Collins, Patricia Hill. *Black Feminist Thought: Knowledge, Consciousness, and the Politics of Empowerment*. 2nd ed. New York: Routledge, 2002. https://search-proquest-com.libproxy.ucl.ac.uk/docview/38929750?accountid=14511.

Cresswell, Tim. *Place: A Short Introduction*. Oxford: Oxford University Press, 2004.

Cubitt, Geoffrey. *History and Memory*. Manchester: Manchester University Press, 2007.

Cuccioletta, Donald. "Multiculturalism or Transculturalism: Towards a Cosmopolitan Citizenship." *London Journal of Canadian Studies* 17 (2001/2002): 1-11.

Dagbovie, Pero Gaglo. "Exploring a Century of Historical Scholarship on Booker T. Washington." *Journal of African American History* 92, no. 2 (2007): 239–64.

de Blasio, Guio, and P. Sestico. "Universalism vs. Particularism: A Round Trip from Sociology to Economics." *Questioni di Economia e Finanza*, Occasional Papers 212 (2014).

de Certeau, Michel. *The Practice of Everyday Life*. Translated by Steven Rendall. Berkeley: University of California Press, 1984.

Dejong, Timothy. "Affect and Diaspora: Unfashionable Hope in Melvin B. Tolson's Libretto for the Republic of Liberia." *Research in African Literatures* 45, no. 3 (2014): 110–29.

Douglass, Frederick, and Harriet A. Jacobs. *Narrative of the Life of Frederick Douglass, an American Slave*. New York: Random House Digital, 2000.

Drabinski, John E. E. "Baldwin's Three Africans." *New Centennial Review* 16, no. 2 (2016): 81–96.

Du Bois, W. E. B. "The Evolution of Negro Leadership." *Dial* 31 (1901): 53–55.

Du Bois, W. E. B. *The Souls of Black Folk*. 1903. Reprint, London: Longmans, Green and Co. Ltd., 1965.

Dudgeon, Pat, and John Fielder. "Third Spaces Within Tertiary Places: Indigenous Australian Studies." *Journal of Community and Applied Social Psychology* 16 (2009): 396–409.

Eakin, John. *Living Autobiography: How We Create Identity in Narrative*. Ithaca: Cornell University Press, 2008.

Ede, Amatoritsero. "The Politics of Afropolitanism." *Journal of African Cultural Studies* 28, no. 1 (2016): 88–100.

Eisenstadt, S. N. "Modernity and Modernization." *Sociopedia.isa* 25, no. 1 (2010): 1–15.

Equiano, Olaudah. *The Interesting Narrative of the Life of Olaudah Equiano, or Gustavus Vassa, the African*. London: G. Vassa, 1789.

Faist, Thomas. Diaspora and Transnationalism: What Kind of Dance Partners?" *Diaspora and Transnationalism: Concepts, Theories and Methods*, edited by Thomas Faist & Rainer Bauböck, 9. Amsterdam: Amsterdam University Press, 2010.

Falola, Toyin. *A Mouth Sweeter Than Salt: An African Memoir*. Ann Arbor: University of Michigan Press, 2004.

Falola, Toyin and Kwame Essien. *Pan-Africanism and the Politics of African Citizenship and Identity*. New York: Routledge, 2013.

Fanon, Frantz. *Black Skin, White Masks*. London: Paladin, 1970.

Farge, Emma. "Gambia President Declares Country an Islamic Republic." *Reuters*, December 12, 2015. http://www.reuters.com/article/us-gambia-politics-dUSKBN0 TU2TA20151211.

Fass, Paula. "The Memoir Problem." *Reviews in American History* 34, no. 1 (2006): 107–23.

Fernandez, Irene P. "Representing Third Spaces, Fluid Identities and Contested Spaces in Contemporary British Literature." *ATLANTIS: Journal of the Spanish Association of Anglo-American Studies* 31, no. 2 (2009): 143–60.

Fiala, Andrew. "On Thinking Globally and Acting Locally: Resurgent Nationalism and the Dialectic of Cosmopolitan Localism." *Dialogue and Universalism—The Journal of the International Society for Universal Dialogue* 29, no. 1 (2019): 37–56.

Flahaux, Marie-Laurence, and Hein De Haas. "African Migration: Trends, Patterns, Drivers." *Comparative Migration Studies* 4, no. 1 (2016): 1–25.

Foster, Christopher, Robert F. Reid-Pharr, Meena Alexander, and Ashley Dawson. "Black Migrant Literature, New African Diasporas, and the Phenomenology of Movement." PhD dissertation, City University of New York, 2015. https://academicworks.cuny.edu/cgi/viewcontent.cgi?article=1942&context=gc_etds.

Fox, Robert Elliot. "Diasporacentricism and Black Aural Texts." *The African Diaspora: African Origins and New World Identities*, edited by Isidore Okpewho, Boyles Davies, and Ali Mazrui, 367–89. Bloomington: Indiana University Press, 1984.

French, David. "Racism and the Indelible Impact of Personal Experience." *National Review*, June 29, 2016. https://web.archive.org/web/20210520014728/https://www.nationalreview.com/2016/06/race-america-personal-experience-changing-perceptions/.

Gates, Appiah, Henry Louis Gates Jr., and Anthony Appiah. *Richard Wright: Critical Perspectives Past and Present*. New York: Penguin, 1993.

Gates, Henry Louis ed. *Bearing Witness: Selections from African-American Autobiography in the Twentieth Century*. New York: Pantheon Books, 1991.

Gates, Henry Louis Jr., Valerie Smith, William Andrews, Kimberly Benston, Brent Edwards, Frances Foster, Deborah McDowell, Hortense Spillers, Robert O'Meally, and Cheryl Wall. "Introduction: The Vernacular Tradition." *The Norton Anthology of African American Literature, Volume One*. New York: W. W. Norton, 2014.

Gates, Henry Louis, and Cornel West. *The Future of the Race*. New York: Vintage Books, 1996.

Georgescu, Elena Anca. "Sites of Personal and Cultural Memories in Doris Lessing's Writings of Africa." *Kultura (Skopje)* 3, no. 4 (2014): 163–72.

Gilroy, Paul. *The Black Atlantic: Modernity and Double Consciousness*. London: Verso, 1993.

Giovetti, Olivia. "The World's 10 Poorest Countries." *Concern Worldwide USA*, July 17, 2019. https://www.corncernusa.org/story/worlds-poorest-countries/.

Glotfelty, Cheryll. *The Ecocriticism Reader: Landmarks in Literary Ecology*. Georgia: University of Georgia Press, 1996.

Graburn, Nelson. "What Is Tradition?" *Museum Anthropology* 24, no. 2–3 (2000): 6–11.

Gruesser, John Cullen. *Black on Black: Twentieth-Century African American Writing about Africa*. Lexington: University Press of Kentucky, 2015.

Hansberry, Lorraine. *A Raisin in the Sun*. New York: Samuel French, 1984.

Harlan, Louis R., and John W. Blassingame, eds. Vol. 1 of *Booker T. Washington Papers: The Autobiographical Writings*. Chicago: University of Illinois Press, 1972.

Harris, Eddy L. *Native Stranger: A Black American's Journey into the Heart of Africa*. New York: Vintage, 1993.

Hoving, Isabel. "Imagined Space/Lived Space, Alienation/Destruction, Singularity/Specificity." In *The Ideologies of Lived Space in Literary Texts, Ancient and Modern*, edited by Jacqueline Klooster and Jo Heirman, 111–24. Cambridge: Academic Press, 2013.

Hughes, Arnold. "'Democratisation' under the Military in The Gambia: 1994–2000." *Journal of Commonwealth & Comparative Politics* 28, no. 3 (2000): 35–52.

Hughes, Langston, and Amos Paul Kennedy. *The Negro Speaks of Rivers*. 1921. Reprint, New York: Disney Jump at the Sun Books, 2009.

Hultin, Niklas, Baba Jallow, Benjamin N. Lawrance, and Assan Sarr. "Autocracy, Migration, and The Gambia's 'Unprecedented' 2016 Election." *African Affairs* 116, no. 463 (2017): 321–40.
Ibekwe, Chinweizu. *Anatomy of Female Power: A Masculinist Dissection of Matriarchy.* Lagos: Pero Press, 1990.
Jacobs, Harriet. *Incidents in the Life of a Slave Girl.* Brooklyn: Sheba Blake Publishing, 1961.
Janis, Michael. "Obama, Africa, and the Post-Racial." *CLCWeb—Comparative Literature and Culture* 11, no. 2 (2009). https://doi.org/10.7771/1481-374.1466.
Jaw, Sait Matty. "Restoring Democracy in the Gambia?: An Analysis of Diaspora Engagement in Gambian Politics." Master's thesis, University of Bergen, 2017.
Jones, David C. "Apart and a Part: Dissonance, Double Consciousness, and the Politics of Black Identity in African American Literature, 1946–1964." PhD dissertation, University of Manchester, 2015.
Joshi, Mani. "Tradition and Modernization (Conflicts and Challenges)." *International Research Journal of Management Science & Technology* 6, no. 6 (2015): 81–82.
Julien, Eileen. "Reading 'Orality' in French-language Novels from Sub-Saharan Africa." In *Francophone Postcolonial Studies: A Critical Introduction*, edited by Charles Forsdick and David Murphy, 122–32. London: Edward Arnold, 2003.
Kalua, Fetson. "Homi Bhabha's Third Space and African Identity." *Journal of African Cultural Studies* 21, no. 1 (2009): 23–32.
Kaplan, Caren. *Questions of Travel: Postmodern Discourses of Displacement.* Durham: Duke University Press, 1996.
Kaye, Jacqueline. "Claude McKay's 'Banjo.'" *Présence Africaine*, no. 73 (1970): 165–69.
Kazeem, Yomi. "Africa's Largest Economies Are Still Struggling to Kick Out Corruption." *Yahoo! Finance*, January 27, 2020. https://finance.yahoo.com/news/africa-largest-economies-still-struggling-180030352.html.
Kehinde, Ayo. "Engaging the Necessity of Multiculturalism and Transculturalism for Africa and African Development." *Journal of Black Studies* 37 (2011): 293–323.
Kehinde, Ayo. "Story-Telling in the Service of Society: Exploring the Utilitarian Values of Nigerian Folktales." *Lumina* 21, no. 2 (2010): 1–17.
Kelly, Philip. "Migration, Transnationalism, and the Spaces of Class Identity." *Philippine Studies: Historical and Ethnographic Viewpoints* 60, no. 2 (2012): 153–85.
Kilbride, Daniel. "What Did Africa Mean to Frederick Douglass?" *Slavery & Abolition* 36, no. 1 (2015): 40–62.
Knox, Paul L., and Sallie A. Marston. *Human Geography: Places and Regions in Global Context*, 7th ed. London: Pearson, 2015.
Koinova, Maria. "Diasporas and International Politics: Utilising the Universalistic Creed of Liberalism for Particularistic and Nationalist Purposes." *Diaspora and Transnationalism: Concepts, Theories and Methods*, edited by Thomas Faist & Rainer Bauböck, 154–59. Amsterdam: Amsterdam University Press, 2010.
Kok, Pieter. "The Definition of Migration and its Application: Making Sense of Recent South African Census and Survey Data." *SA Journal of Demography* 7, no. 1 (1999): 19–30.

Kymlicka, Will. "Multicultural Citizenship: A Liberal Theory of Minority Rights." *Oxford Political Series*. Oxford: Clarendon Press, 1995.

Laakso, Liisa, and Petri Hautaniemi. "Introduction: Diasporas for Peace and Development." In *Diasporas, Development and Peacemaking in the Horn of Africa*, edited by Liisa Laakso and Petri Hautaniemi, 1–10. London: Zed Books, 2014.

Ladele, Omolola A., and Adesumbo E. Omotayo. "Migration and Identities in Chika Unigwe's Novel." *Studies in Literature and Language* 14, no. 3 (2017): 52–57.

Lee, Maurice S. S. "The Old and the New: Double Consciousness and the Literature of Slavery." *ESQ—Journal of the American Renaissance* 49, no. 1–3 (2003): 95–105.

Lefebvre, Henri. *The Production of Space*. Translated by Nicholson-Smith. Oxford: Basil Blackwell, 1991.

Lionett, Francoise. "Geographies of Pain, Captive Bodies and Violent Acts in the Fictions of Gayl Jones, Bessie Head and Myriam Warmer Vieyra." In *The Politics of (M)Othering: Womanhood, Identity and Resistance in African Literature*, ed. Obioma Nnaemeka, 205–27. New York: Routledge, 1997.

Locke, Alain, ed. "Harlem." *The Survey Graphic* 6 (1925): 628–30.

Madsen, Ole. "Modernity." In *Encyclopedia of Critical Psychology*, edited by Thomas Teo, 1199–204. New York: Springer, 2014.

Marable, W. Manning. "Booker T. Washington and African Nationalism." *Phylon (1960-)* 35, no. 4 (1974): 398–406.

Maran, Rene. *Un Homme Pareil Aux Autres A Man Like Any Other*. Paris: Albin Michel, 1947.

Marshall, David, Glenn D'Cruz, Sharyn McDonald, and Katja Lee, eds. *Contemporary Publics: Shifting Boundaries in New Media, Technology and Culture*. London: Palgrave Macmillan, 2016.

Masolo, Dismas A. "Western and African Communitarianism: A Comparison." In *A Companion to African Philosophy*, edited by Kwasi Wiredu, 483–98. Oxford: Blackwell, 2004.

Mazrui, A. M. *English in Africa After the Cold War*. Sydney: Footprint Books, 2004.

Mbiti, J. S. *African Religion and Philosophy*. Nairobi: East African Educational Publishers, 1969.

McCormick, Meghan. "The African Diaspora Network Gives Africans Living Abroad a Pathway to Invest at Home." *Forbes*, March 16, 2020. https://www.forbes.com/sites/meghanmccormick/2020/03/16/the-african-diaspora-network-gives-africans-living-abroad-a-pathway-to-invest-at-home/#2f384610b6f8.

McKay, Claude. *Banjo: A Story Without a Plot*. 1929. Reprint, San Diego: Harcourt, 1957.

McKay, Nelly, and Henry Louis Gates. "From Phillis Wheatley to Toni Morrison: The Flowering of African American Literature." *Journal of Blacks in Higher Education* 14 (1996–1997): 95–100.

Meier, August. *Negro Thought in America, 1890–1915: Racial Ideologies in the Age of Booker T. Washington*. Ann Arbor: University of Michigan Press, 1963.

Menkiti, I. "Community, Communism, Communitarianism: An African Intervention." In *The Palgrave Handbook of African Philosophy*, edited by Adeshina Afolayan and Toyin Falola, 461–73. New York: Macmillan, 2017.

Morley, David. *Home Territories: Media, Mobility and Identity*. London: Routledge, 2000.
Morrison, Toni. *The Bluest Eye*. 1st Plume ed. New York: Plume Book, 1994.
Morrison, Toni. *Sula*. Milan: Sperling & Kupfer, 2012.
Mwaura, Job, Stephanie Newell, Patrick Olooko, John Uwa, Olutoyosi Tokun, Rebecca Onwonga, Ann Kirori, Claire Craig, "Dirty Methods as Ethical Methods? In the Field with 'The Cultural Politics of Dirt in Africa, 1880–Present." In *Routledge Handbook of Interdisciplinary Research Methods 1*, edited by Celia Lury, Rachel Fensham, Alexandra Heller-Nicholas, Sybille Lammes, Angela Last, Mike Michael, and Emma Uprichard, 248–65. New York: Taylor and Francis, 2018.
Nahum, Welang. "Triple Consciousness: The Reimagination of Black Female Identities in Contemporary American Culture." *Open Cultural Studies* 2, no. 1 (2018): 296–306.
Naylor, Gloria. *The Women of Brewster Place*. 1982. Reprint, New York: Penguin, 2005.
Newell, Stephanie. *Histories of Dirt: Media and Urban Life in Colonial and Postcolonial Lagos*. Durham and London: Duke University Press, 2020.
Njie, Cherno M. *Sweat Is Invisible in the Rain*. Austin: Pan-African University Press, 2020.
Nowicka, Magdalena. "Mobile Locations: Construction of Home in a Group of Mobile Transnational Professionals." *Global Networks* 7, no. 1 (2007): 69–86.
Nyang, Sulayman S. "Ten Years of Gambia's Independence: A Political Analysis." *Presence Africaine* 104, no. 4 (1977): 28–45.
Nyerere, Julius. "Ujamma—The Basis of African Socialism." *Journal of Pan African Studies* 1, no. 1 (1987): 4–11.
Nzewi, Ugochukwu-Smooth. "On That Fateful Journey Somewhere: Afropessimism, Afropolitanism and Agency." *Open Space* 1, no. 1 (2014): 95–105.
Obama, Barack. *Dreams from My Father: A Story of Race and Inheritance*. Edinburgh: Canongate Books, 2007.
Olaniyan, Tejumola, and James H. Sweet. *The African Diaspora and the Disciplines*. Bloomington and Indianapolis: Indiana University Press, 2010.
Olney, James. "Autobiography and the Cultural Moment: A Thematic, Historical, and Bibliographical Introduction." In *Autobiography: Essays Theoretical and Critical*, edited by James Olney, 1–27. Princeton: Princeton University Press, 1980.
Olney, James. *Autobiography: Essays Theoretical and Critical*. Princeton: Princeton University Press, 1980.
Ong, W. J. *Orality and Literacy, The Technologizing of the Word*. 2nd ed. Abingdon: Routledge, 2002.
Oppermann, Serpil. "Theorizing Ecocriticism: Toward a Postmodern Ecocritical Practice." *Interdisciplinary Studies in Literature and Environment* 13, no. 2 (2006): 103–28.
Oriaku, R. "Speaking to the Dead about the Living: The Nigerian Newspaper Obituary Publication as Covert Auto/biography." *Ibadan Journal of English Studies* 5&6 (2009–2010): 146.
Parker, Joshua. "Conceptions of Place, Space and Narrative: Past, Present and Future." *Amsterdam International Electronic Journal for Cultural Narratology*, no. 7/8 (2016): 74–101.
Patel, Shailja. *Migritude*. New York: Kaya Press, 2010.

Ralph, David, and Lynn A. Staeheli. "Home and Migration: Mobilities, Belongings and Identities." *Geography Compass* 5, no. 7 (2011): 517–30.

Ramey, Lauri. *Slave Songs and the Birth of African American Poetry*. New York: Palgrave Macmillan, 2007.

Randolph, A. Philip, and Chandler Owen. "The New Negro—What Is He?" *The Messenger*, 2 (1920): 73–74.

Rawls, A. W. "'Race' as an Interaction Order Phenomenon: W. E. B. Du Bois's 'Double Consciousness' Thesis Revisited." *Sociological Theory* 18, no. 2 (2000): 241–74.

Reed Jr., Adolph. "Du Bois's 'Double Consciousness': Race and Gender in Progressive Era American Thought." *Studies in American Political Development* 6 (1992): 93–139.

Relative, S. "Obama Ghana Speech, Cape Coast Castle and Self Determination in Africa." *Associated Content*, July 1, 2009. http://www.associatedcontent.com/article/1933208/obama_ghana_speech_capecoast_castle.html.

Relph, Edwards. "Place and Placelessness." In *Key Texts in Human Geography*, edited by Phil Hubbard, Rob Kitchin, and Gill Valentine, 43–52. London: Sage Publications, 2008.

Ricoeur, P. *Memory, History, Forgetting*. Chicago: University of Chicago Press, 2004.

Rigby, Kate. "Ecocriticism." In *Introducing Criticism at the Twenty-First Century*, edited by Julian Wolfreys, 151–78. Edinburgh: Edinburgh University Press, 2002.

Sadji, Abdoulaye. *Nini*. Montreal: Editions Hurtubise HMH Ltee, 2003.

Saine, Aboulaye. "The Paradox of Third-Wave Democratization in Africa: The Gambia under AFPRC-APRC Rule, 1994–2008." *Africa Today* 56, no. 2 (2009): 106–8.

Samuels, Wilfred, Tracie Guzzio, and Loretta Woodard, eds. *Encyclopedia of African-American Literature*. New York: Facts on File, Inc., 2007.

Sanchez-Arce, Ana Maria. "Changing States: Exile and Syncretism in Bucchi Emecheta's *Kehinde*." *Exile and African Literature* 22 (2000): 77–99.

Sanneh, Alieu. "Culture, Religion, and Democracy in The Gambia: Perspectives from before and after the 2016 Gambian Presidential Election." *Juniata Voices* 17 (2017): 124–36.

Santana, Stephanie Bosch. "Exorcizing the Future: Afropolitanism's Spectral Origins." *Journal of African Cultural Studies* 28, no. 1 (2016): 120–26.

Saul, Heather. "Gambian President Says Gay People Are 'Vermin' and Should Be Tackled Like Malaria-Causing Mosquitoes." *Independent*, February 19, 2014. https://www.independent.co.uk/news/world/africa/gambian-president-says-gay-people-are-vermin-and-should-be-tackled-like-malaria-causing-mosquitoes-9139119.html.

SDGLN. "Gambia's President Says No Gays Allowed; If Caught, 'Will Regret Being Born.'" *SDGLN*, April 1, 2013. http://ilga.org/ilga/en/article/01VLiAB1wR.

Selasi, Taiye. "Bye Babar." *Callaloo* 36, no. 3 (2005): 528–30.

Senghore, A. A. "Press Freedom and Democratic Governance in The Gambia: A Rights-Based Approach." *African Human Rights Law Journal* 12, no. 2 (2012): 508–38.

Shaw, R. Paul. *Migration Theory and Fact (Bibliography Series, No. 5)*. Philadelphia: Regional Science Research Institute, 1975.

Shaw, William. *Migration in Africa: A Review of the Economic Literature on International Migration in 10 Countries*. Washington, DC: World Bank, 2007. http://documents1

.worldbank.org/curated/en/248611468212384547/pdf/430960WP0Migra10Box327347
B01PUBLIC1.pdf.

Sloan, Lacey, Mildred Joyner, Catherine Stakeman, and Cathryne Schmitz, *Critical Multiculturalism and Intersectionality in a Complex World (2nd ed.)* New York: Oxford University Press, 2018.

Solés, Gemma. "Wainaina on Afropolitanism," *UrbanAfrica.net*. April 4, 2014, https://www.urbanafrica.net/urban-voices/wainaina-afropolitanism/.

Sterling, Cheryl. "Race Matters: Cosmopolitanism, Afropolitanism, and Pan-Africanism via Edward Wilmot Blyden." *Journal of Pan-African Studies* 8, no. 1 (2015): 119–48.

Tölölyan, Khachig. "The Nation-State and Its Others: In Lieu of a Preface." *Diaspora: A Journal of Transnational Studies* 1 (1997): 3–7.

Tolson, Melvin Beaunorus. *Libretto for the Republic of Liberia*. New York: Twayne, 1953.

Toosi, Nahal. "Laughter, Frowns and Shrugs: Trump Speaks to the U.N." *Politico*. September 25, 2018, https://www.politico.com/story/2018/09/25/trump-united-nations-globalism-840045.

Verney, Kevern J. *The Art of the Possible: Booker T. Washington and Black Leadership in the United States, 1881–1925*. New York and London: Routledge, 2013.

Walker, Alice. *The Color Purple*. 1st ed. New York: Harcourt Brace Jovanovich, 1982.

Warner-Lewis, Maureen. "The Oral Tradition in the African Diaspora." In *The Cambridge History of African and Caribbean Literature*, edited by Abiola Irele and Simon Gikandi, 118–36. Cambridge: Cambridge University Press, 2004.

Washington, Booker T. *Up from Slavery*. New York: Simon and Schuster, 2013.

Washington, Robert E. E. "Obama and Africa." *Research in Race and Ethnic Relations* 16, no. 16 (2010): 3–26.

Werbner, Richard P. *Memory and the Postcolony: African Anthropology and the Critique of Power*. London: Zed Books, 1998.

Wright, Richard. *Black Boy: A Record of Childhood and Youth*. 1945. Reprint, New York: Random House, 2000.

Wright, Richard. *Black Power: A Record of Reactions in a Land of Pathos*. New York: Perennial, 1954.

Zeleza, Paul Tiyambe. "The Troubled Encounter Between Postcolonialism and African History." *Journal of the Canadian Historical Association* 17, no. 2 (2006): 89–129.

Zussman, Robert. "Narrative Freedom." *Sociological Forum* 27, no. 4 (2012): 807–24.

INDEX

abiku, 65
abolition movement, 180
abolitionism, 181
abolitionist project, 182
Achebe, Chinua, 142, 144, 159–60
Adejimola, Amuseghan, 91
Afolayan, Michael, 34, 38, 91–92, 107, 161
Africa: idealization of, 25; migration in, 17; postcolonial, 36, 38, 134, 169, 173, 176; romanticization of, 197
African Americans, 28, 182, 186–93, 196, 200–204
African countries, exploitation of, 127
African culture, 69, 83, 101, 156, 184, 188; pillar of, 70
African English, 102
African family system, 103–4; oral tradition in, 104
African identity, 24, 27, 29, 37–38, 90, 129, 161
African indigenous education, 120
African languages, use of, 32
African missionaries, 190
African orality, 104, 203–4
African traditions, 83, 86, 90
African women, 166, 168–69, 176
Afrocentrism, 133
Afrofuturism, 186, 197
Afro-pessimism, 186, 197
Afropolitan model, 142
Afropolitanism, 134, 141
afterlife, 35

alienation, 49, 70, 87, 148–49, 187; pain of, 40; radical, 4
American Civil War, 182
Amnesty International, 54, 56, 138
Angelou, Maya, 39, 189–90
Assensoh, A. B., 37, 109, 134, 144, 200
assimilationist model, 46
Atinga cult, 71
Atlanta compromise, 182–83
Awolowo, Obafemi, 30
Azikiwe, Nnamdi, 30

Babalawo, 73–74
Babatunde, Emmanuel, 32, 63, 90, 166
Baldwin, James, 39, 135, 188–89
Bamgbose, Ayo, 93
Barrow, Adama, 58
Bascom, William, 104
belief system, 65, 73, 76, 136; traditional, 65; Yoruba, 71, 88
belongingness, politics of, 37
Benin artworks, 127
Benin Republic, 34
Bhabha, Homi, 37, 135
Black Americans, 51, 146, 181–85, 188, 190, 200, 203
"black Atlantic," 192
Black Diaspora, 4
Black identity, 19, 183
Black movements, 39
Black Nationalism, 133
Black Power, 186–87, 191

Black rights movement, 28
Black spaces, formation of, 4
Blackness, 182, 190; meaning of, 5
Blassingame, John W., 181
Blauner, Robert, 19
borderlessness, 135
Botswana, 172, 176
Boulukos, George E., 179
Brazil, 34
British Empire, 52
Busia, Kofi A., 111

Camp, Claudia V., 15
canto system, 55
Capecia, Mayotte, 187
capitalism, 64, 105
caste system, 45–46
Catholicism, 82, 86–87
celibacy, 84–85, 89–90
Césaire, Aimé, 39
chants, 97
China, 108–9, 116, 120–22, 131
christening, 72
Christian faith, 54, 179
Christianity, 30, 34, 77, 82–85, 180, 190; introduction of, 73, 83
circumcision, 76, 103; female, 117, 119
citizenship, global, 140
civil rights, 20, 39, 189; movement, 188, 191; violation of, 20
civil wars, 30, 158, 160, 169
civilizing mission, 5
cleanliness, 87
Cole, Ngozi, 134
collective responsibility, 82, 95, 166
collectivism, 14, 31, 35
colonial ideology, 180, 190
colonialism, 90–91, 116, 127, 158–59; demise of, 143; factors responsible for, 5; impact of, 30, 91
communal kinship, 84
communal responsibility, 35
communitarian values, 105
communitarianism, 91, 105–7, 160–61, 173, 176, 195; African, 161, 164, 176

concoctions, 65, 80
conflict: interracial, 152; political, 170
copyright law: in Africa, 131; infringements, 127; lack of, 127
corruption, 16–17, 21, 159–60, 169–73, 176
Corruption Perceptions Index (CPI), 17
cosmopolitanism, 38, 134–35, 141, 156
Cresswell, Tim, 14
Cuba, 34
Cubitt, Geoffrey, 178
Cuccioletta, Donald, 149
cultural adjustments, 28
cultural attitude, 53–54, 56
cultural awareness, 19
cultural beliefs, 62
cultural customs and rites, 35
cultural differences, 27–28, 126, 169, 174, 176
cultural entrepreneurship, 51, 143
cultural expressions, 51, 62, 143
cultural heritage, 25, 39, 46
cultural hostility, 149
cultural hybrid, 51, 142
cultural identity, 36, 54, 102, 157, 194–96; importance of, 195
cultural integration, 156
cultural membership, value of, 45
cultural nationalism, 21
cultural orientation, 156, 198
cultural ownership, 196
cultural pluralism, 19, 196
cultural politics, 29, 31, 42–43, 51–52, 54–55, 58, 60, 135
cultural politics and religion, 54
cultural relativism, 46
cultural schisms, 19
cultural shift, 175
cultural systems, 46
culture, 44; Black, 184, 186–87, 203; concept of, 42; interrelation of, 174
culture gap, 51
culture shock, 25, 38, 49, 60, 108, 131, 148, 160, 174

De Certeau, Michel, 10–11, 15, 207
Deoxyribonucleic Acid (DNA), 67

diaspora, 3, 23, 26–27, 50; ideas of, 26; significance of, 59
diasporic communities, formation of, 50
diasporic taxes, 9
diversity, idea of, 36
divination, system of, 55
divorce, 76–77
Doe, Samuel K., 111
double-consciousness, 186–87; theory of, 183
Douglass, Frederick, 38, 180, 198, 200, 202–3
Drabinski, John, 188
dress code, 48
Du Bois, W. E. B., 39, 147, 182, 197, 202–4

ebo (sacrifice), 80
Ede, Amatoritsero, 141
education system, indigenous, 117
educational values, traditional, 155
Egungun festival, 74, 83
Eisenstadt, S. N., 64
elders, 31, 77, 117–18, 155
Encyclopedia Africana, 147
English language, adoption of, 93
Equiano, Olaudah, 38, 179, 197–98, 200
essentialism, 14–15
Esu, 74
Ethiopianism movement, 183
ethnic groups, 45, 52, 58, 143
ethnocentrism, 46
Europe, 184, 197
European culture, 83
exclusivist sentiment, 16
"existential twoness," 19

facial marks, 84
Faist, Thomas, 8
Falola, Toyin, 143
family lineage, interconnectedness of, 48
family system, 37, 85, 93, 103, 165; extended, 118; Yoruba, 104
Fanon, Frantz, 187
feminism, 86, 167, 169, 193
feminist philosophy, 191; African, 167
festivals, 65, 74–75, 83, 101, 120
Fiala, Andrew, 153

fluidity, 21, 26, 84, 86, 145–46
folktales, 30, 45, 85, 102
fortune telling, 73–74
France, 52, 81, 127, 143, 184–85, 187
Francophone Negritude movement, 133, 141
freedom of the press, 57
Freud, Sigmund, 88–89

Gagalo festival, 74
Gamble, D. P., 52
Gates, Henry L., 201, 203–4
Gelede cult, 73
gender equality norms, 8
gender roles, 86
geomancy, system of, 73, 89
Ghana, 92, 129, 147
global identity, 29, 38, 133, 143
globalization, 21, 29, 37–38, 50, 59, 134–36, 145; globalisation, 8
glocalisation, 38
Graburn, Nelson, 62
griots, 46, 155. *See also* elders
Gruesser, John, 183
Gustavus Vassa, 179. *See also* Equiano, Olaudah

Hansberry, Lorraine, 187
Harlem Renaissance, 39, 184–86
Harris, Eddy, 138, 191–92
Hautaniemi, Petri, 59
healthcare policy, 130, 132
healthcare system, 130
hedonism, 65. *See also* modernity
herbs, 65, 80–81
home, 17, 20, 68, 145; conception of, 26–27, 37; fluidity of, 145–46; mobility of, 22; natal, 58, 140
homemaking, dynamic, 23; process of, 25
homosexuality, 55; discrimination against, 56
host spaces, 21–22, 25–27
Hoving, Isabel, 14
Hughes, Arnold, 39, 53, 171, 183, 185, 187–88
Hughes, Langston, 39, 183, 185, 187
human existence, duality of, 88
human rights: abuse, 58; denial of, 55

Human Rights Watch, 54
humanism, 30–31, 38, 105–6, 149, 164
hybridity, 49, 134–35, 148, 154, 156, 196

Ibekwe, Chinweizu, 167
ideal spaces, 16, 26–27
identity, 24, 37; formation of, 149; politics, 50, 56, 145; significance of, 141
identity crises, 41
idioms, 75, 78, 98
Ifá cantos, 162; divination, 73
Ifá system of knowledge, 89
Ijala, 104
"ikola-abe," 76. *See also* circumcision: female
immigration, 16, 59, 135–36, 174; laws, 153–54
imperialism, 91, 152
individualism, 30, 32, 78, 82; criticism of, 166; negation of, 28; principle of, 105, 161; radical, 84
interethnic relationships, 143
internal wars, 147
interracial marriages, 143; tensions, 5

Jamaica, 34, 179
jambur, 46
Jammeh, Yahya, 30–31, 53, 56, 171–72
Jawara, Dawda K., 52–53, 56, 171
Joshi, Mani, 62

Kalua, Fetson, 26–27
Kaplan, Caren, 198
Kehinde, Ayo, 109, 145
knowledge system, 120
Koinova, Maria, 8
Kyerematen-Darko, Bridget, 114
Kymlicka, Will, 44

Laakso, Liisa, 59
language: nodes of, 96; patterns, 93–94; politics of, 37, 91
languages, indigenous, 93, 101, 155
LGBTQ advocacy, 55; community, 53, 56; legal barriers against, 55; trampling on, 55
liberalism, 45, 105
Liberia, 110

Libya, 17
life after death, 67
liminal space, 3, 6, 12, 23, 26; feature, 21
liminality, conception of, 12
literacy, 101, 107, 180, 182
Locke, Alain, 184
London, 111–12, 125, 137–38, 149

Madsen, Ole, 64
Malcolm X, 147
Mali, 16
Mandela, Nelson, 142, 144
Mao Zedong, 121
marriage, 35, 68, 72, 86, 97, 102, 131; polygamous, 118, 131
Marx, Karl, 162
Marxism, 186
Masolo, D. A., 105
material possessions, 23, 75, 79
Mazrui, Alamin, 93
Mbiti, John, 160, 172
McKay, Claude, 39, 184, 201
medical practices, 81; traditional, 80
memory, 178
migration, 25, 136; drivers, 21
migritudinal tendencies, 40
military misrule, 21
modernity, 64, 86–87
Moley, David, 22
monogamy: serial, 108, 118–19; Western, 86
Morrison, Toni, 190
mother figure, 71–72
motherhood, 33, 35, 38, 72, 167
motility, 17, 21
Mozambique, 16
multicultural tendency, 47
multiculturalism, 46, 106, 129, 196, 199

names, 32, 35, 70, 72–73, 96, 100, 163; as identity, 66
nationalism: dual, 25; levels of, 16
Naylor, Gloria, 190–91
negritude, 185–89, 192–94; ideology of, 39; movement, 133
Negro, 184–85

negro spiritual, 202
neoclassical approach, 60, 139
Newell, Stephanie, 43
Nigeria-Biafra war, 143
Nigerian Civil War, 52, 171. *See also* Nigeria-Biafra war
Njie, Cherno M., 40–41, 133–34, 164, 175, 194, 200
Nkrumah, Kwame, 30, 124–25, 143, 146–47, 161
Nyang, Sulayman S., 170
Nyerere, Julius, 30, 161, 164
Nzeogwu, Kaduna, 53
Nzewi, Ugochukwu, 134

Obama, Barack, 192
Odu Ifá, 73
Ofun Irete, 55
Olaniyan, Tejumola, 134
Olodumare, 74, 162
"olohun-iyo," 76
Oluwole, Adunni, 169–70
Omoluabi, concept of, 88
Omolúwàbí, 173
Ong, Walter, 101
oral tradition, 101
orality, 36; essence of, 103; use of, 94, 101
Ori, 34
oriki, 74–76
Orunmila, 73–74

Pack, Robert, 19
pan-African movement, 141, 144, 183, 192
pan-Africanism, 37–39, 89–90, 140–41, 192, 196, 204
panegyrics, 32, 34, 75, 104
particularism, 29, 38, 135, 140, 148
patriarchal system, 85, 88
personality disorder, 49, 148
personhood, 42, 105, 133, 165
pidgin English, 100, 103
place, 14
pluralism, 19, 36, 196; electoral, 8
poems, 74–76, 81–82, 85, 94, 184, 186
political instability, 59, 137

political rights, 182–83
polygyny, 35
power of unity, 154
praise poetry, 97
press freedom, 57
propitiation materials, 80
proverbs, 75, 78, 98
pull factor, 44, 49, 137
purification rite, 67–68
purity, 42, 87–88, 133, 149
push factors, 137

race relations, 18–19
racial discrimination, 28, 175
racial hostility, 149
racial philosophy, 183
racism, 130–31, 135–36, 143, 149–54; argument for, 123; structure of, 125; workings of, 122
Randolph, Philip A., 39, 184
reconstruction, 156, 172, 178, 182, 184–85
reincarnation, 32, 35, 67, 83
religion, 32, 54, 72, 74; foreign, 83; Western, 182
religious tolerance, 54
remembrance ceremonies, 70
repetitive songs, 98
resources, mobilization of, 5
return-aggression approach, 60–61, 139
rites of passage, 62, 117
ritual murders, 112, 149
rule of law, 38
Rushdie, Salman, 41
Rwanda, 56, 147

Sadji, Abdoulaye, 187
Said, Edward, 24, 40, 146
Saine, Aboulaye, 53
Sanneh, Alieu, 54
Santana, Stephanie, 143
Selasi, Taiye, 51, 134, 142
self-determination, 51, 182
self-help, 182
Senegal, 44, 47, 137, 143, 171
Senegambia, 52

INDEX

Senghor, Léopold S., 39, 143
Senghore, Aboubacar A., 57
separatism, notion of, 54
slave songs, 202
slavery, 4; abolition of, 179; aftermath of, 28; impact of, 29
social belonging, 19
social borders, 48
social remittances, 8
social-capital-network theory, 61, 139
societal cultures, 43, 45
solipsism, 105; acts of, 161
songs, 75, 98
sorrow songs, 202
Southern Africa, 34
Soyinka, Wole, 144, 160
space, 10, 13, 177; lived, 15, 25–26; real, 14; subaltern, 11
spirituality, 69, 83, 173, 204
spirituals, 183
Sterling, Cheryl, 141
structuralists, 61, 139
Sullivan, Harry S., 181
superstition, 65
Sweden, 112–13, 130, 140, 151
syncretism, 49, 54, 148

taboo, 65
Thiong'o, Ngugi Wa, 159
Third Space, 3, 20, 26–27, 137
tolerance, 30–31, 45–47, 54, 69, 106, 175, 196
Toloyan, Khachig, 50
Tolson, Melvin B., 186
tradition, as a reservoir, 63
traditional purification rites, 67
transatlantic slave trade, 4, 29, 158, 192, 199
transculturalism, 48, 129, 154
transnationalism, 134, 184
tribal marks, 84
Trump, Donald, 125, 153–54
Trumpism, 135–36, 149
Tubman, William V. S., 186
Turner, Victor, 3, 12
tyranny, 59, 154, 159–60, 170, 173, 176, 204

Ubuntu ideology, 69
UNESCO, 178
United Kingdom, 51, 112, 140, 179–80, 194
United States of America, 17, 19, 109, 125
universalism, 38, 133

values, imported, 83
violence, ethno-religious, 20

Wainaina, Binyavanga, 144
Walker, Alice, 190
Washington, Booker T., 38, 182
"we-social," 160
West, Cornel, 203
West Africa, 17, 34, 44, 111–12, 115, 134, 146, 155
Western cultures, 33–34, 66
Western ideology, 105
westernization, 32–33
white supremacy, 28
Wight, David, 199
witchcraft, 32–33, 71, 73
witchcraft cults, 71
Wolof culture, 31
Wolof society, 45
Wolof traditions, 45
womanhood, 32–35, 38, 167
women, significance of, 168
Wright, Richard, 38, 183

"Yanmiri," 56
Yoruba cosmology, 71, 80, 102
Yoruba cults, 73
Yoruba cultural mosaic, 93
Yoruba culture, 32, 34–35, 84, 98, 101; on sexual relationships, 89, 103
Yoruba deities, 83
Yoruba language, 70, 98; phonology of, 99
Yoruba names, 32; naming process, 100
Yoruba people, 55–56
Yoruba tradition, 32, 66, 71–72, 80, 83, 87–90, 166
Yorubanglish, 102

Zeleza, Paul, 42, 133
Zussman, Robert, 179

ABOUT THE AUTHOR

Toyin Falola is professor of history, University Distinguished Teaching Professor, and the Jacob and Frances Sanger Mossiker Chair in the Humanities at the University of Texas at Austin, and, most recently, the Kluge Chair of the Countries and Culture of the South, the Library of Congress in Washington, DC.

He is a celebrated author, editor, writer, poet, academic leader, organizer, teacher, and pan-Africanist. He is author and editor of over one hundred books on Africa and the African Diaspora, and many of his books have received awards, defined various fields, and inspired the writings of various critical works. He manages six distinguished scholarly monograph series and serves on the board of many journals.

Toyin Falola has received over thirty lifetime career awards and fifteen honorary doctorates and has written extensively on the African Diaspora, including *The African Diaspora: Slavery, Modernity, and Globalization*, *A Mouth Sweeter than Salt*, *Counting the Tiger's Teeth*, *Etches on Fresh Waters*, *Scoundrels of Deferral*, and *Wole Soyinka: Literature, Activism, and African Transformation*.

www.ingramcontent.com/pod-product-compliance
Lightning Source LLC
Chambersburg PA
CBHW030618230426
43661CB00053B/2049